'Karen Evans's latest book, *Community and the Problem of Crime*, represents an excellent analytical and empirically grounded guide to this highly contested and massively important area of social scientific inquiry. This challenging yet accessible monograph will become an invaluable "must-have" text for students of sociological criminology in particular. Evans makes significant contribution to our cumulative sociological knowledge of the crime–community "nexus".'

Gordon Hughes, Chair in Criminology, School of Social Sciences, Cardiff University, UK

'The concept "community" is much used and abused in studies of crime, disorder and crime prevention. The language of community is frequently deployed as cause, location, symptom and solution for all manner of social problems. Fortunately, at last there is a book which brings a splendid, constructively critical, perspective to bear on this many-faceted phenomenon, even engaging with the diverse and contrary tendencies of real communities – marginalisation, stigmatisation, privatisation, securitisation and militarisation – as they reshape the social contexts through *which we move/in which we live*. A refreshing and original read.'

Peter Squires, Professor of Criminology & Public Policy, University of Brighton, UK

'This terrific book provides an exploration of the paradoxes and contradictions of "community" as these relate to crime and social justice. It demonstrates how community is seen to be both a source of social problems and the solution to it, and how it is strategically applied in ways that incorporate and/or marginalise specific population groups. Providing a theoretically informed analysis of concrete cases, trends and issues, the book makes a wonderful contribution to critical appraisals of the dynamics of contemporary society. A vital resource.'

Rob White, Professor of Criminology, University of Tasmania, Australia

COMMUNITY AND THE PROBLEM OF CRIME

The relationship between crime and community has a long history in criminological thought, from the early notion of the criminogenic community developed by the Chicago sociologists through to various crime prevention models in research and policy. This book offers a useful theoretical overview of key approaches to the subject of crime and community and considers the ways in which these have been applied in more practical settings.

Written by an expert in the field and drawing on a range of international case studies from Europe, North America, Australia and Asia, this book explores both why and how crime and community have been linked and the implications of their relationship within criminology and crime prevention policy. Topics covered in the book include:

- the different crime prevention paradigms which have been utilised in the 'fight against crime',
- the turn to community in crime prevention policy, which took place during the 1980s in the UK and US and its subsequent development,
- the particular theoretical and ideological underpinnings to crime prevention work in and with different communities,
- the significance and impact of fear of crime on crime prevention policy,
- different institutional responses to working with community in crime prevention and community safety,
- the ways in which the experience of the UK and US have been translated into the European context,
- a comparison between traditional Western responses to the growing interest in restorative and community-based approaches in other regions.

This book offers essential reading for students taking courses on crime and community, crime prevention, and community safety and community corrections.

Karen Evans is a senior lecturer at the Department of Sociology, Social Policy and Criminology at the University of Liverpool, where she has been employed since 1999. Immediately prior to this lecturing post she was Community Safety Co-ordinator working for the Moss Side and Hulme Partnership in Manchester, UK. With a first degree in Economics and Politics and an employment history, which involved working with the homeless and as a welfare rights advisor, Karen was a somewhat reluctant criminologist. Her research into urban transformations alongside the late Ian Taylor in the early 1990s led her into research into experiences of crime and victimisation in various cities in the Northwest of England, collaborating with Sandra Walklate and others in Liverpool. Karen's work since that time has focused, although not exclusively, around communities in excluded neighbourhoods and their responses to marginalisation and deprivation. She has taught the module Community and the Problem of Crime in Liverpool for the last ten years.

COMMUNITY AND THE PROBLEM OF CRIME

Karen Evans

Routledge
Taylor & Francis Group

LONDON AND NEW YORK

First published 2016
by Routledge
2 Park Square, Milton Park, Abingdon, Oxon, OX14 4RN

and by Routledge
711 Third Avenue, New York, NY 10017

Routledge is an imprint of the Taylor & Francis Group, an informa business

British Library Cataloguing in Publication Data
A catalogue record for this book is available from the British Library

Library of Congress Cataloging-in-Publication Data

Evans, Karen,
Community and the problem of crime / Karen Evans.
   pages cm
   1. Crime—Sociological aspects. 2. Communities. 3. Sociology, Urban.
   4. Community policing. 5. Crime prevention. I. Title.
HV6025.E8155 2015
364.2'5—dc23   2014040816

ISBN: 978-0-415-74855-1 (hbk)
ISBN: 978-1-138-88691-9 (pbk)
ISBN: 978-1-315-79654-3 (ebk)

Typeset in Bembo
by codeMantra

To VK and Alan

CONTENTS

ACKNOWLEDGEMENTS

This book arises out of a module Community and the Problem of Crime which I designed in 2003 and have been leading at the University of Liverpool in the Department of Sociology, Social Policy and Criminology for the last decade. For a number of years I have shared the teaching of this module with other experts in their field who are based in my department. I would like to acknowledge the significant contribution they have made to my understanding of the subject. In particular, I would like to thank Lynn Hancock for her sustained contribution to the module, for her tireless enthusiasm for teaching and for sharing her expertise in this area.

This book has been written at a particularly difficult period of my life during which I have lost a number of people who have been very important to me and who have helped to develop my confidence and abilities. To those who remain and who have supported me throughout this time I give my thanks – to Dave in particular who has had his own troubles to bear at this time but who has remained a fantastic source of strength to me. I must also thank my good friend Ivor Smith for inspiring me with his enthusiasm for my subject and his love of the work of John Clare and Andrew Davies. Thanks also to my copy editor, no other than my mother Barbara Evans, who checked my references as I packed her house into numerous boxes. If any references or indeed tableware are missing or broken, then I take full responsibility.

I would also like to acknowledge the part Microsoft has played in the production of this book. Without the global dominance of this corporation and the contribution of its Windows 8 software writers in particular, the writing of this book would have been made so much easier.

INTRODUCTION

This book has emerged from the module Community and the Problem of Crime which I have been delivering as module leader since returning to Liverpool University in 2003 from a postdoctoral fellowship overseas. The idea for the module was informed by my work as a Community Safety Co-ordinator in the Moss Side and Hulme Partnership in Manchester, UK, a post I held from 1996 to 1999 while I was working on my doctoral thesis based at the University of Salford. I had previously worked with Sandra Walklate on an Economic and Social Research Council (ESRC) funded project Community Safety, Personal Safety and the Fear of Crime, which was one study in the ESRC's *Crime and Social Order Programme* directed by Tim Hope. This programme was expertly run with many seminars and events which brought the successful award-holders together with experts in the field; the arguments and conversations which I was involved in during that time have stayed with me and shaped my understanding and approach to my subject in the intervening years. I was lucky enough to spend a great deal of time with academics such as Tim Hope himself, Adam Crawford, Tony Jefferson, Evi Girling, Richard Sparks and Ian Loader and many more who have continued to write and work in the same area and to have therefore continued to shape the development of my ideas. It was this group of academics who introduced me to so much relevant criminological theory and helped me to transition from a welfare rights and housing advisor with a Master's in Applied Social Research to become an academic teaching, researching and writing around crime and social order well into the twenty-first century. These are the lessons I took into my role as Community Safety Co-ordinator in 1996. I was somewhat disconcerted to find that practitioners and funders who presided over the expenditure of millions of pounds in local areas had little idea of, or recourse to, the theories which shaped the practices which they were implementing. In my own way during that three-year period, I attempted to ensure that the work carried out in Moss Side and Hulme - which was as my job description required to ensure that it was 'a safe place to work, visit and play' – was informed by academic research and theory, and I vowed that I would always teach the subject at university as a theoretically informed module.

Having taught the module for over ten years now, and having witnessed the major changes which have taken place in both academic understanding and in the practice of delivering community safety and crime prevention on the ground, I have realised that it is more important than ever to ground our comprehension of the subject within a clearly argued academic framework. The claims made by policy-makers about, and on, community have become ever more boldly stated and widely framed as if they were universal truths. I hope this book will demonstrate that there is no such thing, and instead that our thinking about community and the uses to which it has been put have changed significantly over the last century and will alter fundamentally in the future too. I have also been concerned that students are even more removed today from the critical way in which we first met the invocation of community in policy discourse. This is unsurprising, as in the more than two decades which have passed since the ESRC programme was first conceived, much of what we then questioned has become a truism in everyday discourse. I was very pleased then when I was approached by Routledge to write this book and saw it as an opportunity to re-engage with the ideas which were so significant at that time and to test how far they had maintained significance over the ensuing decades.

Having said this, I should note that the book has become in the writing less about what community is or is not and more about how the state uses the term 'community' to confer rights upon some groups and to exclude others from exercising those rights. This is not a book about crime prevention either as many authors have addressed this subject in more authoritative ways. It is a book, however, which questions the ways in which the concept of community has been utilised within agendas of crime control and how perspectives forged in the West have gone global. It is particularly concerned, too, with how the problem of crime has come to predominate and to persist as one of the most significant organising problems of national governments in the West, even at a time when recorded crime figures have steadily dropped year upon year.

I have tried in my writing not to fall into the everyday, accepted language of crime and criminality, but this goal has been very difficult to achieve. I am uncomfortable with terms such as offender and victim but have had to make use of these terms in order to write about the concerns which have predominated in government and popular discourse. Community, too, is a problematic concept. John Bruhn has written that 'community enjoys the rather dubious distinction of [being] one of the most frequently and variably used terms in social science' (2011:14). There is no standard definition of the term which could usefully limit and focus its use. Notoriously, Hillery, investigating the concept in 1955 found 94 different definitions had been applied to the term (Konig 1968:22) yet it remains an enduring concept, peddled by politicians and policy-makers as a desirable, almost, ideal state of existence to which we all should aspire and is used widely and largely uncritically in common parlance. Community has been studied to some extent within every academic discipline concerned with human (and some animal) behaviour and has been found in the interactions of like-minded or co-located people, but also in the ways in which organisations or businesses can cluster together for optimal effect. In criminology, the concept of community has generally referred to place-based community, rarely occupational community, although of course there are occupations which might be useful to research as far as crime and social harm are concerned. Further interrogation of the financial community, for example, would be in order at this time, as would interrogation of occupational cultures which sustain harm upon various publics.

The meanings attached to community have been many and varied, but at its most basic the term is used to refer to 'people having something in common' (Crow and Allen 1994:3), and that shared 'something' is in some way acknowledged and realised in practice by some proportion of those who would constitute its members. Communities are not limited to the place-based, realised through a common territory, but can also be interest-based and realised through some form of collective endeavour – whether this is apparent in collective action or less tangible in a sharing of common interests. It is perfectly possible therefore to be a passive member of a community; to feel attached to either an interest or a residential community but without actually becoming involved in common activity with other members of that community. We must be more careful, however, about our use of the term 'community' and must not invoke its use where it does not exist. Where shared interests exist but are not acknowledged, or acknowledged but not realised in some small way, then this does not merit the conferring of the status of community; to do so would render the term almost meaningless. Yet the status of 'community' is often conferred on social and territorial groupings of people who do not acknowledge or realise their 'community' in these ways. The term 'community' can thus be (mis)applied to particular neighbourhoods and geographical localities or in a very sweeping way to denote social groupings where the user of the term believes they do or should share common interests or attachments. Indeed, political and social policy interventions throughout the twentieth century and beyond are littered with such misappropriations of the term 'community'.

As Anthony Cohen (1985) reminds us, 'community' is bounded and also relational. Implied in the term are relations of inclusion but also of exclusion, of the 'we' as opposed to the 'them'. It is not surprising then that in recent decades the concept of 'community' has also become central to many aspects of criminological study where the construction and fear of 'the other' has been a recurring theme. In the sub-discipline of crime prevention, however, community has been used in a less defined and more nostalgic manner to evoke ties that bind residential neighbourhoods together in shared experiences and common interests. In order to make sense of the multiple uses – and abuses – of the term 'community' within criminology, it is important to trace the ways in which 'community' has been incorporated into the discipline over time and to chart the many ways in which the concept has been put to use in theory-building and in practical policy-making. Rather than offering a new definition to add to Hillery's long list, it is hoped that a study of the way others have developed the concept and generated interest in it will reveal more about what is perceived to be the essence of community and why it has become so widely idealised and used as an organising concept in government and policy-making.

The book is organised as follows.

Chapter One looks at the various ways in which academics and policy-makers have worked with the concept of 'community' over different periods. It looks first at classic community studies of the early to mid-twentieth century and how these studies have informed late-twentieth-century understandings of community and which underpin the turn to communitarianism much later in the twentieth century. The chapter reveals that the concept of community has retained a power and significance despite whole-scale economic, social and political upheaval. At times and under certain social conditions, community has been rejected as an organising force within society, but it has been returned to repeatedly and held up as a social good which must be preserved or rebuilt.

Chapter Two considers the place which the concept of community has played in techniques and systems of crime control and prevention. The chapter recounts the move from community to state control of the problem of crime and the various interventions which the state has deployed in its struggle to reduce and contain rates of recorded crime. From this point onwards, community played a secondary role in crime control, called on in different periods to collaborate with the state and contribute to the maintenance of order. Rather than being seen as a solution to crime, communities were initially blamed for harbouring and disseminating the wrong values and were subject to particular scrutiny. Since the 1970s, however, communities have increasingly been brought into the crime control arsenal and have been called upon to play a significant role in crime prevention.

Chapter Three examines ways that the problem of disorder has been conceived. It explores in particular the construction of the 'problem community' and the different ways in which this 'problem' has been perceived and acted upon. From the early theorists of crime and community, working-class neighbourhoods have been cast as socially disorganised, but this chapter questions some of the assumptions upon which this representation of economically disadvantaged communities has been based, suggesting that some communities are differently organised but that this difference need not be perceived of as problematic. From Chapter Four, with much of the work done in sketching out the theories which have been significant in shaping understandings of both community and the problem of crime in previous chapters, the remainder of the book looks at the ways that these theories have informed the more substantive and policy-based agendas which have developed as a consequence.

Chapter Four considers the debates which have proved important in rebuilding community and neighbourhood, which began after the Second World War but which changed in emphasis and focus after the end of the postwar economic boom. Postwar reconstruction changed into post-boom regeneration agendas. These increasingly looked to the restructuring of local neighbourhoods as a means of solving problems which had arisen at a more global level. The chapter includes two case studies outlining problems of flight from the city and possible solutions which have been put in place to reverse the declining fortunes of cities and rural economies in both Japan and Spain. The chapter explains that communities have been co-opted into this regeneration practice and held responsible for their ultimate success or failure.

Chapter Five explores differences within and between what are loosely termed 'communities' beginning with a consideration of the differences between and within cities which can give their neighbourhoods a distinct character. The chapter then goes on to discuss the different fractures which exist within what can be considered place-based communities and the difficulties which these have posed in the construction and maintenance of cohesive communities in the present day. This chapter reveals multiple perspectives within the city, that not all social groups experience their neighbourhoods and social environments in the same ways. It looks at the complex networks of inclusion and exclusion which shape our experiences and have to be acknowledged and understood if any positive changes are to be made to improve access to the city and the right to the city for all. Three more case studies are introduced in this chapter which address the different issues faced by ethnic minority groups and women in the city as well as the presence of 'illegitimate' communities.

Chapter Six starts with a discussion of Hillyard's concept of 'suspect communities' and then considers ways in which, not only the state, but also popular discourse has coalesced around suspicion of certain minority groups, cultures and ways of life. Hillyard developed the concept of suspect communities after doing research on Irish people arrested on suspicion of committing terrorist offences in the 1970s, and Pantazis and Pemberton updated his analysis to include the treatment of Muslims after 9/11. They show how both groups have been targeted for unwelcome attention and considered as responsible for their own isolation and the stereotypes which abound concerning their values and lifestyles. This suspicion, rather than culminating in a myriad of 'communities' living side by side, has created tensions at a national and local level. The chapter looks at the ghettoization and stigmatisation experienced by other groups from the Jews in medieval Europe to the black population in the United States today. The chapter also asks whether the concept of 'suspect community' could be further extended to aid our understanding of the state's treatment of the poor in neo-liberal economies.

Chapter Seven reflects on the policing of communities – their monitoring, regulation and control – which is carried out at a number of different levels and by various organisations. The chapter starts with a look at the ways in which the state interacts with communities through the formal organisation of the Police but then moves on to include more recent insights into governance which have created the expectation that communities will monitor, regulate and control themselves. This chapter introduces in more detail the strategy of responsibilisation, which has been highlighted by David Garland and which has helped criminology to understand the drive to co-opt communities into the crime control agenda in the late twentieth century. It looks further, however, to the increasing militarisation of policing local neighbourhoods perceived as troublesome, and the gap between the rhetoric of community involvement and the reality of communities which are coerced into order through targeted state surveillance and over-policing.

The final chapter returns to the theme of community itself. It explores the limitations of community as an organising concept while arguing that the concept still has relevance today, especially in those areas which are increasingly abandoned by the welfare arm of the state. The chapter also considers the inherently exclusionary qualities of community and the tendency of communities to separate as well as to unite. While 'community' is held up as a positive social formation, this chapter uses case studies from the UK and abroad to demonstrate how the building of communities can produce barriers to progressive policy-making. This chapter explores how competition for resources and influence can result in the formation of separate communities occupying adjacent or shared spaces. It also examines how the dynamics of the relationships between them can be factors which exacerbate rather than reduce criminogenic tendencies. It concludes with a look at how post-exclusionary discourses of community might be framed and the possibilities this might introduce for crime prevention/community safety in the future.

While my own knowledge base is firmly located within the UK and has developed from a Western perspective, I have attempted in this book to include case studies from further afield in order to demonstrate the global reach of the ideas and the policies which have dominated the agenda of crime control within nation-states and increasingly internationally. I ask my students to reflect in their study on a number of processes which have become almost universal in their application to the problem of crime; first stigmatisation, followed by responsibilisation and privatisation. In recent years I have added securitisation to this list, and I fear also that in the coming years the militarisation of responses will also need to be more clearly emphasised.

There are many areas that I have not been able to touch upon in this book, and I fear that my treatment of some issues has been too cursory, but the limitation of this medium for the dissemination of ideas has dictated a certain brevity. I have added questions and suggested further reading to each chapter in the hope that the reader's appetite will be whetted by my initial round-up of the issues and that the reader will take the time to reach further into the debates of their own free will.

References

Cohen, A. (1985) *The Symbolic Construction of Community* London: Routledge.
Konig, R. (1968) *The Community* London: Routledge and Kegan Paul.

1
THE MEANING AND USES OF COMMUNITY

Classic and premodern 'community'

Aristotle in Book 1 of *Politics* claimed that '[a] social instinct is implanted in all men by nature' and […] human life cannot be conceived as existing outside of the social … he who is unable to live in society, or who has no need because he is sufficient for himself, must be either a beast or a god'(Aristotle 2012). Humans are not solitary creatures but co-operate with one another to produce food and shelter and to reproduce future generations. They therefore live in close relationship to others, building codes, rules and laws which govern their social relations and make such close co-existence possible. In doing so, they are building a common way of living and being. These shared experiences lead to commonly held understandings and belief systems which become a shared culture as ways of being and thinking are passed down from one generation to the next. Social organisation is forged through a need to belong and to get along with others using common frames of reference and common understandings in inherently collective enterprises. Hence, the concept of commonality, of 'community,' is considered as 'natural' to humanity and is based on the co-operative relations necessary to ensure survival.

The types of social institutions which people build change as societies acquire new knowledge, systems of production and technological expertise. Hunter/gatherer societies developed social relationships which aided a transitory and unsettled existence. The technologies which they had to aid their survival were basic – weapons with which to hunt, tools to build shelter and pots to cook with. A shift to farming and cultivation around 20,000 years ago demanded a different set of social relationships to reflect a more settled way of life, but co-operation was still key to their survival. As pastoral and agrarian societies began to emerge in the Middle East and Europe, people developed more complex divisions of labour and role differentiation. These societies became less egalitarian (Engels [1884] famously referred to hunter/gatherer societies as 'primitive communism') and more hier-archical as the concept of private property emerged and became institutionalised in systems of law. The accumulation of property in private hands, Engels argued, allowed the generation of profound inequalities of material wealth and power and the development of a class-based system whereby those with shared power and interests collaborated to rule over others. Where power was passed down family lines and aristocratic and monarchical systems were established to aid this process, familial ties took on particular significance. These inequalities in power were deeply established by the time the classical civilisations of the Middle East and southern Europe were firmly established and private ownership was extended to the own-ership of people as well as land and goods. Agricultural workers were tasked with feeding growing cities, and slave labour was put to work for the powerful to enable successful war-making and empire-building.

It was in the Classical period, Konig (1968) argues, that the Greek city-state first developed the concept and practice of building 'community' as a form of social organisation which was separated from ties of kinship. The city-state developed a form of rudimentary democracy which functioned only for the elite groups in society and which was deemed necessary for 'modern' political and social organ-isation to develop. It also required a collective defence to protect the city against attacks by outsiders. The term 'community' which we use today is derived from the Latin prefix *com* together with the verb *munire*, meaning "to fortify, strengthen, or defend." Thus, from the start the idea of community was linked to a political pur-pose and to the exclusion of others, but in its formation it also bound otherwise unconnected people together in a powerful, affective bond through which those included were strengthened and protected.

Before the idea of nation brought people together under a common institu-tional and legal framework, the concept of community acted as a form of social glue at a local level. While the power of city-states in classical civilisation eventu-ally diminished and new political and economic systems took their place, local allegiances remained paramount. However, as Sharpe has described, 'Contrary to popular myth' people did not live together in 'idyllic village settlements' (Sharpe 2001:134). Indeed, as he points out, class divisions were a truly salient feature of pre-industrial society. Sharpe writes of England that:

> [t]he early modern small town or village was as likely to be riven by problems, albeit of a different nature, as any modern city. Legal records, criminal and civil alike, contain ample evidence of social tensions and interpersonal malice. Indeed by the eighteenth century, most English villages, although capable of showing community spirit on occasion, were often so socially stratified as to make it possible to speak of a number of 'communities' within their boundaries.'
> (2001:134)

The most salient division within these settlements, Sharpe argues, was a division of class, between the rich – the 'respectable' middle-class landowners, clergy and tradesmen – and the poor who were surviving through subsistence lifestyles by farming or labouring without education or other resources to help them escape their fate. The 'respectable' elites, however, were very much involved in the policing and monitoring of the behaviour of the poor. The notion of community under these circumstances in reality 'looks very shaky' (2001:134); however, different regions were still organised by local customs and values, and the penalties and sanctions brought to bear on the 'unrespectable' and 'the offender' were shaped by local tradition. Until industrialisation forced specialisation in production and manufacture of goods and necessitated the forging of economic connections between regions and towns, these local areas were organised to local rhythms of life, even in some cases, local time-zones, currencies and laws which differentiated one community from the next.

Prior to mass industrialisation, the world, as Hobsbawm describes it 'was at once much smaller and much vaster than ours' (1962:7). The global population, being so much smaller, was also much more sparsely distributed than today. The major-ity of people lived and died within an extremely small physical area perhaps only spanning one or two square miles. The English poet John Clare (1793–1864), the son of a farm-labourer who wrote eloquently of the disruptive effect of indus-trialisation on the English countryside, was said to be so unnerved by a move of three miles which uprooted him from everybody and everything familiar to him that this precipitated an episode of severe mental illness (Bate 2003). According to Hobsbawm, the costs and physical efforts associated with travel of more than a few miles overland meant that transport by water was the most common form of travel and port cities were more connected, even internationally, than town and country within national boundaries;

> in a real sense London was closer to Plymouth or Leith than to villages in the breckland of Norfolk; Seville was more accessible from Veracruz than Valladolid, Hamburg from Bahia than the Pomeranian hinterland.
>
> (Hobsbawm 1962:9–10)

Under these circumstances, locality and neighbourhood, together with their local customs and traditions, were particularly significant to the rural and disconnected poor. For those with the time and money to travel or for those involved in the business of trade, commerce or indeed war, which necessitated the cultivation of national and global connections, lives were much less connected to locality and place of birth. Hobsbawm (1962:9) estimates, as an example, that at the beginning of the nineteenth century 20 million letters passed through the British postal sys-tem with perhaps ten times more than this number by the middle of the century. Once again, then, the experience and salience of 'community' depended very much on a person's class background.

All that is solid melts into air – community versus society

A fascination with the growing urbanisation of society and how this would affect social relationships of the future inspired social thinkers during the nineteenth century. Between them they published a number of significant texts which continue to influence subsequent work in the understanding of community and society. These writers came from a variety of different perspectives, but each was attempting to grapple with the impact of a whole-scale reorganisation of society away from traditional locally-based social systems which had developed over centuries and towards a more amorphous, seemingly disorganised, city-based life which began to attract people in the tens of thousands and to transform physical and social landscapes. New forms of social organisation found in the rapidly developing urban settlements were surprising, shocking to some and liberating to others, but whatever response these writers had to the cities exploding before their eyes, they recognised that they offered a challenge, not just to the established way of life but also to old ways of thinking and demanded that social life be theorised anew. The following section looks at the work of a number of key theorists who made significant contributions to this body of work. It cannot encompass all those who contributed, nor does it cover the total extent of any one thinker's contributions, but it draws out salient points from a brief exploration of a number of participants in these discussions.

The industrialisation of society rips a people from the land and requires a large-scale shift to cities and an urban landscape. The organisation of social life in cities and around the different rhythms and patterns of life required by industrial rather than agricultural labour also requires different ways of living and thinking about social relationships. The whole-scale and fundamental change from agriculture-based economies and the 'take-off' to a system of production based on manufacturing which we now call the Industrial Revolution is generally located in the north of England in the 1780s but was much more widely felt outside of England in the 1830s and 1840s (Hobsbawm 1962:27). Historians have written of the shock of the developing industrial cities in the nineteenth century in particular, which necessitated radically different orderings of space and of the provision of food, water and transport. The 'great cities of the Industrial Revolution' grew from established places and communities, they 'took root in the countryside' and 'grew up around it' (Saunders 1981:23) but took on fundamentally different forms from those which preceded them. Harold Platt (2005) writes of the newly emerging 'industrial ecologies' which led to physically and socially divided cities; creating filthy, overcrowded and polluted slums as well as leafy suburbs located away from the noxious fumes and stench of industrialisation. Engels described and further analysed these spatial divisions in 1842 using Manchester, England – arguably the first industrial city – as his exemplar – and writing that 'the working people's quarters are sharply separated from the sections of the city reserved for the middle-class' (Engels 1987:85). Such a degree of spatial segregation had not been a feature of previous cities or settlements but industrialisation brought about a deeply divided physical and social structure in which the economic and cultural interests of the different classes became further opposed and entrenched and took on particular forms. Despite their divisive nature, these spatial developments were much copied, and by the end of the nineteenth century 77 per cent of the population of England and Wales lived in cities (Saunders 1981:14). Much of the rest of the world urbanised in the twentieth century. At the beginning of the twenty-first century, it has been estimated that for the first time in history, more than half the world's population live in cities. This proportion is expected to rise to three-quarters of the world's population by the middle of the century, with around one billion living in slums without proper sanitation or services (The Guardian 2014). The 'shock cities' of today continue to be built. They have exploded in numbers most recently across Asia, South America and Africa. In their divided and divisive physical form, they seem not to have the learned the lessons of the nineteenth-century cities but have largely followed similar patterns of spatial segregation, re-creating the slum conditions and inequalities of old.

Classical sociology and the study of community

Ferdinand Tönnies

So the decades around the turn of the twentieth century saw transformations in the social world which were revolutionary in character and which overturned centuries of tradition and have become embedded as accepted social ordering. Industrialisation, the birth of capitalism, the rise of the city, the unleashing of productive forces and global trade networks which fed imperialist appetites were all intimately linked. These decades also saw the birth of sociology as an academic discipline, so it is unsurprising that the earliest sociologists attempted to understand the significance of these transformations. The emergence of the city and the transition from a rural to an urban way of life were considered to have incomparable social significance, inspiring a great deal of interest in the constitution of a social order in the modern world and in the basis of new forms of association. Hoggett (1997) writes that, following Elias (1974), sociologists usually locate the origin of a sociological interest in the concept of 'community' in this time period and more particularly in the work of Ferdinand Tönnies, a sociologist and philosopher born in Schleswig, Denmark (which was later incorporated into Germany). By the time Tönnies began his academic research, the economic system of capitalism was firmly established. According to Hobsbawm, 'It was the triumph of a society which believed that economic growth rested on competitive private enterprise' (Hobsbawm 1975:1), but more than this the transition to capitalism, he argued, created not only division but also:

> a world of suitably distributed material plenty … of ever-growing enlightenment, reason and human opportunity, an advance of the sciences and the arts, in brief a world of continuous and accelerating material and moral progress.'
> (Hobsbawm 1975:1)

Tönnies's work must be located in this political and social context and forms both an exploration and a critique of these changing times. According to Braeman (2013), two key themes shaped the early work of Tönnies – first, the distinction Hegel made between *Gesellschaft* ("society") and *Staat* ("state"), both of which were modern social organisations, and second, an interest in the concept of the *Volkgeist* or 'spirit of the people,' which has more traditional and premodern roots in the shared customs, traditions and beliefs of former eras. These themes informed his most influential work, originally published in 1887, entitled *Gemeinschaft und Gesellschaft,* which was later translated as 'Community and Society'. Much of Tönnies's work explored the essential elements of these fundamentally different types of social organisation. He distinguished between two different kinds of relationship which people engage in – the voluntaristic and the rational. The first is based in emotion and psychology and can be found in the ties that bind family and intimates, whereas the second is more commonly perceived as the basis for contractual relationships and business associations. Underlying Tönnies's work was an interest in the emergence of capitalism and the forms of relationship which are entered into – whether freely or not – for the pursuit of material advantage. In his work can be seen an implicit preference for Gemeinschaft which he considered to be the most enduring and preferable of the two. In his later years, Tönnies even hailed himself a social democrat and developed a sympathetic interest in collective social organisations such as the emerging trade union and socialist movements, workers' education and cooperatives (Braeman 2013). It is clear from Tönnies's work that he believed that Gemeinschaft and Gesellschaft coexisted, that Gesellschaft did not replace Gemeinschaft but that the new social forms were grafted on to preexisting relationships. So it was possible to distinguish the structures of 'community' within the structures of 'society'. In Tönnies's life and work, therefore, we can identify the idea that capitalism was more responsible than urbanism for the predominance of the rational sentiment over the affective represented by 'community'.

Emile Durkheim

Another key contributor to the study of community was the French sociologist and contemporary of Tönnies, Emile Durkheim. Durkheim also explored the changing social relationships of the period, and although his work appears to complement that of Tönnies, Durkheim approached his study from a somewhat less critical perspective. Durkheim, unlike Tönnies, hailed from a scholarly family and had grown up in the city rather than a rural community. He was more influenced by the philosophy of Rousseau than of Hobbes (whom Tönnies cited as influential to his thinking) and was more wedded to the ideas of scientific rationalism and progress. Like Tönnies, however, he was interested in exploring the nature of the 'ties that bind individuals to one another, the connectedness among individuals that has been argued … to be the core meaning of community' (Somerville 2011:6). Durkheim identified two types of social solidarity – 'mechanical' and 'organic'. Mechanical solidarity, he argued, flows from conditions in which people think and act alike, sharing common values and perspectives. He saw mechanical solidarity as a function of homogeneity within social organisation and a collective morality, transgression of which is perceived as transgression against the social and which can result in harsh and repressive response. Organic solidarity, on the other hand, derives from more heterogeneous social relations in which individual difference is accepted and expected. Durkheim argued that while mechanical solidarity is assured through collective social censure, organic solidarity requires the institution of a set of more objectively constituted laws which proscribe what is and what is not harmful to society or a transgression of societal expectations.

Modern society, for Durkheim, was characterised by relations of organic solidarity which arose in conditions where traditional ways of life and traditionally-held values were replaced as people were uprooted from their villages and travelled to cities in search of work, education and a better way of life. In these first, mass, societies, he argued, social differentiation becomes the key to survival. Industrialised and urbanised societies require division of labour and the development of specialisation. Only under these conditions, he believed, can the sum of human knowledge be expanded and continued progress sustained. In these societies people recognize that they are interdependent – small cogs in a bigger system or 'organ' in which all play their part. Each person's work affects everyone else in a complex web of production and exchange. In this way, the 'material density' of modern life in which people live crowded together in urban environments is accompanied by a 'moral density' where a variety of ways of life coexist in close proximity. In modern, urbanised societies, Durkheim argued, mechanical solidarity withers in effect both within and outside of the city, as the weight of tradition acts as a bloc on progress and is surpassed by organic solidarity as new ways of living and thinking are adopted in society as a whole. Durkheim's view of the modern forms of social organisation are less critical than those of Tonnies; he welcomes the progress which the replacement of mechanical by organic solidarity heralds. Durkheim's views, however, presage a later tradition of thought which considered 'community' as backward-facing and oppressive, whilst forms of social organisation formed by modernity are more progressive and liberating for the individual.

Durkheim considered that modern societies would cohere around difference. Whereas traditionally communities were built on shared characteristics and similarity of approach, Durkheim argued that modernity, built as it was on mass migration, could encompass different cultures and that this reality should not be considered as a threat to social solidarity. Indeed, Durkheim welcomed the mass movement of people and the mingling of culture and experience as necessary to ensure social progress. According to Durkheim, members of a cohesive social system do not need to share a common religion and common histories, but for a cohesive social order to be maintained a "conscience collective" – the recognition of shared interests and values – is key. In this way, all persons are free to choose their own philosophies and moralities and to live life the way they choose as long as they do not violate the commonly accepted codes of the society in which they are positioned. Durkheim did not reject the importance of a collective consciousness but located it in the intellectual rather than the affective realm. The ideas of both Tönnies and Durkheim have been read as positing a crude dualism in their typologies and therefore implying opposition between 'community' and 'association,' but a more careful reading of their work demonstrates that they both recognised the enduring significance of social bonds in the change from traditional to modern social formations. Durkheim saw the breaking down of traditional morality and its replacement by new forms of solidarity as bringing about improvement in the general social condition and perhaps resulting in stronger social connections than traditional codes would allow as people chose their affinities rather than being born into them.

Max Weber

The German sociologist, Max Weber, also influenced the discussion of city and community. In his work *The City*, published posthumously in 1921, Weber outlined the various city formations throughout history, arguing that as a result of the development of industrial capitalism in the West, cities became gradually separated from the countryside around them, constituting 'urban communities' which differed markedly from the rural (Weber 1960). In much of the rest of the globe, however, stronger links between the city and rural villages were maintained, and the differentiation between the city and the countryside was not so stark. Using Chinese society as an example, Weber remarked that '[t]he Chinese urban dweller legally belonged to his family and native village in which the temple of his ancestors stood and to which he conscientiously maintained affiliation' (Weber 1960:81–2). Indeed in Russia, Japan, India and China, he suggested, power and administrative control remained located within rural villages rather than moving to cities. In Western capitalism, however, the city garnered a particular significance and importance. This transformation was aided by the predominant religion of Protestantism, which he argued in his influential essay, *The Protestant Ethic and the Spirit of Capitalism,* was peculiarly compatible with the rise of capitalist enterprise, promoting rationalism, a particular work ethic and the pursuit of business and profit-seeking as a social good.

Similar to Durkheim, and contrary to Marx, Weber argued that people shape and transform society through their ideas, not that their ideas are shaped by social forces largely outside their control, For Weber, then, as for Durkheim, the emergence of capitalism signalled the triumph of rationalism over superstition, sentimentality and adherence to tradition and custom (Weber 1905). Weber further argued that under Calvinism adherence to the ethical doctrine to 'love they neighbour' was replaced by the ethical imperative to use work, professional competence and money as tools to build a better society for all. Modern society, he argued demanded a belief in science and in the importance of technological change. Concomitant to this growth in rational organisation, capitalist societies were dominated by scientism, the rise of professionalism and bureaucratic organisations which could oversee and deliver progressive change as well as devise and maintain controls over emerging and disparate social groups. The rise of these autonomous and supposedly neutral organisational forms was instrumental in solidifying the transference of power and autonomy away from the local and towards the national state, justifying strong governmental controls over local populations.

During Weber's lifetime the nation-state emerged as providing a dominant means by which to maintain social order and also as engendering a further layer of collective consciousness through the development of nationalist loyalties. These developments seemingly moved the locus of human attachment away from the locally based 'community' of attachment and further to a more amorphous and generalised 'community of interest' and to an identification with, and the exercise of common purpose felt at, city, regional and national rather than local levels. Weber's work builds an understanding of the conditions under which capitalist economic relations could take root, but in doing this he suggests that progress in the West was based on the coming together of individuals for rational purposes, rather than being based on loyalties of kin, tribe and religion as they remained in the East (Turner 2014:72). Weber described the dominance of Christianity in the West as contributing to this individualisation of association in newly emerging cities within which relationships were based on contract rather than emotional affect. These societies were imbued with the 'spirit of capitalism' perceiving the pursuit of profit as a rational and progressive driving force which would improve humanity. According to Weber's analysis, traditionally-based societies held progress back and the ties of kinship – and tribal loyalties – the communities of old – were considered anachronistic and regressive: rationalism, science and technology were superior in both effect and impact.

Weber's championing of scientific rationalism and individualism diverted attention away from community, which was no longer considered the epitome of human relationships, and towards the more impersonal and legal, contractual basis upon which society would flourish in the future. Weber considered this a paradigm shift which heralded a new, modern era in which humans were liberated from the superstitions and traditions of the past, and, in this unfettered existence they could begin to find the true nature of humanity. Urban life in the modern city was thereby considered as a preferred form of living which allowed the flourishing of ideas and social experimentation. Rural life had remained basically unchanged for centuries, on a long road of gradual improvement in efficiency which allowed some improvements to social conditions but the key area of growth and wealth creation was now thought to be found in commerce and trade. In Hobsbawm's words:

> A secular, rationalist and progressive individualism dominated 'enlightened' thought. To set the individual free from the shackles which fettered him

was its chief object: from the ignorant traditionalism of the Middle Ages, which still threw their shadow across the world, from the superstition of the churches (as distinct from 'natural' or 'rational' religion), from the irrationality which divided men into a hierarchy of higher and lower ranks according to birth or some other irrelevant criterion. Liberty, equality and (it followed) the fraternity of all men were its slogans.

(1962:21)

So the move away from the country to the city, from the stifling chains of 'community' to the freedom of 'association,' was considered as breaking down the class distinctions which had riven rural life. Away from the hierarchical relationships of lord and manor and the petty distinctions and prejudices which characterised country living and stifled the individual's progress, in the city a person might re-invent him- or herself and forge more egalitarian relationships. Meritocracy replaced aristocracy – an individual (at least a male individual) could progress in life and improve his status on the basis of his talents rather than be defined by the accident of his birth. The city therefore attracted a great many people who were eager to improve their individual lot in life. Cut off from the suffocating ties and social networks established over centuries of feudalism and differentiation and of the established aristocratic systems of class domination, the new city residents could seek out others who could help them in their endeavours. The new ideology which dominated urban life proclaimed that all men [sic] were equal, whereas in truth it was the men of the 'middle-ranks of society' (Hobsbawm 1962:22) who were able to take advantage of these changes and who thereby mainly profited from the emergence of the new 'bourgeois' occupations, establishing a new layer to the social division – the middle class.

Georg Simmel

Georg Simmel, an associate of Weber, nevertheless took a different approach to the study of social life in the city. He was interested in the ways in which increasing complexity in social organisation affected people's relationship to the city and to each other. He theorised that the division of life in the city can result in different groups adopting an attitude of indifference or antipathy towards each other, almost as a protective or defensive mechanism and as a way of reducing amazingly complex societies to a level at which the individual can feel comfortable. As societies grow more complex, he argued, this complexity can heighten individual consciousness and self-interest rather than collective understandings and empathies. This does not, he argues, help societies cohere together but aids the formation of societies within society. Simmel argued that life in the metropolis, as he referred to the city, disrupts previous patterns of social relationships and is an onslaught to the senses which overstimulates the human mental capacity. This disruption requires and creates new forms of psychic adaptation – a 'mental life' which is not found in rural and small-town spaces. In his essay *The Metropolis and Mental Life* published in 1905 he explained that:

> The metropolis extracts from man as a discriminating creature a different amount of consciousness than does rural life. Here the rhythm of life and sensory mental imagery flows more slowly, more habitually, and more evenly. Precisely in this connection the sophisticated character of metropolitan psychic life becomes understandable – as over against small town life which rests upon more deeply felt and emotional relationships.
>
> (Simmel 1950:436)

Simmel is interested in understanding the effects of life within the multitude in which the sum of possible relationships is too much for one person to comprehend and to engage in. There is no possibility that the city-dweller can form personal, meaningful relationships with everyone they come into contact with. For Simmel, the metropolis is full of strangers who cannot be known but who nevertheless remain close, sharing the same physical spaces. These strangers must be guarded against, and this is done, Simmel concludes, through the development of intellectual understandings and appreciations which act as a buffer to the emotional so that the threats which the stranger in the city might present to the emotional life of the individual are rendered less psychologically damaging. The money economy and the means of economic exchange between individuals, he argues, aids the objectification of personal relationships, which can now be reduced to a simple monetary exchange of 'How much?' – placing exchange value before all other values. This is the ultimate rational calculation, reducing all reciprocal relationships to that which can be expressed as a number. The economy of the small town, Simmel went on to argue, is based more on the provision of a direct service to the customer, whereas in the money economy which predominates in the metropolis everything is reduced to the production of units which are then bought by an unknown consumer. The modern mind, he posits, becomes akin to a calculating machine, weighing the costs and benefits of contact with others, and loses the significance of personal attachments which dominated life outside the metropolis – the triumph of an 'objective' over the 'subjective' spirit. For Simmel, a fundamental contradiction in modernity is that as we are forced, or choose, to live with the many rather than the few, we exaggerate our individuality and lack of similarity and connection with others; we take on personas which adapt to anomic conditions rather than try to overcome them and assert our commonalities with others.

Sociology and community in the twentieth century

While the sociology of the dying decades of the nineteenth century sought to engage with the shift from rural to urban living and from feudal to industrial capitalism, that of the twentieth century was exercised with the rapid progression of what were becoming globally established capitalist relations of production and exchange. As R. S. Lynd and Merrell Lynd explain in one of America's most influential studies of community, *Middletown. A Study of Modern American Culture* (1929), the early twentieth century was experienced as 'one of the eras of greatest rapidity of change in the history of human institutions' (1929:5). This period of history saw fantastic technological breakthroughs, such as the development of the internal combustion engine, together with advances in mass communication which transformed social life, further disrupted established neighbourhoods and communities and widened social landscapes. At a very basic level, these technologies removed physical restraints which had limited human contact and thereby significantly broadened possible social ambits. The impact of these technologies was felt even by those who, as a consequence of poverty and limited economic resources, could only act as witness to transformations which they were not able to partake in as consumers.

The wholesale transformation of social life at the beginning of the twentieth century inspired an exploration of the impact of change which can be traced in the rise of 'community studies' which either documented actually existing communities or explored the changing nature of social life through the lens of the 'community' or 'neighbourhood'. Some of these studies were authored by residents of the community in question (see Robert Roberts, *The Classic Slum,* published in 1971 but documenting life in the 'slums' of Salford in the first quarter of the twentieth century) or approached by outsiders in the manner of social anthropologists (such as the Lynd's work cited above). These studies differed from those classic urban studies written in the last years of the nineteenth century such as Engels's description of working life and living, *The Condition of the Working Class in England,* published in 1892, or Charles Booth's study published in 1902, *Life and Labour of the People in London,* in being more sociological in nature. These studies were less concerned with the economic conditions in which people lived and more interested in the social institutions and cultures which sustained their existence. What all works did have in common, however, was a focus on the working-class neighbourhood forged in the Industrial Revolution but living in rapidly changing times. These studies looked for evidence of enduring social relations which seemed to survive in difficult times, as well as turning an eye to the ways in which the people studied must adapt to the changing social, economic and technological landscape of their times. In Chicago this interest in adaptation spawned a new type and method of sociology developed and practiced by what came to be known as the Chicago School of Sociology and whose methods and philosophies have been much imitated since.

The Chicago School – community as a function of 'human ecology'

The Chicago School was made up of a number of scholars collaborating in the first designated Department of Sociology in the world, which was founded in 1892. It is commonly viewed that the department really began to develop significant new approaches under the leadership of Robert Park (Sinclair 2009) and his collaboration with the Canadian sociologist Ernest Burgess. Together with McKenzie, Park and Burgess wrote *The City*, a foundational work which formed the basis of much of the Chicago School's research for the next twenty or so years. Park began his analysis of the city with the presumption that the city is more than its physical manifestation – that orderly and artificial construction of streets and 'blocks' which characterize so many U.S. cities – but must be recognized as a product of both the natural environment and the human environment. The city is therefore the sum of the customs, cultures and traditions which people bring to it, as much as the bricks and stones which shape its spaces. The physical and the 'moral' organization of the city, Park argued, interact and shape each other so that the built environment is an expression not only of the geography of the city – of its natural formations and attributes – but also of the nature of the people who live within it, and consequently the city cannot be easily controlled or formally planned. In an approach which he dubbed human ecology, Park advocated detailed study of the city and its neighbourhoods – its 'natural' growth (births over deaths), patterns of migration, the distribution of the population and the forces which shape this as well as the economic and social forces which shape and limit the settlement of people within the city. The School's embrace of human ecology, while focused on the social processes which make up a city, was steeped in the scientific methodologies dominating enquiry in the late nineteenth and early twentieth centuries and reflect a biological determinism fashionable at the time.

The eventual form of the city and its future evolution, Park argued, were unplanned, being the result instead of biological processes which shape the formation of any ecosystem – those of competition for resources, concentration and selection. The early Chicago sociologists were particularly interested in studying these natural processes of neighbourhood formation. Quoting a paper written by Robert Woods in 1913, Park agreed that:

> [t]he neighbourhood is a social unit which, by its clear definition of outline, its inner organic completeness, its hair-trigger reactions, may be fairly considered as functioning like a social mind.
>
> (Woods in Sennett 1969:96)

For Park then, the formation of neighbourhood, who ends up living next to whom and under what conditions, is an example of spontaneous organisation which should be studied in detail in order to understand the growth and significance of community in the city. Like Simmel, Park was also concerned with the psychological consequences of the fact that the direct, face-to-face and intimate 'primary associations' of church, school and family were replaced in the city by less personal and intimate 'secondary associations.' He saw primary association as generating sympathy and mutual identification and as providing natural forms of social control which are eroded as primary associations become substituted by more impersonal secondary associations which weaken restraints and inhibitions. As a consequence, cities experience higher rates of crime and deviance and necessitate more developed formal social control mechanisms involving legislation, courts and policing and the bureaucracies which sustain order and control. His interest also lay in understanding how informal social control was sustained at the level of neighbourhood through the changing nature of primary association in the city. For Park and his students, folk traditions and customs did not disappear in the cities but endured under changing conditions and were altered as a consequence. His interest in the shape of local neighbourhoods, the communities formed within them and also in the criminogenic qualities of city-life contributed to a heavy emphasis on studying the lives of the poor who were thrown together in rapidly expanding working-class districts. The Chicago School offered no exception to the general rule that criminology has focused primarily on the lives and crimes of the powerless.

Following Park's emphasis on the principles of competition and the natural processes by which the strongest outdo the weak, Burgess (1925) traced the city's development as a series of zones, each incorporating differing roles and population groups. The ecological principles of invasion and succession by different populations, he argued, ensure that the city is constantly in flux and that there is movement of the population across these zones. Starting from its core – the central business district – the city forms in a series of concentric circles. Surrounding the core is the 'zone of transition' – what we might also call the inner city. Here, according to Burgess, live the poorest groups in the most disorganized conditions – those who have as yet been unable to gather the resources to move into other zones but who are working to 'transit' out to a better area or those who have chosen to reject the competitive processes which shape the city and therefore stay put. Outside this circle are the more stable, working-class homes, perhaps inhabited by those who have escaped from the zone of transition but are unable to move to yet more desirable neighbourhoods. Outside of this zone is the fourth circle of 'Better Residences' of the middle and aspiring middle classes with shopping centres and leisure facilities such as bars, restaurants and cinemas to keep them entertained. Further outside lies the more suburban, commuter-belt with one eye to the city and another to the countryside – populated by the winners of the competitive process, powerful people living in desirable properties with land and space around them. Within all of these zones, natural and manufactured boundaries aid the formation of smaller, segregated communities which can place their own particular cultural stamp on an area and attract incoming residents who connect with the cultural spaces they have created. Burgess's plan became a classic model for understanding city development, which many adapted to help understand their own cities, but which others eventually dismissed as too limiting and restricted to patterns of development in the early industrializing north of America.

Louis Wirth, another sociologist trained in the Chicago School but writing from the perspective of an economically fragile 1930s America, was more concerned with the social disorganization brought about by the explosion of urban life than with the social customs and mores which brought humanity together. He used Park's approach of human ecology, which in turn leaned heavily on Darwin's theory of evolution and Malthus's writing on overpopulation, to reach particularly gloomy predictions. Wirth argued that men [sic], being basically animals, are so much shaped by their social and physical environment that the practice of urban living creates new personality types. The urban dweller, he posited, is a function of a hitherto unknown 'large, dense and permanent settlement of socially heterogeneous individuals' (Wirth 1938:190). The sheer density of settlement found in cities, Wirth argued, resulted in a reserved, indifferent and blasé character 'released from any obligations or expectations', having lost 'the capacity to relate to other people as if they were part of a community' (Massey et al 1999:44). For Wirth then, the city is a place which is fundamentally socially disorganised, but it is also a space where strangers jostle to find a place they can call home and to surround themselves with like-minded people, building communities and social networks as buffers to the difficult circumstances in which they are placed. Wirth's writing on the city was somewhat ambivalent – city-spaces offered a rationalized and secular environment free from the constraints of traditional community but in doing so created conflict and tension between the different groups competing for space and requiring new community formations to mediate relationships between disparate groups. As a consequence, the communities which make up the city offer, at one and the same time, both inclusion and exclusion. The writings of Simmel, Park and Wirth and their theoretical work on the effects of the urban environment laid the basis for much of the criminology of the mid-twentieth century, and this crucial link will be further explored in Chapter Two. It was an analysis which was largely devoid of consideration of competition between classes, assuming that the move through the different city zones was both desirable and achievable. Instead, much of its focus was on intrazonal competition for resources and social relationships and largely within the poorer districts of the city.

Beyond human ecology – the emergence of the critical lens

Park's work has been hailed as the beginning of a sociological study of community, but it was the later Chicago School of the 1950s and beyond which moved the Chicago model away from human ecology and towards a truly social understanding of community and its making. While the theory of human ecology was critiqued as early as the late 1930s, it was not replaced until much later. In the 1940s, the 'neo-orthodox ecology' of James Quinn and the 'sociocultural ecology' of Firey (see Poplin 1972:91–96 for a fuller description) took the position that economic, social and cultural organisation had also to be considered alongside the purely biotic processes described by the sociologists of Chicago. These writers downplayed the central role of competition in shaping the city however they sought to add to, rather than abandon, the model of human ecology. It took the postwar critique of scientific positivism and the introduction of a more anthropological approach to the study of community in the 1950s and 1960s to fully overturn the idea that cities and communities developed in a perfectly natural process of selection, evolution and competition to form universally recognized neighbourhood types such as the slum, the ghetto, the inner city and the suburbs. The later sociologists of the Chicago School, following the perspective of symbolic interactionism, emphasized human subjectivity, social meaning and decision making, and the need to fully understand human, social, behaviour (Sinclair 2009). The studies which emanated from this tradition highlighted significantly different aspects of community which were of interest to sociologists.

The spread of National Socialist ideologies before the outbreak of the Second World War highlighted ways in which the concept of community could be put to an exclusionary and deadly purpose. Nazi ideology sought to build the purest of national communities by denigrating and ultimately attempting to destroy those considered to lie outside its bounds (Pine 2007). It was inevitable, therefore, that after the war the idea of community would be subject to close critical scrutiny. While many early writers on community considered community as antithetical to society, by the mid-twentieth century community was instead 'defined in opposition to the state' (Delanty 2003:28). National states had proved that they could spiral into totalitarianism and total power over their population. Nisbet, in his influential publication *The Quest for Community* written in 1953 and in his subsequent work, warned of the rise of what he came to call the 'total community' through which the state and society become fused in a totalitarian purpose, harnessing the idea of a national community to achieve fundamentalist political ends. For Nisbet the grassroots communities of voluntary association should be strengthened as a buffer to the rise of the overarching state. Nisbet's arguments, Turner posits, were particularly agreeable to those of the American liberal persuasion who saw 'local, small and intimate communities as a counter-balance to the larger structures of the state and its administrative and coercive arms' (Turner 2014:69).

The first fifty years of the twentieth century had seen two global wars, significant revolutionary upheavals and in Russia, the overturning of a centuries-old dynastic monarchy, economic collapse, mass unemployment and the rise of totalitarian dictatorships. By the end of the war in 1945, two opposing political camps were settling into entrenched positions in a Cold War which was to last for another four decades. At the same time, anti-imperialist campaigns forced a redrawing of global maps as nationalist movements began to make inroads into Empire and to reclaim land from their conquerors. It was, as Hobsbawm noted, 'an age of extremes' (1994), so it is unsurprising that people turned to what they perceived as the traditional and enduring qualities of local community to deliver stability in their lives.

Community offered an alternative set of social relationships built on mutuality and respect for others which was distinctly missing from an economic system devoted to self-interest and exploitation of others – to represent the heart in an increasingly heartless world. As Delanty frames it:

> community came to be seen as the residual category of social, namely that which is left when society becomes more and more rationalized by the state and economic relations.

> (2003:29)

For yet others, the rebuilding of community was proposed as a bulwark against the rise of the modern state and the seemingly irresistible slide into mass consumer capitalism which postwar economic recovery made possible from the 1950s onwards. It offered instead a realm in which mutuality rather than profit could blossom, people might realise truly social relationships and could work together to build consensual and meaningful social organisations built on trust, respect and civility (Robson 2000).

The loss of community

The idea that in some way traditional communal relationships might have endured far into the twentieth century despite macroeconomic and other changes at a societal level led to a body of work in the midcentury which sought to explore different types of local community. Neighbourhoods from rural to urban settings in the US and Europe were subjected to close, almost anthropological scrutiny in order to uncover the patterns of social relationships which combined to form local community networks and to discover the ways in which they had adapted to pressures of urbanisation, industrialisation and bureaucratisation (Bell and Newby 1975:38–39). From this process it was hoped that new theories and understandings of social transformation in the twentieth century would be developed and that lessons could be learned concerning ways to maintain strength in community relationships. In this way, the approach of the Chicago School, that communities provide sociologists with a significant 'social laboratory,' had certainly not been abandoned, yet these works were more influenced by a cultural sociology than the previous positivist perspective provided by human ecology. So these were studies which sought to uncover the social processes whereby people constructed their identities, beliefs and value systems and were able to make sense of a rapidly changing world, yet still find shared understandings and live in close proximity to others.

Maurice Stein, writing in 1964 in *The Eclipse of Community*, suggested that these postwar community studies showed that the primary ties of family and community were weakening fast in the face of structural forces which were pulling local neighbourhoods apart. Central authority, he argued, was taking precedence over local power structures, families were disintegrating as local employment opportunities disappeared, people had to leave their familial neighbourhoods to find work and local social ties similarly withered. As a consequence, by the end of the 1960s Margaret Stacey called for abandoning the term 'community' altogether, arguing that the term 'local social system' should replace this outdated concept that had outlived its usefulness in modern social conditions. Understanding the replacement of community by various local social structures, she argued, would allow the researcher to see the complex network of ties which are active within the locality but also those which are present between the local area and national structures of power. For these writers, the local area was increasingly oriented to extra-local systems – for example, in employment, business interests, political associations and cultural attachments, so that meaningful social relationships were often to be found outside of the geographical boundaries of residence. Furthermore, the complex and changing nature of local social relations was shown to involve intersecting elements of both tradition and modernity, and the rural/urban divide which exercised the early writers on community was said to have all but disappeared (Bell and Newby 1975:51). This was confirmed by the work of Bensman and Vidich (1958) which became a classic of community studies, *Small Town in a Mass Society: Class, Power and Religion in a Rural Community,* in which the authors concluded that any particularities of local ways of life and value systems which the residents of the small town of Springdale felt as being still central to their lives had long been replaced by the more generally held values and behaviours found in urbanised, mass society.

The theme of the 'loss of community' was particularly apparent in the 1970s, and many, harking back once again to the early Chicago School studies, saw this loss as leading to the creation of socially disorganised and problematic neighbourhoods akin to those discovered by Burgess in the 'zone of transition'. Such areas were considered ripe for criminality, if not a causal factor in the rising crime rates which had been recorded in many industrialised countries since the 1960s (see Chapter Two for a full discussion of this perceived link between crime and loss of community). In addition the loss of community was linked to an array of social problems – the loss of local employment, the decline of businesses, the numbers of older people turning to the state for help in the absence of familial support and a growing feeling of isolation and alienation in the city. As a consequence, urban planners charged with postwar urban renewal, were criticised for having created a multitude of soulless landscapes which had destroyed local social structures in their haste to achieve the clearance of the physical slums which were thought to blight the lives of the poorly housed. The theme of rebuilding community was raised as a serious solution to urban blight, a subject that is further explored in Chapter Four.

The rediscovery of community

At the same time as the academy was abandoning the idea of community, it was being rediscovered at the grassroots, political level. The call to rebuild community came from a number of quarters. First, a growing number of theorists began to consider community as a site from which to analyse the possibility of change – giving members of residential communities an agency which had been lacking in community studies that had previously concentrated on description. Poplin outlines the perspective of these 'community action theorists' who focused on the study of 'local residents as they attempt to solve the problems which inevitably arise when man [sic] lives in proximity to his fellow man' (1972:180). Through this exercise, these activists hoped to uncover the extent to which individuals in a residential locality were able and willing to work communally to solve shared social problems and the forms which such action could take. Their work fed into the study and practice of 'community development' which sought to actively engage residents in improving economic and social conditions and in helping to plan services locally (Mayo 1975). While as Robson (2000) demonstrates, community development was initially envisaged as a tool to give back some form of democratic control to populations living in formerly colonised countries, it was adapted to fit the circumstances of deprived urban areas in the West which, it was felt, had similarly suffered from an over-wieldy state interfering in day-to-day lives and entrenching inequalities of power locally and nationally. Some proponents of community development had also been inspired by the radical social movements of the 1960s, which had seen an upsurge in grassroots organisation against state repression and discrimination across the globe. Community development was designed to empower communities by building residents' associations, pressure groups and voluntary services embedded in the local area and familiar with local problems which would become part of the planning process to deliver change. How successful or otherwise these practices proved to be is explored in Chapter Four.

Neo-liberalism, exclusion and community

The latter part of the twentieth century – dubbed late modernity – was greatly affected by a disintegration in social conditions which has continued and heightened in the first part of the twenty-first. Inequalities in income and opportunity became more apparent as social mobility stalled and then reversed. This period involved, as Jock Young has outlined, a 'cultural revolution of individualism and the economic crisis and restructuring of the labour markets of the advanced industrial world' (1999:6), which he argued represented a fundamental shift from an inclusive society to an exclusive society. The former is informed by the principle of the social contract and offers a state dedicated to the welfare of its citizens as long as they offer it a degree of loyalty and conformity to shared ideals. The exclusive society, however, downplays the role of the state and replaces it with the organising principle of market forces and fierce competition whereby the weak go to the wall. This fundamental shift in economic and social conditions has been significantly destabilising to the psychological as well as the economic well-being of those who have experienced these changes. Life is full of risks and precarious in all its elements, and there is little stability with which to anchor one's life (Beck 1992). Under such circumstances, the search for some kind of anchor has stimulated a desire amongst some to find a place of belonging and security – perhaps symbolically, if not in reality – and the idea of community has taken on added significance. Bauman (2001) has argued that throughout the twentieth century society continually searched for and turned to community because people were yearning for something that modernity had apparently destroyed. It is almost irrelevant that the social cohesion and together- ness offered by the turn to community may have never existed in the first place. It is enough that the chimera exists, that people feel that we do not have this cohesion in the present and that it appears to be a state to which we aspire. Cohen (1985) outlined the mechanisms by which people seek and imagine belonging, construct- ing sub-cultural forms of community which may lie outside traditional place-based structures. These communities appeared particularly appropriate to the conditions of late modernity, based as they were around individuals seeking new forms of attachment in an increasingly fractured social world. Famously, Benedict Anderson in *Imagined Communities* (1983) outlined the nature of many of these communities, the reality of their social construction and the key part they played in maintaining difference, boundaries and inclusivity through ideas of nationality and belonging.

The last decade of the twentieth century saw another, more conservative, use of community emerge. Developed by writers such as Amitai Etzioni (1995), the phi- losophy of communitarianism suggested that the neo-liberal turn of the 1980s had pushed a culture of excessive individualism in opposition to collective responsibility, and in their eyes the balance between individual rights and collective responsibil- ity had to be restored. Not comfortable either with the state as the sole arbiter of morality and social control, communitarians advised that community could func- tion as an effective mediator between the individual and the state and that com- munity could serve as a tool to promote social order and control. This perspective led to state attempts to engage and indeed engineer 'successful' communities which would play a significant role in social policy and governance. Somewhat paradoxi- cally, the engineers of economic and social change which had been so instrumental in claiming the benefits of individualism embraced communitarianism and pro- posed a rebuilding of community relations in order to combat some of the worst excesses of the recent past, using shared norms and values to rebuild shattered com- munities characterised by fear, inaction and lack of political participation. Then, in 2000, the American political scientist Robert Putnam added to this debate with the publication of *Bowling Alone,* a work which was to be hugely influential in the debate on the nature of community in late modernity. Putnam argued that informal voluntary and civic association had declined dramatically in the US and that the bonds of community had similarly withered. He called for a rebuilding of 'social capital' – those networks and ties which ensure that individuals can forge meaningful relationships with others to ensure a healthy civic and community life.

Putnam's work gained popularity outside the narrow confines of academia. It was used extensively in policy and practice, even informing the approach of the World Bank in global economic development strategies. The relevance of communitarian philosophies and the role they played in debates around the problem of crime will be further explored in later chapters.

Community-building in virtual spaces

Outside of governmental discourses, new expressions and forms of community emerged at the turn of the century. Writers such as Barry Wellman (1999), Claude Fischer (1982) and Manuel Castells (2012, 2001, 1996) considered the impact of computer-mediated communication on the formation of community. They posited that, with the rise of the Internet and with the ubiquity of information and communication technology in the advanced economies, people would no longer build their meaning in local societies but had already begun to develop new forms of networks unconnected to physical space. Rheingold in his 2000 work, *The Virtual Community*, was one of the first writers to detail their rise, and his ideas inspired much speculation on the futures of community in electronic spaces (Evans 2004). Communities which are liberated from place, it was argued are 'purer' than those built on land, based fully upon active choices rather then chance encounters, stretching globally rather than remaining parochial and bounded. Wellman (1999) saw these more 'personal' global communities as safe, free of discrimination and as both sociable and informative spaces which are likely to grow in popularity and may take prominence over the disorderly and frightening urban spaces in which community was forged in the twentieth century. Castells has gone further in claiming that sociability in complex societies has been transformed and that networks, which can be experienced at the global, regional or local level, have substituted for spatial communities as major forms of sociability. His position holds that although place-based sociability and territorially defined community have not disappeared, they now play a minor role in structuring social relationships for the majority of the population in developed societies.

In this conception of community, residence is only marginally important in the construction of friendships and social groups, and we choose instead to spend more time with people whom we have identified as sharing common interests rather than merely common spaces. The transformation of Western societies from predominantly rural to urban began this process, and increasing global networks, migrations and widening frontiers of experience have strengthened it in recent decades. As people migrate across the globe in increasing numbers, a need has arisen for transnational networks which connect emerging diasporas. The domestication of the Internet has meant that it has become possible to maintain important interpersonal relationships over great distances for all with access to a networked computer. Enhanced communication devices have been perceived as breaking down any remaining barriers of space and time which have hitherto hindered communication across the globe. Castells has argued that the Internet is the most appropriate medium of communication in a global network society and that it will play an increasingly important role, not only in the way that people choose to communicate with each other but also in the ways they form significant social relationships.

Some concluding comments and questions

This chapter has recorded the different ways in which 'community' has been perceived in various historical periods. It reveals the enduring interest in community which has exercised philosophers, academics, policy-makers, politicians and the public more widely for more than a century. The concept of community has retained a power and significance despite whole-scale economic, social and political upheaval. At times and under certain social conditions, community has been rejected as an organising force within society, but it has been returned to repeatedly and held up as a social good which must be preserved or rebuilt.

1. What is the significance of community to life in the twenty-first century? Does it play a 'social-ordering' role in your own life, and if so in what ways?
2. Consider the different arguments which have been put forward to claim 'community' as a progressive or anti-progressive force in society. Where do you stand in this argument and why?

Further reading

The literature on community is vast, and it could take an entire career to fully understand it. While there is no substitute for reading the key contributors to this subject in their own words, their views have been usefully summarised by various authors. Bell and Newby's *Community Studies. An Introduction to the Sociology of the Local Community* (1975) is a classic text which covers much of the key contributors of the first half of the twentieth century and in some detail, but it is somewhat dated now, whereas Crow and Allen's *Community Life. An Introduction to Local Social Relations* (1994) has brought the discussion further up-to-date.

For a more applied consideration of community, Somerville's *Understanding Community. Politics, Policy and Practice* (2011) is a very useful book, although focused on the British experience. Robson's *The State and Community Action* (2000) takes a more international perspective, blending critical theories and their application to explore and understand radical conceptions of community and community activism. For a more theoretically informed discussion of the significance of community at the beginning of the twenty-first century, it would be useful to read Bauman's *Community: Seeking Safety in an Insecure World* (2001).

References

Anderson, B. (2006) *Imagined Communities: Reflections on the Origin and Spread of Nationalism* London; Verso.

Aristotle (2012) *Politics. Translated by Benjamin Jowett* The University of Adelaide http://ebooks.adelaide.edu.au/a/a8po/index.html [Accessed 01.01.14].

Bate, J. (2003) *John Clare: A Biography* London: Picador.

Bauman, Z. (2001) *Community: Seeking Safety in an Insecure World* Cambridge Polity Press.

Beck, U. (1992) *The Risk Society: Towards a New Modernity* London: Sage.

Bell, C., and Newby, H. (1975) *Community Studies. An Introduction to the Sociology of the Local Community* London: George, Allen and Unwin Ltd.

Bensman, A. J., and Vidich, J. (1958) *Small Town in a Mass Society: Class, Power and Religion in a Rural Community* Princeton, NJ: Princeton University Press.

Booth, C. (1902) *Life and Labour of the People of London* http://www.stgite.org.uk/booth1902.html [Accessed 15.02.14].

Braeman, J. (2013) 'Ferdinand Julius Tönnies' *Salem Press Biographical Encyclopedia*, January 2013.

Burgess, E. W. (1925) 'The Growth of the City' in Park, R. E., Burgess, E. W., and McKenzie, R. D. *The City* Chicago: University of Chicago Press.

Castells, M. (1996) *The Network Society* Oxford, UK: Blackwell Publishers.

Castells, M. (2001) *The Internet Galaxy. Reflections on the Internet, Business and Society* Oxford, UK: Oxford University Press.

Castells, M. (2012) *Networks of Outrage and Hope: Social Movements in the Internet Age* Cambridge: Polity Press

Cohen, A. (1985) *The Symbolic Construction of Community* London: Routledge.

Crow, G., and Allen, G. (1994) *Community Life. An Introduction to Local Social Relations* Hemel Hempstead, UK: Harvester Wheatsheaf.

Delanty, G. (2003) *Community* London: Routledge.

Durkheim, E. (1933) *The Division of Labour in Society* Toronto: Macmillan.

Elias, N. (1974) 'Foreword – Towards a Theory of Communities' in Bell, C., and Newby, H. (eds), *The Sociology of Community: A Selection of Readings* London: Frank Cass.

Engels, F. (1884) *The Origin of the Family, Private Property and the State* https://www.marxists.org/archive/marx/works/1884 [Accessed 14.01.14].

Engels, F. (1987) *The Condition of the Working Class in England* London: Penguin.

Etzioni, A. (1993) *The Spirit of Community: Rights, Responsibilities and the Communitarian Agenda* New York: Crown Publishers.

Evans, K. F. (2004) *Maintaining Community in the Information Age. The Importance of Trust, Place and Situated Knowledge* Basingstoke, UK: Palgrave MacMillan.

Firey, W. (1945) 'Sentiment and Symbolism as Ecological Variables' *American Sociological Review* 10 pp. 140–48.

Fischer, C. (1982) *To Dwell Among Friends* Chicago: Chicago University Press.

The Guardian (2014) 'What Future Urban Living?' *Guardian Online* [Accessed 21.02.14].

Hobsbawm, E. J. (1962) *The Age of Revolution: 1789–1848* London: Weidenfield and Nicholson.

Hobsbawm, E. J. (1975) *The Age of Capital: 1848–1875* London: Weidenfield and Nicholson.

Hobsbawm, E. J. (1994) *The Age of Extremes: 1914–1991* London: Weidenfield and Nicholson.

Hoggett, P. (ed) (1997) *Contested Communities. Experiences, Struggles, Policies* Bristol, UK: Policy Press.

Konig, R. (1968) *The Community* London: Routledge and Kegan Paul.

Lynd, R. S., and Merrell Lynd, H. (1929) *Middletown. A Study in Modern American Culture* New York: Harvester Books.

Massey, D., Allen, J., and Pile, S. (eds) (1999) *City Worlds* London: Routledge.

Mayo, M. (1975) 'Community Development. A Radical Alternative' in Bailey, R., and Brake, M. (eds), *Radical Social Work* London: Arnold.

Nisbet, R. (1953) *The Quest for Community* Oxford, UK: Oxford University Press.

Park, R. E., Burgess, E. W., and McKenzie, R. D. (1925) *The City* Chicago: University of Chicago Press.

Pine, L. (2007) *Hitler's "National Community": Society and Culture in Nazi Germany* New York: Bloomsbury.

Platt, H. L. (2005) *Shock Cities. The Environmental Transformation and Reform of Manchester and Chicago* Chicago: University of Chicago Press.

Poplin, D. E. (1972) *Communities: A Survey of Theories and Methods of Research* New York: Macmillan.

Putnam. R. D. (2000) *Bowlingalone: The Collapse and Revival of American Community* New York; Simon & Schuster.

Quinn, J. A. (1950) *Human Ecology* New York: Prentice-Hall.

Rheingold, H. (2000) *The Virtual Community: Homesteading on the Electronic Frontier* Cambridge, MA: MIT Press.

Roberts, R. (1971) *The Classic Slum. Salford Life in the First Quarter of the Twentieth Century* London: Pelican Books.

Robson, T. (2000) *The State and Community Action* London: Pluto Press.

Saunders, P. (1981) *Social Theory and the Urban Question* London: Unwin Hyman Ltd.

Sennett, R. (ed) (1969) *Classic Essays on the Culture of Cities* Appleton: Century Crofts.

Sharpe, J. (2001) 'Crime, Order and Historical Change' in Muncie, J., and McLaughlin, E. (eds), *The Problem of Crime* London: Sage.

Simmel, G. (1950) 'The Metropolis and Mental Life' in Wolff, K. (ed), *The Sociology of Georg Simmel* New York: Free Press.

Sinclair, N. (2009) 'Chicago School of Sociology', *Research Starters Sociology* Chicago: Great Neck Publishing.

Stein, M. (1964) *The Eclipse of Community* New York: Harper Row.

Somerville, P. (2011) *Understanding Community. Politics, Policy and Practice* Bristol, UK: Policy Press.

Tonnies, F. (2001 [1887]) *Gemeinschaft und Gessellschaft (Community and Civil Society)* New York: Cambridge University Press.

Turner, B. S (2014) 'Robert Nisbet and the Problem of Community' *American Sociologist* 45 pp. 68–83.

Weber, M. (2002) [1905] *The Protestant Ethic and the Spirit of Capitalism* Oxford, UK: Blackwell.

Weber, M. (1960) *The City* London: Heinemann.

Wellman, B. (1999) *Networks in the Global Village* Boulder, CO: Westview.

Wirth, L. (1938) 'Urbanism as a Way of Life' *American Journal of Sociology* 44(1) pp. 1–24.

Young, J. (1999) *The Exclusive Society* London: Sage.

2

COMMUNITY AND CRIME

John Lea argues in *Crime and Modernity* crime that the control of crime is performed against the background of a complex set of social relations involving what he has described as the square of crime:

> … a system of interaction between four participants; the state and the criminal justice agencies, offenders, victims, and the various publics and communities involved in the control of various types of crime.
>
> (2002:14)

This complex consideration of crime and its prevention, however, were not always recognised, and one or other of these four elements have been considered as key to understanding crime at different periods of time. 'Community' was the first system involved in the control of crime. This chapter charts the stripping out of community from crime control within early modernity and its re-emergence as a key tool in the crime prevention armoury in the last quarter of the twentieth century.

From community regulation to state enforcement

Before the emergence of the modern state in the eighteenth century, the small towns and villages in which the majority of the population resided were, in effect, 'self-policing communities' (Sharpe 2001:110) bound by common law which was modified locally to fit the particular customs, traditional practices and local understanding of what constituted an infraction of social mores. Sharpe relates that while more serious crimes such as murder, burglary and rape were dealt with by royally appointed judges, the trials of petty offenders were heard in manorial or church courts or before justices of the peace. These courts were involved in much activity which does not trouble criminal courts today, such as the reading and settling of wills, upholding the laws of the church and policing sexual relationships. During this period, there was no professional police force in existence, so it fell to members of the local community to bring any offences and possible offenders to the attention of the local enforcers of the law. With the gradual growth in significance of the central state, however, the community's role in setting moral boundaries and in the regulation of social behaviour diminished as a national criminal justice and prison system emerged (Sharpe 2001:142). This was further achieved with the introduction of a professional, paid police force beginning in the UK with the Metropolitan Police in 1829, although intelligence from the local community remains a significant source of information for the police today (this is further discussed in Chapter Seven).

The formation of modern forms of crime control could be said to have stripped out any role for the community. As Lea writes: '[t]he social foundation of modern crime control is that various types of conflicts have been handed over to the state to sort out' (2002:14). However, this does not mean that the general population has had no part to play at all in the design and practice of modern criminal justice systems. As Lea later goes on to explain, actors within the criminal justice system must deal with crime and dispense justice in ways which are broadly acceptable to the general population of any country if the state and their systems are to have any credibility and legitimacy. A democratic state can only govern if it carries out the will of the people, and 'the categories of criminal law deployed by the state must bear sufficient correspondence to popular conceptions of guilt, justice and harm' (Lea 2002:14) or it risks losing the support of the general population and their trust in the rule of law. The views of 'the general public', while formally absent from modern systems of criminal justice, therefore still could be said to play a significant role. To what extent and in what manner the public plays a role in the control of crime is dependent on complex relations of power, control and governance in particular nations and regions of the world.

The modernisation of crime control in the UK took place at a time when there was increasing concern over the problem of crime as the numbers committed for trial in England and Wales increased four-fold in fifteen years, from 5,000 committals in 1815 to 20,000 by 1830 (Sharpe 2001:142–43). The concept of a 'criminal' or 'dangerous class, Sharpe argues, gained ascendancy during this period. The social changes brought about as a result of rapid industrialisation, urbanisation and the loss of traditional class structures and social controls (discussed in Chapter One) only served to reinforce this perspective. Early industrialisation brought with it social upheaval, resentment, resistance and revolutionary ferment in the emerging working classes across the developing world. Unsurprisingly an increase in numbers brought before the courts can be linked to these disruptions in social life.

Premodern perspectives on crime were based around religious teachings and, in the Christian world on the concept of sin, and it was the responsibility of the entire community to uphold the strictures of commonly-held religious teachings. It was therefore perceived as normal that there was a community response to infractions of the law. Indeed, community responses were encouraged as a way of maintaining local order – hence the public nature of much punishment where the offender was held up to public ridicule and condemnation. Crime was considered a result of the moral weakness of the individual, reflecting possession by evil spirits or a rejection of God and religion, and punishments were designed accordingly. More secular approaches to crime and punishment were developed throughout the eighteenth and nineteenth centuries as the institutions of government and state took on added significance and the power of religion began to wane. Whilst secular approaches became gradually embedded in everyday life, the rational and measured approach to crime championed by the Enlightenment philosophers of the period such as Beccaria (1738–1779) and Bentham (1748–1832) also began to rise to the ascendancy. Even so elements of pre-Enlightenment, premodern crime control measures were not replaced overnight and co-existed for some time after 'modern' measures of trial and punishment were introduced. The impact of religion and shared morality similarly remained a significant pressure in shaping both public opinion and legislation, and arguably they still play a significant role today in our understanding and practice of the law and criminal justice. What the centralising role of the state in defining law and setting acceptable levels of punishment did remove, however, was any local discretion in the definition of crime and punishment. To all intents and purposes then, the community no longer played a role in setting national systems of criminal justice, but it continued to act as a witness to the practice of the law and execution. While punishment (including execution) is largely carried out in private in modernised systems of criminal justice, public galleries are still widely available in court rooms.

Maintaining the offender at the centre of crime control

What the traditional and more 'modern' understandings of crime had in common was their focus on the offender as the problem of crime and its control. The weak-minded or evil individual was seen as the source and problem of criminality in premodern periods, and this focus on the individual was maintained by Enlightenment thinkers. For Enlightenment philosophers, however, criminality was a product of personal agency, rationality and the poor choices made by an individual which led to their decision to commit crime. The choice to break the law was considered as motivated by individual self-interest and a rational calculation on behalf of the individual, weighing up the possible costs and benefits of the breaking of the law, and the decision that their interests could be best served by following the particular course of action they had freely chosen. Crime was to be deterred by a system of punishments 'fitted' to the crime in their level of severity and the individual's loss of freedoms. As a consequence, the control and punishment of crime focused on the individual who had to be persuaded against breaking the law and re-educated should he or she commit crime, and it was through the treatment of individuals that crime was to be controlled. Under these formulations of criminality, the community had to be protected from the offender by their temporary removal to prison or in some cases permanent sanctions (through life sentences, execution or deportation). Criminals were considered to be acting outside of community mores; therefore punishment was designed to isolate offenders from their neighbourhood and family and to leave the law-abiding majority untainted by their presence.

During the nineteenth century, a paradigm shift in intellectual development saw scientific studies and endeavour soon applied to aid an understanding of society. Comte's 'social physics', considered the foundational work of sociology, encouraged the use of scientific analysis to understand the social world. The positivist perspective which Comte pioneered was put to use to promote an understanding of the criminal individual. The categorisation of the offender as 'a criminal type' was based on the discovery of physical or psychological pathology in the individual, which further distinguished the offender from the wider 'normal' community. The control of criminality was firmly located in the control of the pathological individual, the breeding out of defective genes or finding a way to heal sick individuals and so reduce their propensity to criminality. In this period, the offenders and their criminal traits were catalogued and categorised, leading to stereotypical views of the criminal as uncivilised and brutish. The responsibility for detecting, treating and rehabilitating such 'types' lay with the educated professional in particular cases and the state system of criminal justice more generally. Professionalization of systems of policing, crime detection and criminal justice were entrenched during this period and have been maintained ever since, as have the ideas that the state is responsible for defining crime, running a criminal justice system, providing punishment and rehabilitation opportunities for offenders and generally responding to concerns about the extent of crime nationally.

Crime as a social phenomenon

The focus on the individual offender as the problem to be 'solved' in controlling crime persisted into the early twentieth century. However, the Chicago School of sociologists, as outlined in Chapter One, did much to re-shape research and writing on the problem of crime, shifting the focus away from the individual towards the social environment. Although the Chicago sociologists were not the first to link crime and place, Park's framework of 'human ecology' set the benchmark for further study of crime and criminality, which was not based in the individual pathology of offenders but in the social circumstances in which they were found. For the Chicago sociologists, crime was a function of *social disorganisation* created by the rapid development of the city. The neighbourhoods where crime was concentrated were characterised, according to the Chicago researchers, by an eclectic mix of social groups formed of recent migrants to the city and a rapid population turnover.

In such neighbourhoods, they argued, the heterogeneity of populations and their transitory nature undermined the neighbourhood's ability to develop and enforce the basic social controls necessary to provide an environment relatively free from crime. Their work paved the way for an understanding of crime as a social phenomenon rather than the aggregation of the decisions of numerous individuals. It was followed by a host of theories which sought to understand the social circumstances in which crime takes place. Criminal behaviour was seen as a function of the pressure of larger social forces, of 'faulty social conditions' (Tierney 2010:102) which must be addressed if rates of crime were to fall.

In the 1940s, Clifford Shaw and Henry McKay introduced the idea of 'cultural transmission' to explain their theory that in certain areas crime becomes a normalised response to certain social conditions. According to Shaw and McKay's (1942) research, in high-crime areas the community did not function as a tool of order maintenance but instead transmitted transgressive behavioural patterns to its youth. Shaw and McKay demonstrated that juvenile delinquency was spatially patterned and that numbers of young offenders and their rate of offending decreased as distance from the city centre (and the 'zone of transition' [Burgess 1925]) increased. In suburbia and the outer reaches of the city they found rates of crime to be considerably lower. They argued that criminal activity can become an established and for some an accepted behaviour and way of life in socially disorganised neighbourhoods as young people become socialised into criminal cultures. For these early Chicago theorists then, the problem was not so much the existence of a pathological 'dangerous class' as dangerous areas which were a problem to surrounding, presumably law-abiding neighbourhoods, and so the idea of the pathological or 'problem' area was born.

Later theorists influenced by the early Chicago School distanced themselves from the idea of the socially disorganised 'problem neighbourhood.' Edwin Sutherland, for example, argued that the actions of the individuals categorised as criminal were not very different from those of any other type of behaviour seen as 'normal'. Sutherland was just as interested in the criminality of the professional, business classes, and he argued, in contrast to Shaw and McKay, that 'crime is in fact not closely correlated with poverty or with the psychopathic or sociopathic conditions associated with poverty' (Sutherland 1939 in Vold 1951:7) and that the sociologist must look elsewhere for an explanation of law-breaking behaviour. Sutherland did agree that criminality was learned from others – not just the techniques of how to commit crime but also the values which underlay the decision to do so. His theory of differential association mapped out the ways in which cultures and values which led to criminality might become normal and accepted in any setting. The early Chicago sociologists were misled in their analysis, he argued, by their focus on officially recorded crime which recorded the crime of the poor and marginalised, not of the powerful and high-status individuals. Despite Sutherland's insights into the problem of white-collar crime the focus on the troubled and troublesome worlds of the blue-collar working class continued to serve as a focus for the attention of mainstream criminology.

The 1940s and 1950s saw the development of a steady stream of influential theories which described the possible social faults leading to criminality, many of which emanated from the US. Merton's strain theory and his development of the concept of anomie suggested that there was a mismatch between the opportunities available to individuals and the goals which society held up as achievable to anyone who worked hard enough to attain them. Strain theory was further developed by Albert Cohen in his work *Delinquent Boys* (1955) and Cloward and Ohlin in their 1960 work *Delinquency and Opportunity*. Sykes and Matza (1957) contributed a further critique, demonstrating that the use of labels such as 'delinquent' and 'criminal' to describe those who had come into conflict with the law and systems of criminal justice, falsely suggested that these were especially troublesome and dangerous people who inhabited a totally different world with different values. Sykes and Matza demonstrated that many people so labelled led perfectly moral and 'normal' lives not dissimilar from those of the 'law-abiding'. Indeed, their work on techniques of neutralisation suggested that people can simultaneously hold mainstream values while engaging in actions from time to time which appear to go against their stated moral codes. In the UK in the 1950s and 1960s, this US-dominated work was translated into what became a British take on subcultural theory, especially in the hands of academics working from the Birmingham School of Contemporary Cultural Studies. The 'cultural turn' in sociology was reflected in work which held up to scrutiny the construction of crime in the media, the significance of youth sub-cultures, the racialization of the problem of crime and its masculinity.

The sociological emphasis which was placed on criminology at this time and which stressed the social conditions which were seen to contribute to criminality did have a significant impact on the ways in which law-breakers were perceived and the ways in which they could subsequently be treated. Henceforth crime and the criminal could be seen as a product of an imperfect society which needed to reform itself if there was to be any chance of solving the problem of crime. The negative consequences for the individual of being labelled a 'criminal' or a 'delinquent' were also much debated and discussed. The harsh vocabulary associated with the punishment and treatment of the individual criminal gave way to a more forgiving and empathetic lexicon associated with the offender or the law-breaker. The idea that offenders might also be victims of unequal social conditions, of lack of opportunities to thrive, of being labelled as a problem, discriminated against and over-regulated or simply being misunderstood by a system dominated by a different set of values and by criminal justice professionals who had had very different choices and chances in life, allowed more caring and welfare-oriented attitudes towards individuals involved in crime to surface. As Tierney (2010:189) has argued, this period was one in which deviance was politicised and in which more radical critiques emerged which questioned the whole concept of 'the criminal' and the basis of the legal system which criminalised so many people and their actions. In policy terms, perceiving crime as a social rather than an individual phenomenon generated a more liberal take on the problem of crime and helped to foster a "correctionalist penal-welfare" (Garland 1994 in Hughes 1998:43) stance committed to offering support to those in need of help to quit a lifestyle which was damaging to themselves and to others.

The irresistible rise of the 'problem' of crime

While academics and policy-makers were debating the causes of crime and criminality and proposing new solutions based on 'a fully social' understanding of crime (Taylor, Walton and Young 1973), recorded rates of crime began to steadily and then rapidly increase in many parts of the developed world. This increase in the recorded rate of crime was initially observed in the US and then, around a decade later, across the UK. A growing backlash against those welfare-based approaches which had begun to impact on practice within the criminal justice system was unleashed in the US as early as the beginning of the 1970s. Research based in the US conducted by Martinson (1974) claimed that there was little evidence to demonstrate the efficacy of treatment-based practice. The welfare model of criminal justice was attacked as fundamentally flawed, and Martinson famously concluded that all previous interventions demonstrated that in reality 'nothing works' in the prevention of crime. A totally different approach to the problem of crime emerged from a distinctly different social arena. As Hughes (2003:61) observes, the US in the late 1960s witnessed a 'growing, increasingly vociferous and influential conservative and neo-liberal critique' of welfare-based approaches to social problems. They called for a return to more discipline and control of social groups considered as problematic. Under conditions of increasing crime rates and a growing fear of victimisation, the return to a fundamentally conservative approach to crime gradually gained ascendancy. The welfare approached was replaced by one which was based in a more economistic view of the world in which individuals would be tasked with the responsibility of protecting themselves against a rising tide of crime and the market would furnish them with the means by which to do so. Situational crime prevention was born.

Situational crime prevention

Alongside the return to a harsher environment of social control, the conservative approach to the control of crime turned to the task of finding a technical fix to the problem of crime, abandoning the liberal view that crime should be tackled as a social problem. The situational theory espoused by the conservatives was not concerned with crime causation but instead focused on reducing the opportunities for crime to be committed. Situational crime prevention sought to alter the environment (or situation) in which crime might take place in order to deter potential offenders away from their possible targets. Ron Clarke (1980), a British academic who championed this approach, grouped the measures available within situational crime prevention as measures which either:

1. increase the effort of committing a crime
2. increase the likelihood of a crime being detected
3. reduce the available rewards

The tools in its armoury are many and varied from burglar alarms, CCTV, security fencing, locks, screening and tracking devices, employing security personnel but also the redesign of buildings and estates to increase natural surveillance of properties to deter offenders away from their chosen 'target'. Together these are known as 'target-hardening' measures. Today adopting these technical solutions to the problem of crime is considered just 'common sense', but this view demonstrates how powerful the 'industry' which has been built around situational crime prevention has become. As O'Malley (1992) has demonstrated, it has become a 'normal' and taken-for-granted practice to surround oneself with the paraphernalia of the security industry, and this practice is largely viewed as unproblematic. Thus, the theory which lies behind target-hardening measures is rarely considered. It is towards a consideration of these aspects of situational crime prevention that we now turn.

Situational crime prevention – some problems and principles

Misunderstanding motivation: Situational crime prevention measures are based on a particular understanding of what motivates a person to break the law – the theory of rational choice. This theory harks back to the classical school of criminology which paints the individual as *homo economicus*, a rational actor who weighs the costs and benefits of all possible actions before deciding on which course to follow (O'Malley 1992). This perspective reflects a utilitarian understanding of human nature which flourished at the dawn of capitalism and which has been used to justify continued reliance on an economic system which is based on the pursuit of individual profit and suggests humanity is motivated by selfish desires. The idea of the individual, rational actor represents an inherently conservative ideological viewpoint which has been challenged from many liberal and radical viewpoints. It has been suggested instead that committing a crime can be an act motivated by emotion, political sensibility or desire for excitement and that it can also be a collective, social endeavour. The techniques of situational crime prevention will have little effect if crime is not motivated by a rationally calculating individual.

Limited focus: The tools of target-hardening were first developed with the very specific focus of protecting property. When they are adopted for personal protection, for example, employing security guards or round-the-clock monitoring of CCTV, they become quite expensive to maintain and lose their force as cost-effective techniques. Situational crime prevention measures therefore tend to be utilised for particular types of crimes which are easily recognised and inexpensively resolved, but they leave more complex crimes untouched and unmonitored.

Limited effect: Although many proponents of situational crime prevention techniques have recourse to literature which demonstrates their effectiveness in particular situations, the almost universal adoption of target-hardening has taken place over a period in which crime continued to rise and seemingly uncontrollably, but this is rarely mentioned. It has been suggested that target-hardening merely 'displaces crime' on to another less well-protected target (Crawford 1998). Despite the countless millions spent by individuals, businesses and public-sector organisations in protecting their chosen targets, this has left many people, places and situations unprotected and vulnerable.

A pessimist's view?: The situational approach to crime prevention has discarded the notion that the social world could be improved so that people could be turned away from criminality altogether. This is an inherently pessimistic lens from which to view the problem of crime, but it has nevertheless gained support because of its practical applicability. Target-hardening measures have nevertheless been eagerly adopted by governments keen to be seen to be doing something about the problem of crime. These measures are often insisted upon by insurance companies, and they have been embraced by individuals who can feel reassured by the protection they are seen to afford them.

A technique of responsibilisation: Situational crime prevention measures are particularly apt in a period which has seen the rise of conservative and anti-welfare forces. As David Garland reveals in *The Culture of Control* (2001), neo-liberal philosophies have sought to minimise the role of the state in providing public services. Instead, government withdraws into the indirect role of enabler, encouraging the private-sector, third-sector organisations and individuals to take responsibility for themselves. In the realm of crime prevention, rather than provide the measures itself, the state plays a part in promoting the ideology of self-help and educating people in what they must do in order to ensure their own safety and security. In this respect, communities can have a role to play as the site in which locally appropriate situational crime prevention measures are selected and put into place. If the costs can be borne by individuals, communities and organisations rather than the state, then this is considered preferable and a sign of community and citizen engagement. Where the state steps in to fund such measures, this is likely to be completed as a one-off grant of funds with the assumption that responsibility for the ultimate effectiveness of the measures and their ongoing care, monitoring and maintenance remains firmly with interested parties within the locality.

A constant reminder of the need for vigilance: As target-hardening measures are designed to deter the potential offender, they will be most effective when they can be clearly seen. As a result, our landscapes are now cluttered with signs of potential disorder averted – gates, high fences and locks are all barriers which impede progress through public spaces. In our private domain, we are reminded daily of the problem of crime when setting burglar alarms before leaving home or being careful to lock all windows and doors and to keep valuables out of sight. CCTV cameras also function as a constant reminder of a society which must be forever vigilant. While these security measures are intended to protect and reassure, they can also disrupt our sense of safety and security. Innes (2004) has introduced the idea of 'signal' crimes and disorders, arguing that some especially 'visible' crimes and disorders serve as 'warning signals' about the risky people, places and events that might be encountered. Target-hardening measures, however, increase the visibility of the problem of crime, and it is therefore arguable as to whether they improve security or in fact increase our sense of fear and foreboding.

Architectural determinism: The proponents of situational crime prevention have attempted, quite literally, to 'design out' crime. Based on the work of US theorists such as Jane Jacobs (1961) and Oscar Newman (1972) and in the UK, Alice Coleman (1989), a particular theory which became known as 'architectural determinism' suggested that certain configurations of space are criminogenic. While Jacobs concentrated her ire on the soulless nature of postwar planning and architecture which she argued stifles community and creative solutions to social problems, Newman and Coleman contended that concrete high-rise office and residential developments have encouraged criminality to flourish. Newman argued that this architecture included too much space that was 'public' and cared for by public authorities rather than private individuals. In its stead he advocated the provision of 'defensible space' – pockets of land surrounding private homes and institutions which must be maintained by the individual 'owner' and which create visible barriers. In the UK, Coleman in an influential publication 'Utopia on Trial' went further to argue that the postwar architectural style directly led to criminality arguing that:

> [a]rchitectural situations that are highly vulnerable to crime can teach children to adopt criminal decisions and this learned disposition can then cause them to see all situational weaknesses as rational opportunities for crime.
>
> (Coleman 1989:109–10 quoted in Crawford 1998:77)

Newman and Coleman's ideas were firmly rooted in the rise of the ideologies of the conservative, neo-liberal right. They were anti-state, anti-public proponents of individual responsibilisation and privatisation. Their work contributed to a general demonisation of public housing and, in the UK a policy focus which saw the demolition of many publically-owned residential tower blocks and their replacement with more traditional housing with private gardens, picket fences and lockable gates. While Jacobs' work celebrated heterogeneity, complexity and social mixing in the city, Newman and Coleman turned to individual defensiveness, cutting away the individual from the public world – a retreat into private hearth and family.

Abandoning the social: Perhaps the most significant criticism of situational crime prevention is that it rejects a collective or social solution to the problem of crime and leaves individuals who are grappling with the problem of crime isolated and alone.

Situational crime prevention decontextualizes crime, its causes and solutions, from the social world in which they are embedded. Furthermore, it demands individually motivated action, but some people are more able to cope than others and have more economic resources to purchase and install their 'crime-fighting' equipment. This is also a problem for communities wishing to take action in a collective way. As Matthews has revealed, '[s]ome neighbourhoods may have the economic or political resources to withstand or endure 'signs of decline' (1992: 32), while others may struggle for various reasons. However, those individuals and communities which find themselves unable to act (or unwilling to adopt this particular model of crime prevention) are hailed as inadequate (or even obstinate) and therefore to blame for their situation.

In conclusion, situational crime prevention demonstrates the neo-liberal project adapted to the problem of crime. As Crawford so ably summarised:

> The installation of governments committed to a neo-liberal ideology – emphasising the free market, a minimal state and individual free choice and responsibility – dovetailed with and promoted criminological ideas which shared the same basic propositions. As a consequence, the spread of situational crime prevention needs to be understood as connected to the political programmes with which it is aligned.
>
> (1998:65)

Social crime prevention

Measures which have become known as 'social crime prevention' take a different theoretical and practical perspective than situational measures. Social crime prevention is based on the idea that crime is a social problem and that it should therefore be dealt with accordingly. There are a number of different aspects to this approach, but in the main it explores the social context which impacts on law-breaking as well as the social environments in which this occurs. Put simply, therefore, social crime prevention aims to intervene in the social world in which crime occurs as well as the social mechanisms which might be put in place in order to help to bring about a reduction in crime. Those social crime prevention measures which focus on the individual's propensity to commit crime are referred to as 'dispositional' (Hughes 2007) in that they are concerned to understand the individual's motivations to break the law, but for social crime prevention the individual's actions are considered in their social context. Two theories which have played a significant part in informing social crime prevention are control theory, especially as outlined by Gottfredson and Hirschi (1990), and stake in conformity theory, as outlined by writers such as Cloward and Ohlin (1960) and Cohen (1955) (see Crawford 1998:104–8 for a fuller discussion). Control theory focuses on informal and formal mechanisms which guide or direct the individual towards conforming behaviour, while stake in conformity theory is more concerned with ensuring that individuals feel that they have a positive part to play in society and that in 'following the rules' they can achieve their goals.

In its earliest manifestations, social crime prevention was closely allied to social policy and the goal of social improvement. It was recognised that decisions made in providing social goods such as housing, welfare, and schooling can have unintended and undesirable outcomes which may contribute to rising crime rates. Social crime prevention is therefore much more closely linked to welfarist agendas, suggesting that the state has responsibility to enact social policies which help to create crime-free environments, and as such it has been somewhat marginalised by neo-liberal ideologues. As Crawford has concluded:

> Over the last two decades situational crime prevention initiatives have been the subject of substantial government funding and research, while dedicated social crime prevention has survived on poorly researched, piecemeal and usually 'one-off' local projects.
>
> (1998:103)

Nevertheless, social crime prevention has not been entirely abandoned, even if it is poorly funded. Many organisations involved in working with young people especially have seen the benefit of projects based on its principles – supplying young people with their 'stake in conformity' and opportunities for leisure, training and employment which might otherwise be missing from their lives.

Social crime prevention has not been immune to the neo-liberal shift and individual responsibilisation. In the 1980s and 1990s, social crime prevention became more 'developmental' in nature (Gilling 2007), focusing on the individual's adaptation to the social environment. Hirschi and Gottfredson's *A General Theory of Crime* (1990) typifies the change to this direction. In this work, the authors define crime as resulting from self-interested behaviour, arguing that all crime can be explained as a combination of criminal opportunity and low self-control. Rather than interrogating the larger structural forces which deprive the individual of the possibility to engage fully in mainstream society, their theory relies more on a critique of parenting techniques which they identify as the most decisive factor in determining the likelihood that a person will commit crimes. This particular take on social crime prevention has proved popular amongst certain conservative thinkers. Charles Murray's work, for example, was extremely influential across both sides of the Atlantic. Murray (1990) posited that an emerging underclass was responsible for dysfunctional cultural adaptations leading to rising crime rates.

Social crime prevention measures are unlikely to produce immediate results as the changes which they aim to bring about can be slow to materialise and their impact may take years to take effect; this can mean that funding is difficult to secure for these projects. The Head Start and Sure Start centres are models of social crime prevention which were introduced in the US in the 1960s and in the UK in the

1990s, respectively, and are an example of initiatives which take time to develop but were nevertheless state-funded. These centres were set up to provide preschool care and education for children in deprived neighbourhoods. Gilling (2007:25–26) reports that longitudinal cost-benefit analysis of Head Start has demonstrated that these centres save thirteen dollars on reduced welfare payments and spending on criminal justice for every dollar spent on the centres and that the arrest rate for children who have gone through the programme was 40 per cent below that of their peer group who had not benefited from this intervention. These figures suggest that social crime prevention could be considered good value for money, but of course there will be many other benefits flowing from the existence of the centres which were not or cannot be measured – for example, impact on the families whose children are accepted into the centres or the positive benefits they may provide for mothers who might otherwise be isolated in their homes. Some social crime prevention then could be seen as positive social interventions in their own right, not just in terms of their impact on future rates of offending.

Social crime prevention – problems and principles

Socially disorganised or differently organised? Social crime prevention can also be closely linked to the concern of the early Chicago School sociologists with social disorganisation in the zone of transition. However, the assumptions which lie behind social disorganisation theory have been challenged by various theorists. Jane Jacobs (1961) suggested that the city is considered disorganised and fearful by those who do not know it intimately – people who come in as outsiders, the ethnographers who misread the hustle and bustle of the city and its multicultural neighbourhoods and cannot see the order and patterns within them. What they fear, she argues, are the heterogeneity and social mix which cities represent. As Mooney concurs:

> Disorder only emerges out of a vision of order: one cannot have order without some sense of disorder. Both concepts are highly ambiguous reflecting particular interpretations of urban life and wider social arrangements.
>
> (Mooney in Pile et al 1999:55)

Others have written of how seemingly disordered neighbourhoods can actually incorporate elements of close supervision and surveillance by residents (Hope and Foster 1992), including those who might be organised outside of commonly accepted and legitimate frameworks (Walklate and Evans 1999). It is also possible for neighbourhoods to be highly organised, with strong interpersonal networks but also relatively high rates of crime (Snell 2001).

The tyranny of social control: Social control has always been poorly defined and is itself a contested concept which can take on many different meanings depending on a person's particular perspective (Hudson 1997). The liberal view considers it as essential for maintaining stable, secure social relationships, but it can also be used to label those who do not conform and to monitor and surveil social groups which appear to position themselves outside of 'normal' cultural values. As we will see in Chapter Five, this can lead to denigration of innovative and creative adaptations and to discrimination against those groups seen to be somehow 'different'. Elizabeth Wilson has argued that the soi-disant 'social disorganisation of the city' can be experienced as a freedom from the petty tyrannies and stifling social mores of village life. Writing of the period of rapid urbanisation in the nineteenth century, Wilson has argued that the relative anonymity afforded by city-life gave women a new autonomy and control over their lives which had not been previously possible and that it provided a new way of life and liberation for many women. She explains as an example that:

> Most of the male modernist literary figures of the early twentieth century ... drew a threatening picture of the modern metropolis (an exception being James Joyce), but modernist women writers such as Virginia Woolf and Dorothy Richardson responded with joy and affirmation. In *Mrs Dalloway*, Virginia Woolf exulted in the vitality of a summer's morning in London, in the swing, tramp and tread; in the bellow and uproar ... in the triumph and the jingle and the strange high swinging of some aeroplane overhead.
>
> (1991:158)

For writers such as Wilson, the idea of the city as a dangerous space is conceived by those who hold a particular, conservative viewpoint. For conflict theorists too, 'social control' can signify state control, the suppression of dissent, the labelling of 'problematic social groups' and the disciplining of individuals and populations into an acceptance of hegemonic ideologies (Foucault 1975).

A focus on youth: Social crime prevention measures have often set out to strengthen institutions of informal social control, especially those working with the primary socialising institutions of family, schools and neighbourhood. The assumption which lies behind this focus on primary institutions is that positive socialisation needs to happen at an early age; therefore, the subject of many of the social interventions proposed are children and young people. Accordingly, Hirschi's work centred on 'young delinquents'. In his hugely influential and popular work *Causes of Delinquency* (1969), he famously argued that youthful law-breaking can be explained by the absence of social bonds and attachments. Strengthening attachment to family, schools and law-abiding peer groups and ensuring involvement in conventional rather than illegitimate activities, he argued, would be likely to result in young people adopting conventional and crime-free lifestyles in which they would recognise the importance of the law in maintaining the social and moral values to which they had been steered.

Risk-based interventions: Social policy has become increasingly informed by the assessment of 'risk', and from the 1990s crime prevention policy has concentrated on those considered at risk of offending. Policy interventions have been directed at this group of, mainly young, people who might be deterred from offending if they are 'caught' early enough. While such interventions could be informed by welfarism and the protection of 'at-risk' individuals, Crawford (1998:266–67) has argued that an approach which seeks to control and manage risky individuals has superceded previous approaches which emphasised the care and support of the vulnerable. The management of risks approach concentrates on the 'risks' which individuals pose to society, rather than the impact society has on individuals and therefore ends up perceiving the individual, or indeed 'entire social groups', as the problem. Individuals who have been labelled as problematic are held responsible for their actions and perceived as operating outside of acceptable social norms by choice. They are consequently stigmatised and vilified as troublesome rather than treated as vulnerable citizens with rights who need to be understood and helped and are increasingly considered as dangerous and incorrigible individuals from whom society must be protected. Risk assessments are being made far earlier in the life stage of the potential 'criminal', even to the extent that expectant mothers and their partners are assessed in order to predict possible 'offenders of the future' (McCarthy et al 2004).

Community-based crime prevention

Community-based crime prevention is an amalgam of the situational and social crime prevention approaches outlined above, which are developed at the neighbourhood level. The community-based approach was developed in the 1970s and, as with the approaches outlined earlier, is complex and multidimensional. The British criminologist Tim Hope has written that it is difficult to locate the theories which lie behind community crime prevention practices, as 'practitioner accounts of community crime prevention often seem muddled, inconsistent and un-theorized' (1995:22). Its starting point, however is that:

> the crime rate within a given area – or community – may be the result of something more than merely the sum total of individual criminal propensities. This suggests that there is something about a 'community' which itself shapes and influences rates of crime.

> (Crawford 1998:124)

As a result, communities are also subject to risk assessments which 'involve secondary analysis of publically available data at the smallest possible geographical area' (McCarthy et al 2004:xii), with at-risk communities described as containing higher than 'normal' numbers of lone-parent households, rates of unemployment, substandard housing, crime, anti-social behaviour, community norms tolerant of crime, residential mobility, vandalism, economic deprivation and social exclusion. Community crime prevention measures are concerned with changing the social conditions in an area which are thought to be contributing to a high crime rate. As such community crime prevention is fundamentally 'social' in its founding principles. However, later in this chapter an exploration of the approach of community crime prevention in practice will demonstrate that it has not always been fully 'social' in its implementation.

The problem with community crime prevention of course lies in identifying what it is about a community that has led to high rates of crime, and there are as many solutions offered as there are theories as to the causes of crime locally. Hope argues that community crime prevention is *political* in character and that the approaches to the problem of crime do not arise from a rational and theoretically informed body of evidence (although this may be claimed by practitioners). Instead, he states, they are shaped by the dominant policy paradigm of the period in which they are developed. Policy paradigms, Hope argues, are shaped by what is assumed to be the nature of the problem of crime in any particular period, so that the way the problem of crime is understood and the solutions which are proposed reflect the political philosophies dominant at that point in time.

Hope (1995) identifies three distinct paradigms which have characterised community crime prevention policy since its emergence in the 1970s – community crime prevention in the growth city, in the frightened city and in the disintegrating city. Hope's analysis ends in the paradigm prevalent in the early 1990s. However, I will argue that crime prevention in the dysfunctional city could explain a shift in attitudes which was witnessed from the mid-1990s onwards.

Community crime prevention in the growth city

This paradigm owes much to the influence of the early Chicago School's areal analysis of the city. The high rates of delinquency which they identified in the zone of transition were hypothesized as resulting from disordered social relations. The Chicago School sociologists were interested not only in understanding social relations in the developing city but also in intervening to change and improve the conditions of urban life. To that effect, they set up the Chicago Area Project (CAP) with the aim of improving the institutional structure of these neighbourhoods and bringing some kind of order into the chaos. The CAP's interventions were not designed to change individual 'delinquent careers' but rather to co-ordinate local institutions, groups and agencies to work together to bring about positive changes for the area as a whole. The principle of *community organizing* or *community development* was thus borne. However, in concentrating on what were seen to be dysfunctional communities, the Chicago School's legacy also helped to create the idea of 'the problem community' and the 'problem area' in which residents were considered unable to create the conditions which allowed the neighbourhood to prosper and must therefore be helped by outside actors to reach their true potential. This intervention into so-called problem areas was criticised as paternalistic and controlling, with the anarchist and housing activist Colin Ward summing up the attitude thus:

Ours is a society in which, in every field, one group of people makes decisions, exercises control, limits choices, while the great majority have to accept these decisions, submit to this control and act within the limits of these externally imposed choices.

(1985:5)

This radical critique of top-down intervention in community inspired a movement in *tenant participation* which built a momentum globally in the late 1960s and early 1970s. Since then it has evolved outside of the housing sector to influence wider social movements such as the Landless Workers' Movement in Brazil and the struggle for indigenous land rights in formerly colonised areas (Hammond 2009). What these movements have in common is that they force an acceptance of the skill-sets, values and ways of life of people who are marginalised and sometimes demonised by the majority in power. In the UK in the 1970s, tenant participation was attempted as a method of improving conditions within public-sector housing which had faced considerable physical and social deterioration. It was hoped that tenant involvement in the running of these estates would help foster stronger horizontal connections between residents and connect tenants to those with the power to ensure that policy remained acceptable and relevant to the residents of public-sector housing. Finally, this approach to community crime prevention also included an element of *resource mobilisation* – acknowledging that many 'problem areas' had been starved of resources and were in need of inward investment if they had any chance to sustain social cohesion and resident involvement in the face of larger structural forces such as unemployment, lack of opportunities for work and training and poverty wages or benefits.

Community crime prevention in the frightened city

From the mid-1970s, Hope identifies the first paradigm shift in community crime prevention when 'the problem of crime was redefined significantly in public policy making' (1995:41). By this time, in the face of rising crime rates and emerging drug markets, the 'problem neighbourhood' had become 'dangerous'. Increasing anxiety about the problem of crime fed into the political sphere in a more overt way, and throughout public discourse discussion of the fear of crime became more difficult to ignore or avoid. In the US, the 1980s witnessed the devastating effects of drugs such as cocaine and crack cocaine on the residents of impoverished and struggling neighbourhoods (Bourgois 1995). During this period, politicians began to use the fight against crime as a political tool and vote winner. Those who wanted to hold office had to be seen to recognise the problem and to be seen to be doing something about it. This is the period in which rhetoric pushing the 'fight against crime' emerged as a dominant trope in crime prevention discourse. This 'fight' was acknowledged in advertising campaigns encouraging the use of situational crime prevention measures, such as the 'Lock It or Lose It' campaign launched in the UK

(Crawford 1998), but also featured in community crime prevention policy in the form of what Hope has termed the 'residential defence' paradigm where 'prevention is better than cure'. Hope identifies two community-based strategies which emerged at this time, namely, *intentional organising of community surveillance*, which encouraged the residents of high-crime and highly fearful areas to become involved in actively maintaining order in their neighbourhoods, maintaining a watchful eye over their own and others' property; and *environmental modification* which would redesign the built environment in order to create the physical conditions in which such surveillance and the informal social control of neighbourhoods could best be conducted. The residential defence paradigm suggested that the best 'defenders' of neighbourhoods were the residents themselves – the potential victims.

The frightened city paradigm was closely linked to the growing recognition of the need to take victimisation seriously and to support those who had become victims of crime. In 1986, the UK criminologists Roger Matthews and Jock Young published *Confronting Crime*, which was to become influential in both academic and policy circles in the following decades. In this volume, they expounded their theory which has become known as 'left realism' through which they argued that radical criminologists must take victimisation seriously, not least because high-crime areas were peopled by some of the most impoverished and marginalised whose fears and concerns around the problem of crime had been sidelined. Matthews and Young argued that it was the task of critical criminology to propose solutions to crime and victimisation which were progressive and positive in their approach and outcomes. Their work encouraged publically-funded victimisation surveys which sought to discover how crime was experienced locally, to tap into local knowledge to assess the problem, to propose and design policy responses to reduce both crime and the fear of crime and to ensure the safety and security of local communities. The 'community safety' approach rather than the more narrowly focused 'crime prevention' approach emerged from this more critical perspective to gain some support in the ensuing decade, mainly within left-leaning local authorities keen to engage local residents in solving the problem of crime and in improving economic and social conditions in their area. 'Community safety' (further explored in the following chapters) looked outside the narrow confines of the courts and the police to call on more diverse elements of the local community – residents, schools, local councils, businesses and beyond – to work together to find local solutions to local problems.

Community crime prevention in the disintegrating city

Hope's third community crime prevention paradigm was, he believed, just emerging at the time of writing in the early to mid-1990s. By the early 1990s, the problem of crime had been redrawn, as a number of studies based on victimisation data demonstrated the significance of the concentration of crime and of repeat victimisation (Gottfredson 1986; Trickett et al 1992). These studies revealed that crime was highly concentrated within high-crime neighbourhoods and that particular individuals and social groups within those areas were highly vulnerable to multiple and repeat victimisation. Crime prevention in the disintegrating city was therefore premised on the view that crime was out of control – at least in certain neighbourhoods – and that these areas had additionally developed significant problems of local disorder (Dennis 1998). The generalised fear manifest in earlier paradigms had become the awful lived reality in areas of concentrated, high crime. The solutions put forward under this paradigm, Hope contends, were those of *preserving order* and *protecting the vulnerable*.

The need to preserve order during this period, Hope (1995) suggested, meant that crime prevention researchers and practitioners steadily moved away from consideration of what might have caused the social conditions in which crime appeared to have increased so dramatically and instead had turned their focus almost exclusively to control of the crime problem as it was manifest in different areas and among the most vulnerable groups. The shift to control of the crime problem introduced a new layer of formal social control mechanisms into high-crime neighbourhoods with the idea of 'zero tolerance' towards crime and disorder, attaining support from police and public authorities. Zero tolerance policing was introduced in the early 1990s in New York, under Mayor Rudolph Giuliani and Police Commissioner Bill Bratton, and in Hartlepool in the UK by their Chief Inspector Ray Mallon (Dennis 1998). It was inextricably linked to Wilson and Kelling's 'Broken Windows' thesis (1982), which is further discussed in later chapters. The term 'zero tolerance' suggested non-discretionary responses to the problem of crime and disorder. While it was not adopted formally as a national policy, it paved the way for the introduction of more overt and visible policing, and tighter control over the behaviour of younger local residents and other groups generally considered 'risky'.

The concept of 'risk' was integral to the paradigm of the disintegrating city. Whereas welfarist approaches were perceived as costly and ineffective, risk-based approaches allowed a focussed intervention on the people and places deemed to be problematic. This risk-based paradigm (Beck 1992) was further extended into the realm of victimisation (Donaghue 2013). Research highlighting the problem of repeat and multiple victimisation published in the late 1980s and early 1990s, complemented by local surveys measuring the extent and nature of crime and victimisation, helped to create the concept of the vulnerable victim in need of protection. Vulnerable victims were said to be located in high-crime areas sharing the same spaces as the offenders who preyed upon them. These offenders were not strange and alien outsiders but 'familiar and [sometimes] the familial' (Walklate and Evans 1999:134), and new techniques of crime control had to be developed to respond to this revelation.

Confronting the problem of crime and disorder under the disintegrating city paradigm revisited the more conservative and anti-progressive tones of earlier periods, reintroducing in their wake a more confrontational policing style, which was clearly crime-focussed and the antithesis of the more liberal agenda associated with community safety. While lip-service was made to community safety and security, at least in the UK this approach was abandoned in reality as the discourse and practices of control of crime and disorder achieved prominence. While across much of continental Europe more welfare-oriented political regimes continued to maintain support for the community safety/security approach (Crawford 1998), this approach was largely abandoned in the US and the UK and in areas of central and southern America where the politics of neo-liberalism held sway.

Community crime prevention in the dysfunctional city

Hope's analysis of community crime prevention paradigms ends in the mid-1990s as risk-based approaches to crime control began to emerge more strongly. Beck's influential thesis on 'Risk Society' was published in 1992, and his argument was readily taken up by criminologists on both sides of the Atlantic. Beck's contention that the risk society is one which is obsessed with the control of future consequences seemed to fit with the ways in which the problem of crime was also envisaged. The 1990s saw criminal justice policy shift markedly towards preventative practices and away from rehabilitation. In the years between 1993 and 1996, for example, the federal government of the US passed the "three strikes and you're out" legislation, adopted by 25 states, which encouraged the courts to pass lifetime prison sentences upon the third criminal conviction (Austin and Irwin, 2001). The Crime and Disorder Act introduced in the UK by a Labour government (which replaced a seventeen-year run in office of the Conservative Party, which had foregrounded law and disorder as a political imperative) also typified a risk-based control agenda, introducing anti-social behaviour orders, compulsory drug treatment and testing and parenting programmes and possible temporary curfews for young people, among other measures of crime control (Evans 2011). These measures, and others like them, have been seen as a product of a more punitive turn in criminal justice, but in addition they are representative of a preventative turn (Ashworth and Zedner 2014) and agenda of control which seeks to target future problems before they have arisen. Prisoners given life on their third conviction are incarcerated in order to prevent the risks of any future harm they might commit, not on the evidence of their actions to that date. It is assumed that those who are three times guilty will forever pose a threat. The 'orders' and curfews handed out by the British courts as a result of the 1998 Crime and Disorder Act can control the lives of those who have not yet committed a criminal offence.

Risk-based assessments individualise the problem of crime so that it is no longer perceived as a consequence of structural forces, inequalities and lack of opportunities. Instead crime is linked to the circumstances surrounding an individual, his or her poor choices and lack of motivation to change. In short crime is perceived as a consequence of dysfunctionality – of the individual's inability to lead a law-abiding life or of the dysfunctional community tainted by counter-cultural norms which has embarked on a trajectory of socially destructive behaviour. The dysfunctional individual or community subsequently passes responsibility for their actions onto the government and the powerful. In the words of the conservative writer Norman Dennis:

> There has been a profound displacement of perception and values, which has left the English population much more prone to react to problems in self-destructive and anti-social ways, with a decline in a culture of responsibility, a rise in a culture of victimhood, and a transfer of attributions of causality from the cultural to the material environment.
>
> (Dennis 1998:4–5)

This perspective stands in stark contrast to the approach of the criminologists who first discovered the existence of 'high-crime areas'. Trickett et al (1992) were careful to conclude that their findings and understanding of the concentration of crime did not require victim-blaming or rely on pejorative views of the residents suffering from high levels of crime and victimisation. By the mid-1990s, however, and as we will see in the following chapter, the problem of crime and disorder had been firmly placed on the shoulders of dysfunctional people and communities, necessitating solution which involved *the close management of problematic individuals and neighbourhoods* and their *responsibilisation*. This new paradigm of crime control has also led, as we will see in Chapter Five, to *policies of securitisation and community control* which reached new and unpredicted heights.

With the responsibilisation of communities came a desire for community involvement in the prevention of crime, which had not been seen as appropriate since the modernisation of crime control with which this chapter starts. Community crime prevention and community safety have been joined by community courts in which members of the local community sit on advisory bodies in order to help establish the court's response to local offenders (Lee 2000). Even punishment has been returned to the community with schemes such as Community Payback which involves outfitting offenders in high-visibility vests, working in teams on projects designed to have them give something back to the community they have victimized (Parfrement-Hopkins 2011).

Some concluding comments and questions

In the early, premodern period, attachment to community was considered key to maintaining acceptable behaviour, which was controlled by a desire to conform to collective values. The role of community in maintaining social order was considered anachronistic and parochial by 'modernisers' who looked to enlightened philosophers and professional elites to replace the rule of the street by the rule of law. The state took on the function of social control, developing a coercive arm which was awarded the right to use violence to attain its aim, while this avenue was removed from the general population. From this point onwards, community played a secondary role in the control of crime, called on in different periods to collaborate with the state and contribute to maintaining order. Communities, however, have often been found wanting in this role. Initially, a loss of community organisation was considered responsible, and various interventions were effected, with the aim of rebuilding or strengthening community in areas which were struggling. Communities have also been blamed for harbouring and disseminating the wrong values and have come under increasing scrutiny in recent decades. As Hope's work reveals, the problems of the nation have been blamed on the community and as these problems take different form, so attitudes to community have altered as a consequence.

1. Do you consider crime a function of lack of community or the wrong kind of community?
2. In what ways do you think community could play a significant role in crime prevention?

Further reading

There are many useful books and articles which consider the ways in which communities have been incorporated into crime prevention policy. Barbara Hudson's chapter on 'Social Control' in (Maguire et al 1997) the second edition of *The Oxford Handbook of Criminology* is a useful starting point for understanding the ways in which social control has been theorised. Hughes (2003) *Understanding Crime Prevention* remains very useful in outlining the theory of situational and social crime prevention techniques and gives a clear overview of the salient debates on crime prevention practices.

References

Ashworth, A., and Zedner, L. (2014) *Preventive Justice* Oxford, UK: Oxford University Press.

Austin, J., and Irwin, J. (2001) *It's About Time: America's Imprisonment Binge* Belmont, CA: Wadsworth.

Beck, U. (1992) *The Risk Society: Towards a New Modernity* London: Sage.

Bourgois, P. (1995) *In Search of Respect: Selling Crack in El Barrio* Cambridge, UK: Cambridge University Press.

Burgess, E. W. (1925) 'The Growth of the City' in Park, R. E., Burgess, E. W., and McKenzie, R. D. (eds), *The City* Chicago: University of Chicago Press.

Clarke, R. V. (1980) 'Situational Crime Prevention: Theory and Practice' *British Journal of Criminology* 20(2) pp. 136–145.

Cloward, R., and Ohlin, L. (1960) *Delinquency and Opportunity* London: Collier Macmillan.

Cohen, A. K. (1955) *Delinquent Boys* London: Free Press.

Coleman, A. (1989) *Utopia on Trial* London: Hilary Shipman.

Crawford, A. (1998) *Crime Prevention and Community Safety* Harlow, UK: Longman.

Dennis, N. (ed) (1998) *Zero Tolerance. Policing a Free Society* London: IEA Health and Welfare Unit.

Donoghue, J. (2013) 'Reflections On Risk, Anti-Social Behaviour and Vulnerable/Repeat Victims' *British Journal of Criminology* 53 pp. 805–23.

Evans, K. (2011) *Crime Prevention a Critical Introduction* London: Sage.

Foucault, M. (1975) *Discipline and Punish. The Birth of the French Prison* New York: Random House.

Garland, D. (2001) *The Culture of Control: Crime and Social Order in Contemporary Society* Chicago: University of Chicago Press.

Gilling, D. (2007) *Crime Reduction and Community Safety* Cullompton, Devon, UK: Willan Publishing.

Hammond, J. L. (2009) 'Land Occupations, Violence, and the Politics of Agrarian Reform in Brazil' *Latin American Perspectives* 167(36) pp. 156–77.

Gottfredson, M. R. (1986) 'Substantive Contributions of Victimization Surveys' *Crime and Justice* 7 pp. 251–87.

Gottfredson, M. R., and Hirschi, T. (1990) *A General Theory of Crime* Stanford, CA: Stanford University Press.

Hirschi, T. (1969) *Causes of Delinquency* Berkeley: University of California Press.

Hope, T. (1995) 'Building a Safer Society. Strategic Approaches to Crime Prevention' *Crime and Justice* 19 pp. 21–89.

Hope, T., and Foster, J. (1992) 'Conflicting Forces: Changing the Dynamics of Crime and Community on a "Problem Estate"' *British Journal of Criminology* 32 pp. 488–504.

Hudson, B. (1997) 'Social Control' in Maguire, M., Morgan, M. and Reiner, R. (eds), *The Oxford Handbook of Criminology 2nd ed.* Oxford, UK: Oxford University Press.

Hughes, G. (2007) *The Politics of Crime and Community* Basingstoke, UK: Palgrave.

Hughes, G. (2003) *Understanding Crime Prevention* Milton Keynes: Open University Press.

Hughes, G. (1998) *Understanding Crime Prevention* Buckingham, UK: Open University Press.

Innes, M. (2004) 'Signal Crimes and Signal Disorders: Notes on Deviance as Communicative Action' *British Journal of Sociology* 55(3) pp. 335–55.

Jacobs, J. (1961) *The Death and Life of Great American Cities* New York: Vintage.

Lea, J. (2002) *Crime and Modernity. Continuities in Left Realist Criminology* London: Sage.

Lee, E. (2000) *Community Courts An Evolving Model* Bureau of Justice Assistance https://www.ncjrs.gov/pdffiles1/bja/183452.pdf [Accessed 06.03.14].

Martinson, R. (1974) 'What Works? Questions and Answers About Prison Reform' *Public Interest* 35 pp. 22–54.

Matthews, R. (1992) 'Replacing "Broken Windows": Crime, Incivilities and Urban Change' in Matthews, R., and Young, J. (eds), *Issues in Realist Criminology* London: Sage.

Matthews, R., and Young, J. (1986) *Confronting Crime* London: Sage.

McCarthy, P., Laing, K., and Walker, J. (2004) *Offenders of the Future? Assessing the Risk of Children and Young People Becoming Involved in Criminal or Antisocial Behaviour* London: Department for Education and Skills Research Report No 545.

Merton, R. (1938) 'Social Structure and "Anomie"' *American Sociological Review* 3 pp. 672–82.

Murray, C. (1990) *The Emerging British Underclass* London: IEA.

Newman, O. (1972) *Defensible Space: People and Design in the Violent City* London: Architectural Press.

O'Malley, P. (1992) 'Risk, Power and Crime Prevention' *Economy and Society* 21(3) pp. 251–68.

O'Malley, P. (2013) *Crime and Risk* London: Sage.

Parfrement-Hopkins, J. (2011) *Perceptions of Crime, Engagement with the Police, Authorities Dealing with Anti-Social Behaviour and Community Payback: Findings from the 2010/11 British Crime Survey, Supplementary Volume 1 to Crime in England and Wales 2010/11* London: Home Office.

Pile, S., Brook, C., and Mooney, G. (eds) (1999) *Unruly Cities? Order/Disorder* London: Routledge.

Sharpe, J. (2001) 'Crime, Order and Historical Change' in Muncie, J., and McLaughlin, E. (eds), *The Problem of Crime* London: Sage.

Shaw, C., and MacKay, H. (1942) *Juvenile Delinquency and Urban Areas* Chicago: University of Chicago Press.

Snell, C. (2001) *Neighborhood Structure, Crime and Fear of Crime: Testing Bursik and Grasmick's Neighborhood Control Theory* New York: LFB Scholarly Publishing LLC.

Sykes, G., and Matza, D. (1957) 'Techniques of Neutralisation: A Theory of Delinquency' *American Sociological Review* p. 26.

Taylor, I. Walton, P., and Young, J. (1973) *The New Criminology. For a Social Theory of Deviance* London: Routledge and Kegan Paul.

Tierney, J. (2010) *Criminology. Theory and Context* Harlow, UK: Pearson Education Ltd.

Trickett, A., Osborn, D. R., Seymour, J., and Pease, K. (1992) 'What Is Different About High Crime Areas?' *British Journal of Criminology* 32(1) pp. 81–89.

Vold, G. B. (1951) 'Edwin Hardin Sutherland: Sociological Criminologist' *American Sociological Review* 16 (1) pp. 2–9.

Walklate, S., and Evans, K. (1999) *Zero Tolerance or Community Tolerance? Managing Crime in High Crime Areas* Aldershot, UK: Ashgate.

Ward, C. (1985) *When We Build Again: Let's Have Housing That Works* London: Pluto Press.

Wilson, E. (1991) *The Sphinx in the City. Urban Life, the Control of Disorder, and Women* Los Angeles: University of California Press.

Wilson, J. Q. and Kelling, G. (1982) 'Broken Windows: The Police and Neighbourhood Safety' *The Atlantic Monthly* pp. 29–37.

3
DISORDERLY COMMUNITIES

As we have seen in previous chapters, since industrialisation the city has been considered a place of both disorder and delinquency. Industrialisation created a working
class, and the industrial cities had to accommodate this newly created social group
on a mass scale. In post-industrial societies, we are still left to contend with the
legacy of industrialisation. Whereas early theorists thought the industrial city had
destabilised the traditional social ordering of the countryside, the post-industrial
city has been identified with a complete breakdown of order. Both these claims will
be explored more fully in this chapter, and the processes by which violent social
transformations have been associated with increased criminality and disorder will
be more closely investigated.

The 'problem' of urbanisation

The rise of industrialisation brought with it the reformation of class society and the
creation of the 'working classes' and with them new forms of social organisation
which had never been experienced before. Industrialisation and the manufacturing
process required centralisation not only of capital but also of labour (Engels 1987),
and thus hundreds of thousands of individuals left behind land-based occupations
to find work in factory-based systems of production with the hope of gaining a
share in the immense wealth industrialisation created. The expanding cities needed
an infrastructure and services which were also provided by these new arrivals. This
process has been replicated worldwide as industrialisation has proved a global phenomenon, so that whereas 100 years ago only 20 per cent of the world's population
lived in an urban area in the early twenty-first century more than half the world's
population are urban-dwellers and by 2050 it is estimated that this proportion will
increase to 7 out of 10 people (World Health Organisation 2014). The conditions

many of those newly arrived in our cities will face will be anything but ideal. The reality is that many will find themselves living in overcrowded slums without electricity or sanitation, which are increasingly a part of the global urban infrastructure. Mike Davis (2006) has estimated that one-third of the world's urban population currently live in slums, and this figure is likely to grow to 2 billion by 2030. The process of urbanisation should therefore not be considered a historical phenomenon but should also be viewed as having genuine contemporary significance. Observing this process today can also help us to understand what the early scholars must have seen and felt about their experiences, and it can also help us to understand why they reached the conclusions they did. At the same time, it will help uncover some of the mistakes they may have made in their initial interpretation of the urban form.

Wherever cities are subject to rapid expansion, this expansion is rarely planned. With the exception of planned economies such as China, where literally hundreds of cities have been designed and built since the late 1970s, the majority of cities worldwide have developed largely unplanned by centralised authorities (Yew 2012). The rapid expansion of production and the sheer weight of humanity moving to newly industrialising areas over the last century has meant that governments and market forces have provided post hoc, if at all, so that services have followed the people rather than having been put in place in readiness for their arrival. This situation has meant that most cities have grown organically but also in a haphazard and sometimes dangerous fashion. From Engels's horror at the conditions of working-class life in Victorian cities to the proliferation of urban slums in much of the developed and developing world today, the built environment stands as testament to the disorder and degradation of day-to-day living which industrialisation has unleashed. However, the disorder created by urbanisation is not the complete picture. While it is this which exercised the minds of the classical scholars whose work was described in Chapter One, there are still other readings of the social life of the city and the urban working classes which are missing from much of their work.

A tale of two cities?

Despite the appalling conditions experienced by much of the urban population today, slum conditions are not universal. While industrialisation resulted in an obvious unsettling of space, a certain stability has also descended on our towns and cities. In many regions of the world, infrastructures have been built which have provided an adequate level of services, and legislation has been passed outlawing the worst excesses of profiteering and exploitation, thus safeguarding the welfare of the population. Of course, the extent to which this has been accomplished has varied significantly across nations, but just as there is a story to be told about the city of slums, so there are many other cities, including the sustainable city, the diverse city, the creative city and the city as a source of wealth and prosperity (Janssens et al 2009). The industrial city can be read as a remarkable human accomplishment allowing millions of people to live close together in relative harmony and enjoying a way of life and a prosperity which was previously unimaginable. Criminology has been largely concerned with the disorderly city rather than with the processes whereby the chaos of the city was tamed and order more or less restored by the very people experiencing this chaos on a daily basis. In this respect then, criminology is a particularly pessimistic discipline in that it is concerned with what appears to go wrong in the social order rather than what is achieved in day-to-day living which keeps the city on its ordered path.

The discipline of criminology largely developed as a consequence of the perceived dangerous nature and the unruliness of the working classes, and it has been dominated by a concern with the law-breaking of this layer of society rather than with the harms created by powerful economic and political forces. Certainly where crime is associated with place, it is working-class neighbourhoods or the spaces in which the working classes congregate which have been the target for attention rather than the suburban spaces of the middle classes or the centres of finance and business, which are also found in our towns and cities. These latter spaces have been considered models of order, regulation and manners in contrast to working-class neighbourhoods which are portrayed as disordered, crime-ridden and unruly, although recent scandals and economic collapse have seen the extent of corruption, financial mismanagement and law-breaking of the powerful shockingly exposed. The powerful, however, are rarely portrayed as acting in pursuance of the interests of their own social group. Instead it is suggested that their individual actions, though undoubtedly self-serving, are also rational and necessary and coincide with the national interest in that they allow the economy to thrive, creating employment and generating wealth, which is considered to work to the advantage of all. It is partly for these reasons that the concept of 'community' takes on a different flavour when it is applied to these social groups.

'Problem communities'

The communities which have exercised the criminologist are those which have been linked to criminality, law-breaking and disorderly behaviour. As we have seen in previous chapters, 100 years of criminological theory, since the early Chicago School, have linked crime to particular urban spaces. Park, his students and those who have followed in their footsteps have maintained a focus on working-class and impoverished neighbourhoods rather than on suburban and rural living. The 'communities' which have therefore persisted as problematic are consequently the working-class communities found in these spaces which have taken on a particular shape in our perception. While the terms 'business community' and 'financial community' are also familiar to our ears, they imply a community of interest based in economically-rational behaviour. Community as it is applied to the powerless is used to denote the more affective relationships connected to feelings of attachment and belonging. The crimes of the powerful are rarely linked to the concept of 'community'. The crimes of the powerless, however, as we have seen in Chapter Two, have been regularly linked to community in a number of ways and so much so that with regard to crime prevention theory and practice the term 'community' has become almost synonymous with poor, marginalised urban neighbourhoods. Crime in these neighbourhoods has been seen as a consequence of too little community (social disorganisation), too much community (differential association) or the wrong kind of community (cultural transmission). As a result, criminology and crime prevention practices have looked to understand and re-engineer the right kind of community in working-class neighbourhoods in order to find solutions to 'the problem of crime'.

Of course, community can be very important to people who live in areas where the struggle for survival dominates lives and mutual co-operation can be an important way to gain access to sources of help and support which are otherwise not available. This is especially important where the state has abrogated its responsibility to play a key role in the provision of welfare and services. Park observed the key role which socially supportive networks played in the lives of the poor in Chicago and other US cities in the early twentieth century, and he contrasted the social relations apparent in the very different neighbourhoods of 5th Avenue and the Bronx in New York, remarking that the financially successful 5th Avenue in New York 'never had an improvement association' whereas the struggling 135th Street in the Bronx was 'rapidly becoming a very intimate and highly organized community' (Park in Sennett 1969:97). The social networks which were built by the more affluent and which are also characterized by shared geographical location, mutual interest, co-operation and no doubt attachment are rarely spoken of as pertaining to 'community'. This underscores, once again, that 'community' is seen as antithetical to 'economic rationality' and the 'success' which can be achieved by participating in the behaviours associated with capitalist enterprise.

So why is community different for the working class? In Park's writing, community is associated with traditional ties of kith and kin and also with the re-imagining of customs and traditions which emanated from pre-urban, rural societies and which are rebuilt in urban conditions by those who might otherwise continue to be strangers to each other. These strangers, Park considered, gravitate within the city to those places where they fancy they will encounter people like themselves, so that they can build new connections and communities which afford them safety, security and affection which the urban landscape on its own cannot provide. The alienation resulting from the proletarianisation of labour, the strangeness of urban existence and living cheek by jowl with strangers is tempered by the solidarity found within the relations of community. However, the choices made by the wealthy and privileged as to where to live and work and as to which social and business connections afford the best results, are imagined differently. These are considered the inevitable consequences of building a new way of life and a modern, progressive society which has, in contrast, eschewed the old ways of living. Of course. the bourgeoisie and the builders of industry do not share the alienation of labour, the forced cohabitation of the city's poorer neighbourhoods and a daily struggle to make ends meet. Their wealth and privilege allow them autonomy at work and an escape from the worst living conditions of the city. These luxuries are not in the purview of the majority who must find their comfort in their immediate surroundings. The search for neighbourliness, place-based community and above all the support of others could therefore be considered more salient to the underprivileged.

In the early twentieth century, attachment to community was criticised as anti-thetical to modernity and as holding back essential progress by tying people to their sentimental attachments to place. The social landscape of industrialised and indus-trialising areas of the world changed fundamentally during that century as national economies boomed and others declined. The twentieth century saw huge disrup-tions to traditional communities as people left the places of their birth to find their futures outside of their established familial and communal connections. From the global economic slump of the 1930s through the deindustrialisation of the 1970s and the post-crash economic restructuring from 2008, those who have lost their employment have been advised to follow the work rather than to stay attached to places and social connections which could no longer provide them with opportu-nities but which might furnish them with social solidarity, help in their old age and the love and affection of their family and friends.

Crime, poverty, disadvantage and the role of community

The social restructuring of the twentieth century saw a concentration of poverty in urban centres, prompting an ongoing concern about the social conditions found in these poor urban neighbourhoods. These areas were regarded with some distaste by the urban commentators from the more privileged classes and were perceived as areas of disease and social contamination. The discipline of criminology has in many ways sustained this fascination with spaces of poverty and with the slums, ghettos and inner cities which have been linked with crime and criminality. Since the early Chicago theorists developed their models of human ecology, the spatial analysis of crime and criminality has played a significant role within the discipline. This is a result of a certain practicality – the high-crime neighbourhood has acted as a social laboratory for many people interested in understanding the problem of crime – but also of an ideological framework which considers the poor as a problem in themselves. So while criminological theory has identified poverty and disadvantage as conditions which may lead to criminal behaviour, the discipline has largely responded not by looking to alleviate the conditions which produce poverty and disadvantage but by attempting to change the behaviour of the people who endure them.

As we saw in the previous chapter, after a brief hiatus in the 1950s and 1960s the spatial analysis of crime re-emerged in the 1970s when Western economies began to falter as the boom years of postwar restructuring began to collapse into ongoing economic and social insecurity. The subsequent rise in unemployment and inflationary increases which ate into the disposable income of many affected families meant that the postwar optimism also began to fade. The effects of the crisis were devastating in areas which lost work, where whole industries disappeared and where future prospects became particularly bleak. Many of these areas spiralled into an economic decline from which many have never recovered. By the end of the 1970s, for example, unemployment had reached nearly 11 per cent of the workforce in the US (*The Washington Post* 2014) and similar levels in much of the rest of the Western economy. Australia followed suit shortly after (Lambert 2012). According to the *Washington Post*, there have been eleven economic recessions in the US since the Second World War, each one of which has added further social costs. As the US remains at the time of writing the world's largest economy, US economic problems have had far-reaching repercussions in other parts of the world. In addition, the global financial and banking collapse of 2008 led to sudden and soaring unemployment, which in some European countries such as Spain and Greece has amounted to a quarter of the workforce unemployed (Lambert 2012).

The loss of current and future prospects was not only individually devastating for those affected but has also had significant social consequences. Amongst these was the creation of the conditions in which a market for the supply of illegal drugs flourished. The increased supply and demand for drugs in the 1970s was perceived as a driving force behind a worsening gang problem and increasing rates of crime, gun use and homicide in the poorest neighbourhoods of cities particularly across the US. By the early 1990s, the Office of National Drug Control Policy in the US was claiming that illegal drug use was the main concern of the US population, prompting George Bush Senior to announce a 'war on drugs'. Although by this point the indicators showed a decline in both illegal and licit mood-altering drugs, a dip in the drug market and the beginning of a fall in recorded crime which has since been sustained (Stimmel 1996), the areas which had suffered in the preceding two decades were now linked in the popular imagination with criminal gangs and violent criminality. While rates of drug use and violence did not reach the same proportions in the rest of the West, the damage wrought by deindustrialisation and the destabilisation of Western economies had similar effects across Europe. Other parts of the world, especially those which were involved in the supply of illegal drugs to the markets in the West, experienced their own social devastation as a consequence of the violence of both the trade in illegal drugs and the war against drugs.

From around the mid-1990s recorded crime rates fell in many Western economies, but the effects of two decades of concern stemming from increasing levels of violence, gangs and the market for illegal drugs and the fear of crime remain stubbornly high. This is hardly surprising given the continued focus on these issues in the media, culture, politics and the popular discourse during this period. Within criminology, and more recently in criminal justice policy too, there has been continued attention on exploring crime and the fear of crime at the level of the neighbourhood. The loss of 'community' has been perceived as pivotal in contributing to higher rates of crime. As Lacey and Zedner suggest, 'rapid social and economic change' has:

> wrested social relations from localized contexts, weakened family and communal ties and ... eroded 'traditional' forms of social cohesion.
>
> (1995:301)

As a consequence, the focus on local social relations has fed into strategies of prevention that have explored the role of community in understanding the problem of crime and, as Hughes reports, somewhat ironically, community is considered as both the breeder and the prophylactic against crime and disorder (Hughes 2007:110).

Critical voices on community and crime

The late flowering of critical voices in criminology is unsurprising given the nature of the discipline, which is steeped in the state's need to control its citizens to its own needs and political ends. The classical 'founding fathers' of criminology were liberal philosophers who considered the modern legal system as a moral good and were concerned with maintaining the individual's responsibility in upholding the rule of law. Other academic disciplines such as philosophy, history and literature have been more open to an understanding and acceptance of the role of dissent in shaping contemporary society and social history, while the role of criminology has been that of condemning and suppressing dissident and law-breaking behaviours. To fully understand the links which have been made between community and the problem of crime, it is necessary to understand the normative framework in which criminology has developed and within which the majority of the discipline continues to work. In the following sections, however, I will introduce some key insights which were developed outside the discipline of criminology but which have enriched the radical understandings of the subject, before then going on to explain how the dominant voices in this subject area have interpreted the problem of crime, community and disorder quite differently.

Informal social controls – the public and the private

The everyday life and activity of the urban poor has had positive and stabilising effects on the city. As outlined in the preceding chapter, premodern forms of justice involved the populace as much as the 'professional' in maintaining the social order, and the day-to-day policing of communities was carried out first and foremost by local residents. These informal practices of social control did not disappear altogether as a consequence of industrialisation and urbanisation but were carried on within urban residential neighbourhoods. Lea, for example, uses the work of Nancy Tomes to argue that working-class communities in industrialising cities 'exercised high degrees of surveillance and autonomous regulation of conflict', in

Tomes's example, by intervening in incidents of domestic violence (Tomes 1978 in Lea 2002:60), but Lea's research has also demonstrated that such intervention also played a part in the regulation of street crime. In the industrialising cities, Lea argues, life was led outside of the home. The cramped, inadequate nature of private space, together with a tradition of a more shared and collective way of life, would have meant that boundaries between public and private life were blurred at this time. As a consequence, neighbours were more familiar and tended to look out for one another, and morality, as life, was collective and shared. Gradually, as conditions in the home improved and social aspirations altered, more of life was lived in the private, domestic sphere, and the nuclear family became the site for the production of morality. The state, as we have seen, took over the policing role, and encouraged self-regulation within the family, criminalising behaviour (for example, infringements of sexual morality such as incest) which threatened the stability of family life.

While a shared, collective morality of the street is accessible to the urban ethnographer, it is questionable to what extent the informal controls which existed more privately within families and neighbourhoods could have been witnessed by the philosophers and writers who judged these communities from afar. It is a well-aired criticism that the ethnography of the Chicago School was street-based and therefore unable to comment to any great extent on the private, domestic lives of their subjects. The Chicago School also had very little to contribute on the policing and social control of women and girls in the home. With such a partial view of the working-class neighbourhood, it is difficult to see how these writers could possibly have understood the complex and nuanced nature of social relations in the working-class city, although this glaring omission was largely unremarked upon. Criminology had to wait until the 1970s and the inclusion of feminist voices in the discipline to include any substantial body of work which could begin to fill this particular gap in its understanding. Ethnographies of city life published after this period, influenced by feminist research methods which give prominence to the experiences and stories of research subjects, have uncovered different ways in which local relationships in city neighbourhoods have acted as stabilising and protective factors (Bottoms and Wiles 1986; Bursik and Grasmick 1993; Hope and Foster 1992). This is not to ignore the important body of feminist work which has uncovered the problematic nature of such 'protection' in stifling women's lives and opportunities, but it does suggest that risk factors for crime, rather than emanating from disorder within communities, may in fact be externally imposed. For women, the risk factors may be just as likely be a function of patriarchal ordering within the 'stable' and seemingly ordered family.

Urban social movements and resistance

Writing only decades after some of the most significant social upheavals in history, Karl Marx famously stated in the *Communist Manifesto*, written with Engels in 1848, that "the history of all hitherto existing societies is the history of class struggle" (Marx and Engels 1998). Yet the writing of scholars such as Tonnies, Durkheim, Weber and Simmel is largely devoid of reference to the class conflicts which shaped the town and country before, during and after the age of industry was established. Yet these conflicts have also contributed to the making of modern society and they suggest, too, that collectivism and communal relations have been as significant as alienation and anomie in the development of our history and the shaping of society. Theories of urbanisation, however, have been more concerned with understanding the development of industry, the physical form of the city and the symbolic landscapes created as a result, rather than engaging with social resistance to industrialisation and the immiseration of social life which it brought in its wake (Harvey 2012). Indeed, capitalism and the productive forces it unleashed were generally considered a source of wealth and opportunities representing a progressive phase in human history. While the agricultural and industrial revolutions of the eighteenth century had their critics 'writing in a well-established tradition of questioning the justice and humanity of commercialised production, economic competition and the private ownership of property' (Jay and Jay 1986:25), the prosperity the new economic system was capable of providing was considered a triumph of human intellect over natural forces. The devastating social conditions, or 'side-effects' (Crowther 2000:34) witnessed in the working-class neighbourhoods of the cities were portrayed then (and to a great extent still are today) by the apologists for capitalism as a product of weak-minded, undisciplined individuals rather than a product of a deeply flawed system balanced in favour of the owners of capital and finance. These attitudes endured in the theoretical contributions offered by classical criminology and in the focus on social disorganisation, first mooted by the Chicago sociologists, but still very much in vogue in contemporary explanations of the problem of crime. In a seeming paradox, but of course eminently understandable to those of us who view life through a critical lens, attempts at self-organisation by those most negatively affected in order to combat the conditions created by rapid urbanisation have been at best ignored and at worst considered problems of disorder in their own right. Invariably, the creation of trade unions, for example, is initially resisted by government forces whenever they first arise in any national context, and those social movements which have successfully raised fundamental questions concerning the current ordering of society and thereby threatened the stability of the existing social order, continue to face censure and ultimately repression (Castells 2012). As the perspective of cultural criminology also contends, everyday actions of resistance to social conformity can also be subject to draconian social controls and criminalisation (Ferrell 2001).

Cities have always been places of confrontation and conflict. As Miller et al assert, city spaces have acted as:

> the central stage for contesting hegemonic power relations in urbanized societies, making broad claims for rights and justice, building and mobilizing

> solidarities among diverse peoples and groups. The city has been the central plat-
> form for elevating these struggles and driving them toward their respective ends.
>
> (2013:452)

Such confrontations and conflict have developed from more than just the concentration of people in one place (as Simmel theorised – see Chapter One), and
the diverse and heterogeneous neighbourhoods constructed by inward migration (as suggested by the sociology of the Chicago School). To understand the
sources of conflict in the city, it is necessary to consider the function of the
city within capitalism. The cities of earlier industrial eras were built to facilitate the accumulation of capital, and their urban founders 'were in the business
of manipulating place for its exchange values' (Logan and Molotch 2006:294)
rather than for ease of use or the safety and security of its residents. Yet those
who are drawn to the city as a place to find work are concerned with more
than just the city's capacity to generate profit and a wage. Those who, in the
words of Karl Marx (1998), have nothing to sell but their labour must also find
within their chosen city, spaces which are liveable and in which they can find
a safe and secure place to call home and maybe raise a family. For the majority
of city-dwellers, the city is their only place of residence, one which they leave
only occasionally, they are concerned therefore with its usability – in Marxist
terms its use-value (Marx 1983). A constant tension exists between use-value
and exchange-value. Use-value requires that money is spent on a city's infrastructure, on providing housing and essential services (collective consumption)
and on providing a rich cultural environment in which to thrive, whereas those
concerned with the need to extract as much profit out of a city as possible want
to spend as little on these projects as they can. Most of the time this tension
remains unseen and unarticulated, but if too much money is extracted and not
enough is spent, a city can become unliveable, and at such times the tension
becomes palpable and can spill out into the streets.

Cities can also become unliveable for certain groups who are denied access
to their 'right to the city' (Lefebvre 1993) for whatever reason – perhaps due to
discriminatory policies, over-policing or lack of resources. As places of resistance,
urban neighbourhoods have played a major part in the making of history. Sociologists such as Manuel Castells, writing on urban social movements in *The City
and the Grassroots* (1983), have demonstrated that throughout history urban social
movements have been major agents of social change and have sometimes had
remarkable impact on our spatial and built environments. In *Networks of Outrage and
Hope* (2012), Castells makes the following argument:

> [A]ll urban forms result from the relentless interaction between the repro-
> duction of urban forms by institutions and resistance, or counteraction, by
> citizens who don't feel included in the processes of automatic reproduction

of the existing urban structure. Urban form results from urban structure and social movements interacting with one another.

(Costanza-Chock 2014: MIT website)

Castells has argued that disorder is therefore inherent in city spaces and urban social movements are most likely to arise as a result of demands for collective consumption, the assertion of cultural identity or demands for political representation.

The local 'structure of feeling'

Urban spaces are created by the people who live within them as well as by the producers and planners of the built environment. Those spaces have been created by a city's people in different social and historical circumstances; some are created in fleeting moments of revolt and dissent such as the Paris Commune of 1871 but endure in the city's folklore and memory (Zederman 2014). Other spaces created from below endure emotionally, physically and politically. The neighbourhood of Haight Ashbury in San Francisco, for example, while much changed demographically, still retains in physical form a reminder of the countercultural movements and lifestyles which formed its alternative reputation in the 1960s. In the UK, Manchester's Gay Village, once a place for clandestine meetings of a criminalised LGBT minority, later achieved a reputation nationally and internationally as a place to celebrate gay culture and leisure and was hailed as an economic as well as a political success (Bell 1991; Taylor et al 1996). Iconic black neighbourhoods such as Harlem in New York and Moss Side in Manchester in the UK (Ward 1975) retain a distinct profile which is rooted in their history as places within which black and minority ethnic groups were able to settle and create safe and affordable spaces in deeply divided countries. The particular nature of all these spaces was created by groups of people who out of necessity or desire sought to create an alternative to that which mainstream society was able to offer, and by doing so they brought about significant social changes too. By their very existence, these spaces proclaimed that alternative and, most unfortunately, often reviled, ways of life and thinking had a right to exist and be heard amongst the clamour of the more mainstream, dominant voices. They were unplanned, growing organically, built from below by those who had been unplanned for and excluded. As Pile et al remark in their 1999 edited collection, *Unruly Cities*':

The differentiation of urban space [italics in original] is not simply about the form that differences take, but about how such differences are produced.

(Pile et al 1999:2)

As a consequence of action and organisation from below, such neighbourhoods did not merely exist but also flourished as cultural spaces and as catalysts for social change – the Harlem Renaissance of the 1920s and 1930s was instrumental in the development of black pride and a politics of the excluded which later rocked the American establishment as the civil rights movement of the 1960s demanded recognition and representation for African Americans across the US. Similarly, the gay rights movement and the emergence of the sentiment of Gay Pride emerged from the spaces which had been built through the clamour of voices of resistance demanding significant social change. It is in such spaces that 'community' has been observed as a living, working social mechanism in the modern age. These are communities which have been said to display all the features of interest, attachment and place which were proclaimed as heralding the existence of particularly strong community feeling in modern social conditions.

A city's people, the communities in which they engage and the cultures which they create do not always conform to normative frameworks imposed upon them by the planners, policy-makers and urban elites who appear as the makers of history. 'Problem neighbourhoods', 'those inner cities', 'sink estates' are all terms used to describe the poor neighbourhoods of our cities. In categorising these areas by use of sweeping generalisations with, more often than not, negative connotations attached, the areas and the people who dwell within them are all lumped together as troublesome and as likely to be disproportionately involved in criminal activity. Yet in order to understand and shed light on contemporary social relations within these neighbourhoods, they should also be read through their own specific histories which can otherwise lie buried and forgotten. The cultural critic Raymond Williams, himself a product of both English and Welsh cultural connections, dubbed this unique adaptation the 'structure of feeling', the socially patterned and actually lived experience of place which develops over time and is formed by social interaction within and between particular neighbourhoods (Williams 1977). This concept was introduced into criminology as late as 1996 by Taylor et al and informed the research of Walklate and Evans (1999) and Girling et al (2000). The research generated from these studies (all funded by the Economic and Social Research Council in the UK) connected patterns of crime and adaptations to crime in different areas in the Northwest of England as being shaped by history and cultural identity which had developed over preceding decades and periods of economic, political and social restructuring. Mainstream criminology and policy-makers concerned with the 'problem of crime' have largely remained ignorant of this aspect of local social relations and have considered any place and any community connected with high rates of recorded crime as more similar than different. As a result, the 'solutions' which are promoted tend to be generated by those who are not intimately connected with the spaces in which they are operating and can create more problems than they resolve.

Back to social disorganisation

Notwithstanding that in recent years more radical and critical voices have emerged within the discipline to question criminology's basic assumptions and to debunk the theory of social disorganisation, mainstream criminology and crime prevention policy has continued to focus on the perceived links between social disorganisation and levels of crime. Areas with high rates of recorded crime or unusually high numbers of residents with criminal convictions have been linked to a number of factors which are seen to contribute to social disorganisation – fatherless families, high rates of population turnover, the presence of groups with different ethnic identities, to name but a few. These social factors have been predicated as highly significant in contributing to rates of 'criminality' and 'delinquency' and have been influential in directing research in the areas of community and crime, whilst they also continue to feature heavily in policy debates and popular understandings as major contributing factors in the problem of crime.

In the 1970s, the deindustrialised inner city which housed the urban working classes was the focus of policy-makers' attentions. The loss of employment hit these areas hard, and residents had to rapidly adapt to changing economic conditions, learning to live without guaranteed work and having to rely, where these were available, on benefits provided by the state. Communities without work will understandably look very different from those in which work is a constant and continuous part of everyday life. It has been argued that the loss of employment in the 1970s hit men particularly hard as they were primarily employed in the sectors of industry which suffered most at this time. Nevertheless, any loss of employment and income will be felt by an entire family, and some areas experienced a whole-scale shift from work to worklessness as entire industries on which their residents depended closed. Writers from both the left (Campbell 1993) and the right (Murray 1994) were concerned to document and explore the impact that years without job opportunities would have on communities, and especially the social impact on young men who were made economically redundant. The conclusion reached was that:

> there is a connection between the economic redundancy of young males, their non-attachment to the nuclear family and high levels of deviant and disorderly behaviour.
>
> (Crowther 2000:5)

By the 1980s into the second decade of a post-industrial employment landscape, the term 'underclass' gained popularity, used disparagingly to refer to a social group living outside of the world of work, on welfare and likely to be involved in crime. When the term was first used, it described those people who had fallen foul of deindustrialisation and were without paid employment, with skills which were no longer relevant to the economy, trapped in poverty and struggling on the bottom rungs of the ladder as a consequence (Wilson 1978, 1987). By the end of the 1980s, however, the meaning attached to the underclass had changed to encompass a more condemnatory attitude which blamed individuals for the position in which they found themselves. In the new use of the term, 'the underclass' was peopled by those who had *chosen* not to engage with work and were therefore responsible for the poor conditions in which they lived. They were welfare scroungers, petty criminals, drug addicts, hustlers, homeless and beggars. These individuals were no longer victims of economic decline but deficient in their attitude and behaviour, believing in their entitlement to resources which the state would provide, rather than having to engage in paid employment (Mead 1986). In the US, the term 'underclass' took on an extra layer of meaning and became almost exclusively linked to the residents of black urban neighbourhoods. Effective socialization and supervision were considered as lacking or severely reduced in 'problem' communities, thus contributing to chaotic and unstable families and communities. This, together with the predominance of anti-normative attitudes, was used to explain a continued reliance on benefits rather than the failure of the economy to provide work for those who needed and wanted to be economically independent.

Relying heavily on Shaw and McKay's earlier characterisation of social disorganisation which was oriented more to social relationships in the inner city rather than individual behavioural traits, Bursik and Grasmick published *Neighbourhoods and Crime* in 1993 which brought much of the work on social disorganisation together to build a 'systemic theory of neighbourhood organisation' (Snell 2001) which they further developed over the next two decades. The authors agreed with Shaw and McKay that rapid population turnover and higher rates of ethnic heterogeneity reduced the capacity of neighbourhoods to influence the behaviour of their residents. The authors argued that the self-regulation of neighbourhoods was a function of the extent and density of formal and informal networks which can bring residents together. However, they then went on to argue that the ability of these networks to develop and function is affected by both the level of crime in an area and the level of fear of crime. Decades of high crime rates had therefore eroded the capabilities of communities to pay a part in the maintenance of order. Bursik and Grasmick concluded that social disorganization and offending were linked at a number of levels; the private, the parochial and the public

The private level: works at the level of interpersonal friendships and peer groups, suggesting that friends and other close relationships are important in helping to control an individual's actions. The fact that friends can withdraw support or express disapproval of behaviour which they find problematic, Bursik and Grasmick argued, means that they can act as a constant check on behaviour. However, they also argued that rapid turnover in a residential population would destabilise peer networks and make significant friendships difficult to sustain. They also claimed that racial and ethnic heterogeneity in a neighbourhood limits the scope of interpersonal networks as individuals prefer to connect with those most like themselves.

The parochial level: refers to the part local social institutions play in influencing a person's behaviour and in encouraging pro-social activities, so that schools, places of

worship and voluntary organisations in the neighbourhood are said to play an important role in the socialisation of youth especially but also in regulating adult behaviour
too. For Bursik and Grasmick it is important to keep individuals connected to these
local social institutions from which they can maintain networks of trust and mutual
self-help.

The public level: Bursik and Grasmick also argued that communities can be influenced and controlled from outside the local neighbourhood through the policies
of local, regional and national governments and other service providers. Good relationships with the holders of the purse-strings, for example, may release funding
down to a local area that might not otherwise be forthcoming. It is important, then,
for communities to build links to outside organisations and to maintain positive
relationships with the locally and nationally powerful.

Bursik and Grasmick's work has been much cited and is still used extensively
today within mainstream criminology to explore social relations in local neighbourhoods andto test the existence and effectiveness of 'horizontal' and 'vertical' social
relations (Hope 1995) within communities. While some of Bursik and Grasmick's
observations appear eminently sensible, they are based on a number of assumptions which should be scrutinised. Their work suggests that areas with high rates
of recorded crime are unstable, with high rates of population turnover, though this
is certainly not true of many areas considered to be 'high-crime' neighbourhoods
(see, for example, the neighbourhood of Oldtown described by Walklate and Evans
1999). It also assumes that the significant and influential relationships in the lives of
individuals who may engage in criminal or anti-social behaviour are those which
they find in their local streets. This emphasises the prominence of place-based community and downplays the importance of interests and attachments which may be
based outside of the narrow confines of the neighbourhood. It is also important to
consider whether the focus on the local has such a pull in contemporary 'network
society' (Castells 1996) within which numerous social networking sites, instant
messaging and access to constant newsfeeds allow the individual myriad ways to
connect outside their own locality.

Bursik and Grasmick's perspective is also troubling in that, as many before them,
they consider ethnic heterogeneity to be a limiting factor in establishing personal
and institutional networks. These claims will be further explored in Chapter Five,
but it is enough now to raise the question as to whether the multicultural spaces of
our cities are indeed fragmented and lacking in connectivity across what some may
see as ethnic boundaries. While personal identity and ethnicity may act as a limiting factor for some individuals, and while communal tensions and conflicts may
arise between particular groups on occasion, it would be a mistake to believe that
the everyday experiences of neighbours are today, or have been in the past, constantly constrained by prejudice, discrimination and segregation. The concentration
of people from very different nations, traditions and religions in urban centres is a
long-established reality which has created a rich diversity of relationships that have

been mutually beneficial in many ways. Bursik and Grasmick's 'systemic theory' may be more appropriate to the US experience where 'race' has a particular historical force and continued significance, rather than replicable across other urban contexts around the globe.

The significance of 'fear'

Where Bursik and Grasmick hit a chord which has resonated further afield, however, is in the idea that informal supervision, which is key to building a stable and sustainable community, is linked to levels of fear in a neighbourhood. Fear of crime first emerged as a policy concern in the 1970s in the US, however, national and international surveys which set out to measure levels of fear were instigated in many countries in the following decades. Fear was linked to social disorganisation in two ways. Initially, residents' fear of crime was linked to the quality of the external environment. It has been generally accepted, for example, that 'highly visible signs of what [the residents] perceive as disorderly and disreputable behavior' contribute to high levels of fear (Biderman et al p.160, cited in Hale 1988). Garofalo and Laub (1978) reversed this observation, claiming that residents who are less satisfied with the quality of life in their neighbourhood, the availability of services, public transport, schools, overall noise levels and so on will express a greater fear of crime than those who are more satisfied. Research in the area of fear of crime prompted concern that signs of disorder, also referred to as the level of 'incivilities' in a neighbourhood, should be limited as much as possible to allay residents' fears. This perspective prompted initiatives which sought to draw resources into an area in order to refurbish and clean up the physical environment, to improve local facilities and services and to find housing solutions for the street homeless. Lewis and Salem conducted research in 1986 which reiterated the importance of local resource mobilisation. They argued that the fear of crime which residents within marginalised and struggling neighbourhoods reported was as much a function of fear for their future as it was of their fear of victimisation in the present. Those communities, they argued, experienced a lack of control over many aspects of their lives, and while this fear could not be easily articulated, it could find expression in concern about crime and victimisation which was all too real and palpable. Lewis and Salem therefore wished to encourage communities to mobilise their internal resources in order to access external help, support and finances.

In the 1980s, fear of crime was also linked to a community's inability to maintain order. Fear was considered a severely limiting factor in any attempt to build or to strengthen a community's capacity to act on its own behalf to ensure the safety of the neighbourhood (Hale 1988). Echoing the work of Simmel and others outlined in Chapter One, this concern was linked to a fear of strangers. Greenberg et al (1982) concluded from their research that neighbours in high-crime areas were unlikely to interfere in disputes between those unfamiliar to them or to feel responsible for looking after the property of people with whom they did not have close ties (Greenberg et al 1982). The academic and policy emphasis shifted away from structural inequalities and the redistribution of financial resources and connections to the powerful and moved towards attempts to build social networks and community feeling within troubled areas so that the community could begin to help itself. This left communities isolated from the structures of power and finance which could really start to make a difference. It is clear that this later perspective focused on the responsibility of the community to act in already disordered places rather than the national or local state's responsibility to create conditions in which social order could thrive.

Left realism and the fear of crime

It was during this period that left realism emerged as a perspective within criminology. Left realists were concerned that radical criminology did not take the experiences of victims of crime seriously. They pointed out that if the left had a responsibility to accurately reflect the experiences of the working class, then they had to acknowledge that many working-class communities had been devastated, not only by poverty and unemployment, but also by life in high-crime areas in which many had been victimised or knew someone close to them who had become a victim of crime. Fear, they argued, was also a destructive element within these communities and had to be tackled. The left realists employed local victimisation surveys to build up a picture of what life was like for the residents of high-crime areas and the ways in which crime affected their everyday life. They were also interested in revealing how formal and informal control mechanisms within an area worked to either increase or diminish residents' sense of security and safety. Crime, they concluded, was harming individuals and social relationships in the working-class city; after all, they argued, research had revealed that most crime is intraclass, perpetrated on the most vulnerable of the working class by other members of the working class. Feminists working within the left realist perspective highlighted the harmful actions of predatory males, which increased levels of fear amongst women and girls (Stanko 1990).

Left realism found some favour among the more liberal and left-leaning local authorities keen to improve social conditions in more marginalised neighbourhoods. They worked alongside academics to develop practical solutions to the problem of crime, which involved engaging with the community and bringing about positive social reforms. In Tierney's words, this engagement with the community 'was seen as forging links with the historical struggle of the working class to improve their lot' (2010:292) and involved the funding of, among other initiatives, self-help groups, neighbourhood networks, tenant participation, victim support schemes and victim–offender mediation. While many of these projects found favour locally, left realism had fallen into the trap of perceiving crime as the primary focus of attention.

This was not surprising given the emphasis which residents of high-crime areas placed on the problem of crime themselves but the approach followed by left realism did not break the causal link which had been made between the dysfunctional community and the problem of crime. By unwittingly reinforcing this relationship left realists were unable to resist the right's onslaught on community which followed on its heels. Right realists also agreed that crime should be taken seriously but they approached the problem from a very different angle.

Broken windows and broken societies – the triumph of right realism

In 1982, the US magazine, *Atlantic Monthly*, published an article by George L. Kelling and James Q. Wilson which was to prove so influential that it has become almost part of folklore (Matthews 1992). The broken windows theory, as it came to be known, began by expressing a concern about levels of public fear, which Kelling and Wilson attributed not just to fear of crime but also to fear of disorderly people and places. It is this fear, they argued, that 'leads to the breakdown of community controls' (1982:31) and which must be tackled head on. Their solution was to swiftly remove signs of disorder from public view and to increase perceptions of security in neighbourhoods through the presence of police on the streets. The popularity of the broken windows theory led to a frenzy of graffiti removal, street cleaning, repairing and maintenance of public-facing property and the forcing of minimum standards onto the owners of private property. It also led to a different kind of 'cleansing', to whit, the removal of those people who were also seen to signal public disorder, so the homeless and anyone begging on the streets or drinking alcohol in public were not to be tolerated and were moved on. This is perhaps the most significant legacy of 'broken windows'. As the resources to clean and maintain the physical environment have been drastically scaled back, the social cleansing has been sustained and has fed into a general condemnation of people who live their life, through either choice or necessity, outside of the bounds of what is considered normal and orderly behaviour and the normalisation of a policy which sweeps them off the streets.

Wilson and Kelling's work is deeply conservative. It is infused with concern for the 'standards' and 'values' associated with a mythical past and 'golden-age' of community (see Ramasinghe 2012). It is part of a tradition of work which is largely devoid of a structural analysis which might consider poverty, discrimination and disadvantage as contributing factors in the existence of 'high-crime' areas and instead which looks to communities to sort out problems which are increasingly seen as of their own making. It is unsurprising that people who live in areas where victimisation and signs of disorder and decay are a regular part of their daily life are likely to feel demoralised, upset and angry (Skogan 1990). Their lack of action might be read as apathy but could equally be a consequence of a realistic assessment that they are safer if they do not speak out or that they have tried and failed to improve matters in the past and can no longer see intervention as effective (Evans et al 1996; Walklate and Evans 1999). It may be, as Matthews argues, that neighbourhood decline leads to disorder rather than the other way around (Matthews 1992). However, this consideration is markedly lacking from the right realist perspective and 'dominant, neo-liberal political thinking, [which] rather than seeing social policy as a means of reducing crime, has come to identify it as the cause of contemporary social ills' (Crawford 1998:108). As Crawford explains, for the right it is welfarism which has led to social disintegration and an over-reliance on the state which has killed the self-reliance of the individual and community.

On disorder ...

The working-class neighbourhoods of our cities have remained a focus of attention since their formation. For the early reformers, it was the poverty and unsanitary conditions in which workers had to live which prompted their concern, but alongside the dangers the industrial city presented to workers was concern that the working class itself posed a threat to the social order which had created it. In industrial cities, workers were physically separated from the locally powerful and therefore were freed from the old ways of living when they had been kept close to the landowning aristocracy with the expectations that they would defer to 'their betters'. In working-class neighbourhoods, freed from the expectations of tradition and forced into cramped and crowded environments, new ways of living necessarily emerged and new allegiances were forged as people adapted to the changed conditions of their lives. This was a brutal existence for many, with long hours of back-breaking work and few employment rights and also a precarious life for those who relied on casual labour. Mayhew (1967), writing of London in 1861, was sympathetic to the plight of the new working classes and also those who, for lack of work, had to live off the streets and off their wits. For others however, the poorest were considered as being without morality, irreligious and 'dangerous' in their capacity to pollute the social body. The idea that the poor could be distinguished in their intent as those who struggled hard in extreme conditions and deserved better and the undeserving who chose indigence or to live their life outside of expected social norms drove punitive sanctions such as workhouses and prison, which to a more enlightened mind appear cruel and unjustified. It is hardly surprising that under such circumstances resistance became one of a range of possible responses. The forms this resistance might take are many and varied, and left realists have criticised critical criminologists for idealising the commission of crime as a form of working-class resistance. Whilst it is true that shoplifting, insurance fraud or smuggling could be perceived as taking back from corporations that have exploited in order to generate profit, and it is also true that graffiti art, pirate radio, and occupations of public spaces can all be read as 'adventures in urban anarchy' (Ferrell 2001), street robbery from the poorest members of society, the sexual harassment and assault of women and the violent clashes of drunk males at the end of a Saturday night are more the symptoms of profound damage and alienation. It is important therefore to consider what criminology and policy-makers consider to be disorderly and to carefully examine the parameters they use when condemning behaviour they consider as anti-social, criminal or harmful in any way.

Mainstream criminologists have generally drawn tight boundaries around what is to be considered a good and social life. Unsurprisingly, the upholding of the law of the land and the lack of law-breaking behaviour have featured prominently in their measure of pro-social behaviour. In more recent decades, however, a focus on the problem of disorder has been added to concern over the problem of crime and law-breaking. Criminologists have defined disorder as 'violation of norms concerning public behaviour' (Skogan 1990:4) or as 'reflections of the erosion of commonly accepted standards and values' (Lewis and Salem 1986: xiv), but of course there are obvious questions to be raised concerning who controls the general understanding of what is 'commonly accepted' and 'normal'. Following Wilson, Kelling and other influential conservatives such as Murray and Dennis, social problems such as homelessness, adaptations to poverty like begging or washing car windows to find the money to survive, drinking alcohol in a public place and a myriad of other behaviours have been redefined as signs of disorder and re-imagined as sources of disquiet and concern. The additional concept of 'anti-social behaviour' which crept into the criminological lexicon around the 1990s has widened almost without limit the range of actions which can be considered as unwelcome and to be condemned. Under UK law, anti-social behaviour is defined as that which is likely to cause harassment, alarm or distress to one or more persons who do not live in the same household as the perpetrator. As Squires (2008) has pointed out, this takes criminologists and policy on crime control into a discussion of what may or may not be offensive to any one individual. Intolerance of difference, of marginal lifestyles and of certain social groups is now woven into the problem of crime and disorder. The repercussions of broadening the 'problem' will be further explored in later chapters.

Some concluding comments and questions

This chapter has looked at the construction of the 'problem community' and the different ways in which this problem has been perceived. Beginning with the early theorists of crime and community, working-class neighbourhoods have been cast as socially disorganised, but this chapter questions some of the assumptions upon which this representation of economically disadvantaged communities has been based. Some communities, as suggested, are differently organised, but this difference need not be perceived of as problematic. This is not to say that social problems do not exist, but they can be seen as either individually or structurally created and crime control policy has considered the problem to be that of the individual rather than the structures of society within which the individual must operate. The problem community is therefore perceived as being made up of problematic individuals. Therefore, it is important to consider the following:

1. Is there such a thing as a 'problem community', and what is the problem?
2. How can communities be perceived as both 'the breeder and the prophylactic against crime and disorder' (Hughes 2007)?

Further reading

A number of interesting and significant books explore social and community relations in areas with high rates of recorded crime. These books are a good place to begin to understand the social and community dynamics of place and how they relate to the problem of crime and other social issues their residents face. A number of these resources have been used in this chapter. Campbell's *Goliath: Britain's Dangerous Places* (1993) is an easy read, presented in a journalistic style. It connects with some key criminological theories, but to understand the problem of crime in a more nuanced and theoretically informed way, Girling et al's *Crime and Social Change in Middle England* (2000), written a few years later, is more reflective and looks at the problem from different perspectives. Crowther's *Policing Urban Poverty*, also published in 2000, gives a comprehensive overview of the control of working-class neighbourhoods and is a significant text in this area.

References

Bell, D. J. (1991) 'Insignificant Others: Lesbian and Gay Geographies' *Area* 23 pp. 332–9.

Bottoms, A. E., and Wiles, P. (1986) 'Housing Tenure and Residential Community Crime Careers' in Reiss and Tonry (eds), *Communities and Crime* Chicago: University of Chicago Press.

Bursik, R. J., and Grasmick, H. G. (1993) *Neighbourhoods and Crime. The Dimensions of Effective Community Control* New York: Lexington Books.

Campbell, B. (1993) *Goliath: Britain's Dangerous Places* London: Virago.

Castells, M. (2012) *Networks of Outrage and Hope: Social Movements in the Internet Age* London: Polity Press.

Castells, M. (1996) *The Network Society* Oxford, UK: Blackwell Publishers.

Castells, M. (1983) *The City and the Grassroots: A Cross-Cultural Theory of Urban Social Movements* London: Arnold.

Costanza-Chock, S. (2014) 'Manuel Castells "The Space of Autonomy: Cyberspace and Urban Space in Networked Social Movements".' *MIT Centre for Civic Media* http://civic.mit.edu/blog/schock/manuel-castells-the-space-of-autonomy-cyberspace-and-urban-space-in-networked-social [Accessed 09.06.14].

Crawford, A. (1998) *Crime Prevention and Community Safety* Harlow, UK: Longman.

Crowther, C. (2000) *Policing Urban Poverty* Basingstoke, UK: Macmillan Press.

Davis, M. (2006) *Planet of Slums* London: Verso.

Engels, F. (1987) *The Condition of the Working Class in England* London: Penguin.

Evans, K., Fraser, P., and Walklate, S. (1996) '"Whom Can You Trust? The Politics of "Grassing" on an Inner-City Housing Estate' *Sociological Review* 44(3) pp. 361–80.

Ferrell, J. (2001) *Tearing Down the Streets* Basingstoke, UK: Palgrave.

Garofalo, J., and Laub, J. (1978) 'The Fear of Crime: Broadening Our Perspective' *Victimology: An International Journal* 3 pp. 242–53.

Girling, E., Loader, I., and Sparks, R. (2000) *Crime and Social Change in Middle England: Questions of Order in an English Town* London: Routledge.

Greenberg, W., William, R., and Williams, J. (1982) *Safe and Secure Neighborhoods: Physical Characteristics and Informal Territorial in High and Low Crime Neighborhoods* Washington, DC: National Institute of Justice.

Hale, D. (1988) 'Fear of Crime and Quality of Life: A Test of Garofalo and Laub's Model' *Criminal Justice Review* 13(1) pp. 13–19.

Harvey, D. (2012) *Rebel Cities* London: Verso.

Hope, T., and Foster, J. (1992) 'Conflicting Forces: Changing the Dynamics of Crime and Community on a "Problem Estate"' *British Journal of Criminology* 32 pp. 488–504.

Hughes, G. (2007) *The Politics of Crime and Community* Basingstoke, UK: Palgrave.

Janssens, M. (ed) (2009) *Sustainable Cities: Diversity, Economic Growth and Social Cohesion* Cheltenham, UK: Edward Elgar Publications.

Jay, E., and Jay, R. (eds) (1986) *Critics of Capitalism. Victorian Reactions to 'Political Economy'* Cambridge, UK: Cambridge University Press.

Kelling, G. L., and Wilson, J. Q. (1982) 'Broken Windows. The Police and Neighborhood Safety' *Atlantic Monthly* March 1.

Lacey, N., and Zedner, L. (1995) 'Discourses of Community in Criminal Justice' *Journal of Law and Society* 2(3) pp. 301–25.

Lambert, T. (2012) *A Brief History of Unemployment* http://www.localhistories.org/unemployment.html [Accessed 15.06.14].

Lea, J. (2002) *Crime and Modernity. Continuities in Left Realist Criminology* London: Sage.

Lefebvre, H. (1993) *Writings on the City* Oxford, UK: Blackwell.

Lewis, D. A., and Salem, G. (1986) *Fear of Crime: Incivility and the Production of a Social Problem* New Brunswick, NJ: Transaction Books.

Logan, J. R., and Molotch, H. (2006) 'The City as Growth Machine' in Fainstein and Campbell (eds), *Readings in Urban Theory* London: Blackwells.

Marx, K. (1983) *Capital Volume One* London: Lawrence and Wishart.

Marx, K., and Engels, F. (1998) *The Communist Manifesto*, introduction by Martin Malia New York: Penguin.

Mayhew, H. (1967 [1861]) *London Labour and the London Poor: A Cyclopaedia of the Condition and Earnings of Those That Will Work, Those That Cannot Work, and Those That Will Not Work* New York: A. M. Kelley.

Matthews, R. (1992) 'Replacing "Broken Windows": Crime, Incivilities and Urban Change' in Matthews, R., and Young, J. (eds), *Issues in Realist Criminology* London: Sage.

Mead, L. M. (1986) *Beyond Entitlement: The Social Obligations of Citizenship* New York: The Free Press.

Miller, B., Nicholls, W., Beaumont, J. (2013) *Spaces of Contention: Spatialities and Social Movements* Aldershot: Ashgate.

Murray, C. (1990) *The Emerging British Underclass* London: IEA.

Park, R. E., Burgess, E. W., and McKenzie, R. D. (1925) *The City* Chicago: University of Chicago Press.

Pile, S., Brook, C., and Mooney, G. (eds) (1999) *Unruly Cities? Order/Disorder* London: Routledge.

Ramasinghe, P. (2012) '"Jane Jacobs" Framing of Public Disorder and Its Relation to the "Broken Windows Theory"' *Theoretical Criminology* 16(1) pp. 63–84.

Sennett, R.(ed) (1969) *Classic Essays on the Culture of Cities* Appleton: Century Crofts.

Simmel, G. (1950) 'The Metropolis and Mental Life' in Wolff, K. (ed), *The Sociology of Georg Simmel* New York: Free Press.

Skogan, W. G. (1990) *Disorder and Decline: Crime and the Spiral of Decay in American Neighborhoods* California: University of California Press.

Snell, C. (2001) *Neighborhood Structure, Crime and Fear of Crime: Testing Bursik and Grasmick's Neighborhood Control Theory* New York: LFB Scholarly Publishing.

Squires, P. (2008) *ASBO Nation. The Criminalisation of Nuisance* Bristol, UK: Policy Press.

Stanko, E. (1990) *Everyday Violence: How Men and Women Experience Sexual and Physical Danger* London: Pandora.

Stimmel, B. (1996) *Drug Abuse and Social Policy in America. The War That Must Be Won* London: Routledge.

Taylor, I., Evans, K., and Fraser, P. (1996) *A Tale of Two Cities. Global Change, Local Feeling and Everyday Life in the North of England, A Study of Manchester and Sheffield* London: Routledge.

Tierney, J. (2010) *Criminology. Theory and Context* Harlow, UK: Pearson Education Ltd.

Walklate, S., and Evans, K. (1999) *Zero Tolerance or Community Tolerance? Managing Crime in High Crime Areas* Aldershot, UK: Ashgate.

Ward, R. (1975) *Residential Succession and Racism in Moss Side* Unpublished PhD thesis University of Manchester.

The Washington Post (2014) 'A Brief History of U.S. Unemployment' *The Washington Post Business Section* http://www.washingtonpost.com/wp-srv/special/business/us-unemployment-rate-history/ [Accessed 30.07.14].

Williams, R. (1977) *Marxism and Literature* Oxford, UK: Oxford University Press.

Wilson, W. J. (1987) *The Truly Disadvantaged: The Inner City, the Underclass, and Public Policy* Chicago: University of Chicago Press.

Wilson, W. J. (1978) *The Declining Significance of Race: Blacks and Changing American Institutions* Chicago: University of Chicago Press.

World Health Organisation (2014) 'Urban Population Growth' *Global Health Observatory* http://www.who.int/gho/urban_health/situation_trends/urban_population_growth_text/en/ [Accessed 05.06.14].

Yew, C. P. (2012) 'Pseudo-Urbanization? Competitive Government Behavior and Urban Sprawl in China' *Journal of Contemporary China* 21(74) pp. 281–98.

Zederman, M. (2014) 'Memories of the Paris Commune in Belleville Since the 1980s Folklorization and New Forms of Mobilization in a Transforming Quartier' *History and Memory* 26(1) pp. 109–35.

4

REGENERATING COMMUNITIES

While the preceding chapter explored ways in which communities have been considered as disordered places, this chapter looks at different attempts which have been made to construct socially ordered places, starting with the physical regeneration of cities and neighbourhoods and then moving on to consider the move to social and community regeneration which predominated from the 1970s. In 1995, Lacey and Zedner wrote that:

> [s]ocial order ... cannot merely be protected and maintained but ... must, rather, be actively constructed and managed if the social and psychological costs of insecurity are to be minimized.
>
> (1995:301)

Many different plans have been proposed as the way to induce necessary changes, but as this chapter will reveal, each plan has been constrained by the historical and political period in which they have been constructed (Fainstein and Campbell 2006:2). From the 1970s, the idea that local and national state interventions into the life of communities were a necessary part of urban governance was established, whereas prior to this point interventions tended to be designed and implemented by individual philanthropists and progressive thinkers eager to establish some kind of 'utopia' amongst urban chaos. The move from benign interference to full-fledged state intervention will be considered over the next few pages.

Shaping the built environment

The poor quality of life and environmental conditions which persisted in newly industrialised cities were, as soon as they took physical form, considered a cause for concern, and they have remained a focus of attention ever since. However, reformers have looked at the problem differently in subsequent historical periods. Initially, reformers were exercised with improving the built environment of the newly emerging cities in order to minimise the effects of poor environmental quality on the physical and psychic health of the urban population. The problems created by industrialisation raise issues concerning sanitation, pollution, over-crowding and substandard housing, and the early reformers looked for solutions in the architecture of the city. In Victorian Britain, which is often held up as a great example of urban reform, valiant attempts were made to provide sewerage sys-tems and clean water to the cities, to build a public infrastructure of roads, streets and housing, and in perhaps the first example of situational crime prevention, to install street-lighting and to build a policing structure which would improve the safety of city streets at all times. Urban design and re-design, however, is never neutral and value-free; instead it can be read as an expression of the way social problems are understood and of a vision of what social relations should look like. In Victor Hugo's words, architecture is a 'granite book' in which the dominant ideas of each generation are written. In that respect, urban planning is value-laden and reflects the moral and political perspective of the planner. In addition, the built environment is the physical embodiment of relations of power – economic, political and social which prevail. It is rare that the built environment expresses an alternative vision for society, although utopian visions of the 'good' city and community have, and continue to be, presented as possible futures in fiction and non-fictional accounts alike; see, for example, the final chapters of both Harvey (2000) and Ferrell (2001).

Garden cities and model towns

The end of the nineteenth century saw the birth of the garden-city movement, developed by the founder of the Town and Country Planners Association, Ebenezer Howard. Howard's vision was to merge the best of town and country in one space – the garden city. He wanted to celebrate the vitality of the urban form while instilling within it the tranquillity and beauty experienced in the rural. This perfect combination, he argued, could only be achieved through planned development and subsequent growth. Howard's vision rested, not only on the planning of the built environment but also in the provision of affordable housing, a supply of local jobs with decent working conditions and the building of strong and sociable communi-ties in which the population was given every encouragement and opportunity to engage in civic life. Garden cities offered a blueprint for social improvements as well as a high standard of living, in beautiful surroundings with access to parks and leisure and in a townscape crafted to delight residents and to bring out the best in every individual personally and socially.

Howard's vision typifies the reforming zeal demonstrated by many reformers of the time. Many, such as the Rowntree, Cadbury and Leverhulme families in the UK, were motivated by their religious beliefs to build ordered environments which would encourage high moral standards in their residents. Their belief that physical environments affected spiritual and moral outlooks coincides with the more contemporary attitudes expressed by Coleman and Newman discussed in previous chapters. Garden cities and bespoke urban and suburban estates proliferated across North America. They were also established in other regions of the globe as models for the perfect city environment, formed from the Western experience, were instigated in colonial and post-colonial contexts. The countryside was never far from these model cities which were to be surrounded by a green lung of agriculture and woodland which could provide high-quality food and clean air to the city. The green spaces of the countryside were brought into the city wherever possible so that each family could enjoy leisure opportunities on their doorstep with gardens to grow their own produce should they desire. In the twentieth century, motivated by a more secular outlook, the modernist architect Le Corbusier advocated the fully planned city, zoned into its different uses, residential, commercial and industrial with wide boulevards, open vistas and affordable and efficient transport so that all could enjoy the facilities and creative opportunities which only the more densely populated city could provide. Howard was keen to promote networks of small, self-sustaining and locally controlled communities, while Corbusier has been criticised as 'an authoritarian centralist' (Cochrane 1999), but both sought to combat disorder through the planning and building of alternative city-spaces, which, despite Howard's anarchist pretensions, involved a top-down approach to managing urban spaces. The vision of both architects involved an inherent rejection of what they considered to be the messy and unwanted outcome of the organic growth of city-spaces. Jane Jacobs, writing in the 1960s, took issue with the sterilising of city-spaces through urban design. Rather than condemning the heterogeneous vibrancy of city streets, she celebrated the diversity and creative forces which she found in encounters between strangers. She argued that, rather than generating fear, the eclectic mix of people and lifestyles found on the city's streets would ensure that individuals were able to create new kinds of social structures and entrepreneurial networks which would bring them closer together and provide for each other's needs.

Postwar reconstruction

After the horrors of the Second World War and the physical destruction left in its wake, a new urgency arose for urban planners and architects across Europe who were charged with creating a workable infrastructure to replace that which had been lost. The cities that were rebuilt postwar incorporated many elements of Corbusier's approach. Densely-populated high-rise neighbourhoods replaced many bomb-damaged inner-city areas which were razed to the ground and completely replaced. The housing of the poorer families and individuals in low-cost, and often low-quality, high-rises provided in many instances by the state became the norm to the east of the political divide as well as the West. Subsequently, this housing solution was normalised in cities across the globe and taken up by private developers too. While these densely-packed and crowded tower blocks afforded a rapid solution to the problem of cities blighted by war, they did not prove to be popular for long. Residents were often forced out of the areas in which they and their families had lived for generations, where communities had developed deep roots and were long established. They now found themselves rehoused in new towns and neighbourhoods in which they were separated from the supportive social networks and shared spaces of the past.

The newly-constructed areas of working-class living might have seemed superficially to resemble the blueprints left by Corbusier, but the leisure facilities, public transport links and opportunities for creative living and employment which were also written into his plans were not forthcoming in these new environments. The newly-constructed estates were not the utopias Corbusier and his followers had envisioned, but they lacked many basic amenities. Moreover, the green areas left between them were poorly maintained and easily degraded, hardly the spiritually and morally uplifting spaces envisioned by former plans. Families on floors above ground level were left with few safe spaces for small toddlers and children old enough to play outside, leaving the children well away from the supervisory gaze of their parents and neighbours. In reality, they did not function as family housing and in many places were instead let to single people and younger childless couples, once again changing the dynamics of community and neighbourhood interaction in these areas.

For critics of modernist urban planning, the newly-created cities and neighbourhoods which sprang up in the second half of the twentieth century embodied within them the functional principles of industrialism and the ordering of society required by capitalism into different classes. The zoning of cities into areas for commercial, employment and residential uses reflected the separation of the self required in a society dominated by mass production, the division of labour and the extreme specialisation of work and the replacement of skilled craftsmanship with the worker as unskilled automaton. They represented, too, the triumph of economic growth over other social values. In the same way, the planned and functional spaces embodied the move from organic to mechanical solidarity, which as we have seen in Chapter One so concerned the early critics of the urban form. The city-blocks and high-rises which have come to dominate every urban landscape demonstrate a homogeneity to city life which to writers like Jacobs were in danger of stifling creativity and difference. It is often remarked that the commercial hearts of twenty-first century cities are all dominated by the same stores, owned by the few multinational corporations which dominate in the world economy, underscoring again that there few spaces owned and controlled by individuals and their visions for the city. Our cities are more than ever planned and shaped by external forces for their own purposes, as 'temples of consumption' and generators of profit rather than to facilitate the building of meaningful social networks and community support. They are planned from above rather than built from below, stripping away the possibility for autonomous and creative solutions to the problems which can, all too often, be faced by their residents.

Economic flight and the destruction of community

Concern about the modern urban form and the destruction of organic community and creativity which it facilitated has been compounded in the postwar period by intense economic slumps which have occurred with some regularity and appear to be deepening in their extent and impact. Every slump has led to economic restructuring which has had catastrophic consequences for those who lose employment and their means of living as a result. The last half of the twentieth century saw a significant stripping out of industry from the so-called developed world and the flight of investment to the 'developing' economies where labour and other costs were lower and the profit-generating opportunities were consequently much higher. These economies have benefitted from this incoming investment in terms of increased opportunities for work and a higher standard of living for many, but they have also experienced similar social changes consequent to structural transformation from agricultural to industrialised production as Britain and North America experienced in the nineteenth century. The architectural forms which they have employed in order to grow their own cities and house their new workforce are similar in form to the densely-packed, high-rise blueprint adopted in the West and have generated similar social problems.

Where capital and investment have withdrawn from national and regional economies, the effects have been widespread. Cities, once built to house workers, now have to house the workless instead. Towns and villages, such as mining or dockland areas, which have been dependent on one main source of work and wages, have faced wholesale devastation as these industries have been shut down. These changes have taken their toll on community and neighbourhood relations as well as on the individuals affected. Social institutions built around work, and the secondary businesses which have relied for their source of income on a local waged workforce, have fallen by the wayside too. As a result of the withdrawal of money from these areas, whole populations have had to adapt to living in conditions of poverty, lack of work and uncertain futures. One solution has been for individuals to leave settled communities to look for work elsewhere, a solution that has fuelled intranational and international migration on a mass scale.

While the extent and nature of internal migration is difficult to assess, international migration figures are more accurately monitored, and they tell a story of some significance. Globally, the Organisation for Economic Co-operation and Development (OECD) has estimated that there are approximately 232 million international migrants in the world in 2014, with around 60 per cent residing in the 'developed' world (OECD 2014). The OECD estimates that around two million people migrated each year in the 1990s and that this figure rose to around 4.6 million each year from 2000 to 2010. After this period of boom, however, their figures show that migration flows have slowed somewhat. Although the total number of migrants globally might appear large, the total migrant population is estimated to account for just over 3 per cent of the world's population (OECD 2014).

Unequal and uneven development

The impact of internal and international migration has been more significant in some areas than in others. The majority of international migrations, for example, occur within economically advanced regions of the world, so that an economically successful city such as London was in 2013 made up of 8.3 million people, of whom 37 per cent were born outside of the country (The Migration Observatory 2014). Outside of these areas which have attracted substantial inward migration, there has been a concomitant emptying out of populations. The old agricultural communities have continued to be severely impacted by rural depopulation, and many are now aging communities with few young people able or willing to make a living in the countryside.

CASE STUDY – RURAL DEPOPULATION AND REPOPULATION IN SPAIN

From 1996 to 2010, 70 per cent of Spain's population growth came from inward migration. In 1996, only 1.4 per cent of its population (just over 500,000 people) were born outside Spain. In 2010, however, this had risen to 12.2 per cent of the population (over 5,700,000 individuals). This international migration has, to some extent, reversed a long-standing trend of depopulation of rural Spain which occurred as those of reproductive age moved to its industrial cities for work. This trend accelerated from the 1950s as traditional, subsistence farming became unviable (partly due to lack of local labour) and intensive farming on an industrial scale took its place. This further added to the depopulation of the countryside as this mode of food production today requires less labour power than it did in the past. This demographic trend slowed in the 1980s as rural economies were restructured to provide opportunities for rural tourism, the development of an improved infrastructure, improved communications and access to Internet technology, the building of second homes and an expansion of public-sector services in rural areas. This restructuring has helped to attract internal and international migration to the countryside. Those of foreign birth now make up nearly 7 per cent of the Spanish rural population. Although the rural population has increased as a result, it has not reached its former strength. These developments have also changed the class composition of rural areas as a new middle class which

(Continued)

is better educated with more disposable income has emerged as key to the sustainability of the rural economy. This has been termed 'rural gentrification'. It has been suggested that the middle-class incomers are more 'urban' in their outlook and that, rather than conforming to the values and traditions of the established communities, they have brought new ideas and lifestyles into rural areas, creating some tension between this group and the indigenous, local population (Bayona-i-Carrasco and Gil-Alonso: 2013).

The phenomenon of shrinking cities has also become apparent in much of the economically developed world since the 1970s. In Europe and North America this has occurred first as a result of deindustrialisation and has had far-reaching social and economic consequences as areas became depopulated and economically precarious. In the postcommunist nations of the East, the transition to economies based on models of Western capitalism have devastated established industries and contributed to migratory flows of the economically active out of these countries. The developed economies have also seen falling fertility rates and an aging population. This situation, combined with falling rates of economic activity, has left cities across the globe struggling to find ways to maintain both their social and physical infrastructures.

CASE STUDY – REGENERATING THE SHRINKING CITIES OF JAPAN

Japan has been losing population since the beginning of the twenty-first century, largely due to a rapidly declining birth rate. It is left with a population which is aging faster than in many other economies. Japan has also suffered serious economic decline. After the Second World War, the country rapidly industrialised to become one of the largest economies in the world. It was less affected by the downturn in global economic activity in the 1970s; however, an economic crash in 1991 precipitated a decade-long decline which was just beginning to be halted when the global financial crisis of 2008 again reversed the country's economic fortunes. The city of Osaka, for example, lost over 16,000 factories – nearly half its entire stock – in the fifteen years from 1990 to 2005. Unemployment rates in Japan have been amongst the lowest in the world but shot to a high of over 5 per cent of the workforce (still low in comparison to many other deindustrialised economies) and by 2014 had fallen to around 3.5 per cent.

The combination of population loss and financial crisis in Japan has seen increasing numbers of vacant houses, the closure of entire shopping areas, an underused infrastructure, public spaces emptied of people and a growing concern and fear for the future. Nearly one quarter of Japan's population was over 65 in 2014, and there is concern that its population will decline by approximately one-fifth by 2050 from its peak in 2005. Well over half of Japan's 2,217 municipalities saw a decline in their population between 2000 and 2005 as their residents moved to its largest cities. Indeed, at the turn of the last century over half of Japan's population lived in these cities, but it is now projected that they will also see a rapid decline in their populations. As Japan has had strict immigration controls in the past and continues with this policy, a solution cannot be found in encouraging inward international migration (Buhnik 2010).

Over the last decade (since around 2004), the 'creative city' movement has gained some prominence globally, with UNESCO promoting global cultural diversity through its 'Global Network of Creative Cities'. Urban theorists have used the work of Jane Jacobs (1984 in Sasaki 2010) on cultural regeneration of urban spaces to adopt the creative city model as a tool to strengthen the economy of cities which have lost their productive base. Jacobs argued that cities which rely on production and export of goods for wealth-creation leave themselves particularly vulnerable to external factors outside their control. They should rebalance their economies, Jacob recommends, by attracting inward investment through the promotion of local cultural industries and cultural tourism using their unique characters as a form of 'cultural capital' which others will buy in to. As a result, cities will develop their own economies based on local cultural industries and hospitality, and thereby build a local workforce which is diversified, more resilient and has generated wealth from within, which can also be spent locally. In Japan, three cities have been registered as creative cities by UNESCO – Kanazawa, Kobe and Nagoya – and others are adopting the creative city model to develop their local infrastructure and economies around cultural industries. In this way, they hope to attract new residents and contribute to economic reconstruction nationally (Sasaki 2010).

Outwardly successful cities have also seen fluctuations in the fate of their residents. In the UK, for example, while London as a whole seems on the surface to be faring quite well, the incomes of the poorest 10 per cent of the population have fallen dramatically since the crash of 2008 and poverty has spread more evenly across the borough of Greater London than previously. This development appears to be a consequence of increasing inequality, with Inner London and its financial, commercial and residential districts doing comparatively well (Lupton 2013), while in its poorer neighbourhoods residents are struggling to meet high rents and the increasing costs of living. This London story has replicated itself in cities and regions across the globe.

The shifting social contract

The sustained global boom which followed immediately after the Second World War seemed to many to demonstrate an end to economic cycles of boom and bust which had previously characterised capitalism. In the West standards of living were on the rise, productivity remained high for nearly thirty years and unemployment remained low. A number of economic theorists heralded the end of crises and predicted continuing growth into the future and the possible end of poverty (Bell 1960). Their complacency was shattered in the late 1960s and early 1970s as the boom came to an end and the US suffered a collapse in the rate of profit. As the dollar lost its value, the postwar economic consensus which had kept Western economies tied to the dollar was dismantled, and national economies floated their currencies independently. The ensuing financial mayhem as national exchange rates fluctuated wildly, together with a collapse in business confidence, saw the return of high-price inflation, a slowdown in production and the beginnings of a rise in unemployment and a subsequent drop in household income. This financial crisis was compounded by what has become known as 'the oil crisis'. In 1973, the oil-producing countries, having grown in confidence economically and politically, began to flex their muscles on the global stage. Oil production was cut by around 20 per cent, the price of a barrel of oil almost doubled and supplies were restricted. In addition, the oil-producing regions demanded that more of the profit from the sale of oil be ploughed back into local economies rather than profiting multinational corporations. The ensuing economic slump had wide-ranging impacts.

The long post-war economic boom had financed a level of state expenditure in the economically developed nations which was unparalleled in human history but after the economic slump of the 1970s it was argued that this level of expenditure could not be sustained. The welfarist project was accompanied by the idea of the 'social contract', which stated that should individuals play their part, get a decent education, look for work and play by the rules, in turn this would result in the availability of 'good work' that paid well and a level of government services providing a level of care and financial support for those who found themselves without work through no fault of their own (Rubin 2012). According to Rubin, the social contract was premised on the understanding that:

> [if] individuals develop skills, invest in human capital, network, show up at work and work hard; they have a reasonable expectation that those investments in their own abilities, in relationships and the social worlds in which they are embedded will translate into a way of life for which they have been preparing.
> (2012:331)

After the 1970s, however, business and the state gradually began to withdraw from their side of the social contract, so that work and social conditions which prevail under contemporary capitalism look very different to those which were normal in the early 1970s. The postwar consensus on employment led to benefits such as paid holidays and sick leave, a plethora of employment rights such as maternity leave, the right to join and actively organise in a trade union, set working hours and a contract of employment which held the employer to certain standards in their treatment of workers. Many, if not all, of these rights have been eroded or withdrawn today. Rubin cites the hyperexploitation of workers, so-called flexible working which actually demands 24/7 availability from workers, technological advances which allow workers to be constantly linked in to work environments and to extend work into private life as characteristics of the contemporary work environment. This environment, she argues, has helped to 'shift' the social contract but could also be said to have all but destroyed it for many. The expectation that governments provide for their citizens has been represented and criticised as a 'sense of entitlement' held by individuals, which holds them back from providing for themselves. Those who are entering the world of work today are likely to be paid less than their parents, to work longer hours with less employment rights and to retire much later, if they can find work at all.

From renewal to regeneration

In the 1970s, the social contract was still more or less intact. The postwar rebuilding of cities was largely achieved with funding from national governments, and urban renewal was largely considered a national and public matter. So the crisis of dein-dustrialisation, rising unemployment and increasing poverty was initially considered the responsibility of the state to attempt to resolve. Subsequently, however, respon-sibility began to shift away from the national state, the problem was pushed further down to local and regional state authorities and then, beginning in the 1980s it was expected that partnerships would be built with the private sector to lever in finance from this sector too. As the financing models have changed, so too has the focus of the partners involved. Postwar urban renewal emphasised the development of society and the provision of infrastructure and housing. It reflected a certain optimism that building the physical infrastructure for future economic and social success would benefit the country as a whole and lead to a general growth in pros-perity. By the 1970s, however, this optimism had faded, and the idea of regenera-tion of failed local economies, rather than renewal of neighbourhoods and society, gained currency. The regeneration discourse is more concerned with responding to and finding ways to adapt to a crisis, whether this is manifest at the level of the economy or community and neighbourhood. Perversely, given that the problem of deindustrialisation and economic degeneration was global in its reach, regeneration has been largely driven at a local level. As we will see later in this chapter, this was in part a move away from the imposition of national solutions onto local communities and a concern to devolve responsibility to the local level (Roberts and Sykes 1999). Regeneration policies also had the effect of fragmenting responses to problems which were manifest nationally and internationally. To be successful, regeneration should include an analysis of factors which are economic, social and related to the built environment which are considered to be holding back a particular local area. It should also formulate a strategy which can address all of these factors. The next section looks at the economic policies considered necessary to regeneration in different periods.

Regenerating economy

The first regeneration strategies were designed to allow adaptations in the industrial environment in which towns and cities operated. Deindustrialisation had left whole areas of cities without an economic function as industries withdrew but left behind buildings and machinery which were now redundant. The devastation left by the retreat of industry was palpable and physical as well as social in its impact. Local councils, aided initially by access to central government funds, encouraged town planning authorities to allow a redesignation and refunctioning of these abandoned spaces to allow emerging industries (often based in the service rather than the production sectors) to sweep away the old and replace with new office and factory spaces more appropriate for their needs. This phase also involved retraining local workers so that they would learn new skill-sets considered more relevant to production needs in the late twentieth century. Schools and colleges were also expected to get involved, adapting curricula to educate young people for the demands of emerging technology and knowledge-based industries. The new industries, however, did not require the large workforces necessary to establish and sustain manufacturing. This led to fears that large sections of urban populations might remain largely economically inactive and that authorities might have to plan for a 'work society that is running out of work' (Dahrendorf 1985:119 in Crowther 2000:182).

In the 1980s, regeneration projects shifted towards the provision of commerce rather than industry. This was the decade of the emergence and then proliferation of the 'out-of-town' shopping mall. The old town centres and local neighbourhood shops had been devastated by economic slump in the 1970s, and rather than concentrate on renewing the old infrastructure the solution was thought to lie in building designated 'temples of consumption' (Taylor et al 1996). The older established shopping areas had been situated close to local amenities, centres of democratic participation such as town halls, health services and housing, but these new shopping centres were dedicated to consumption, offered nothing in the way of public services and were isolated from everyday services. They required the shopper to leave behind community, neighbourhood and locality to travel in order to consume. These were privately owned and managed centres, designed purely for expenditure on shopping and leisure; some included pubs, restaurants and cinemas. Those who were not consuming were not welcome, and as Norris and Armstrong (1999) have revealed, CCTV surveillance was used to eliminate 'undesirables' – often those who were not shopping – from the centres altogether. The development of areas specifically designated for different types of consumption reflected a wider economic restructuring towards producing wealth through commerce rather than through industry.

The 1980s and 1990s also saw a global deregulation of financial services with a relaxation of rules around debt and the availability of finance. The West was going to spend its way out of recession rather than try to recapture its industrial global supremacy. Individuals were allowed to amass higher and higher levels of debt in order to enable this change in economic focus to occur. This period has been associated, at least in the Anglo-American world, with a closer relationship between regeneration strategies and the private sector. In addition, individuals were (and are) encouraged to access private-sector funding to start their own businesses rather than rely on a dwindling stock of employment opportunities in order to become property owners rather than renting from the public or private sector. They were also expected to develop self-reliance rather than wait for the public sector to provide opportunities. Private finance initiatives dominated regeneration in this period within which, in an effort to reduce the burden of public-sector debt, large-scale and extensive projects such as the building of new hospitals and schools were financed almost entirely without public-sector funding but with the promise that the private financers could continue to extract rent and/or profits from the project for many years into the future. Precisely how this will affect the running of these institutions in future years has yet to be fully realised. It is clear, however, that in this last period the removal of public-sector funding and a turn to a reliance on private financing has seen the national and local state institutions taking on the role of 'enablers' rather than 'providers' of many public services (Hancock 2001:6).

Housing as a motor for regeneration

The provision of housing, and the form it takes remains a key area of social policy. It is estimated, for example, that 80 per cent of all development in the UK relates to housing (Edgar and Taylor 2000). In addition, where we live has a profound effect on our quality of life and on opportunities in our present and future lives. The physical conditions in which we live can affect our physical and mental health, overcrowded housing can create real misery and distress and a lack of privacy and quiet space can negatively affect the ability to use home as a site of education, self-improvement and work. The residential neighbourhood can provide access to good schools, efficient transport links and recreational facilities, or it can be devoid of such services and trap its residents into a spiral of decline and social exclusion. Areas can gain reputations, which means that it is difficult for anyone with a particular address to find work (referred to in the UK as post-code discrimination). Housing is also important for any discussion and exploration of residential community. In the latter decades of the twentieth century, demand for housing changed significantly as across the developed world families became smaller, more fragmented and the number of people living on their own across all age ranges increased dramatically. As a consequence, the provision of housing has had to change to accommodate these demands (Edgar and Taylor 2000). So the social, as well as the physical, aspects of housing and how populations are housed remains hugely significant.

Housing has also been a source of some tension in the city, especially where it remains a scarce resource. In the 1960s, John Rex and Robert Moore conducted a study of Sparkbrook, an inner-city area within the city of Birmingham in the UK (Rex and Moore 1967). They argued that housing was a key source of conflict in the city, with certain groups disadvantaged and discriminated against in the housing market. The poorer sections of the population were without the financial means to access decent accommodation, and black and minority ethnic (BME) groups were effectively barred from local authority housing by a prior-residence qualification, which forced them into substandard multi-occupied dwellings supplied by private landlords in the inner city. The struggle over housing was conceptualised by Rex and Moore as one of competing 'housing classes'. While this conceptualisation has come under some criticism, the problems they outlined have resurfaced wherever housing is a scarce commodity. Newly arrived workers are considered as taking what by right belongs to the indigenous population if they are able to access decent housing.

In the 1980s, Anthony Bottoms and Paul Wiles, again as a result of research based in the UK but this time in the city of Sheffield, developed the idea of 'community crime careers' which they concluded were significantly affected by access to different housing markets (Bottoms and Wiles 1986). Some groups, they argued, found themselves unable to access housing in areas with good services, schools and employment opportunities and were as a result forced to occupy less desirable locations. As a result, the more poorly serviced areas developed different social relations. The authors suggested that the amount of crime recorded in an area therefore resulted from more than just the number of people living in an area with a propensity to commit crime, but that the demographic constitution of an area and the social relations active within it would lead to some areas being more criminogenic than others. Bottoms and Wiles argued that:

> [t]he interactive effects within and between groups, the development of particular cultural patterns, or both may be more criminogenically important than any initial propensity to offend. Furthermore, once the population of an area is allocated and its community crime profile established, this will be further influenced by the wider social response to that community.
>
> (1986:122)

For Bottoms and Wiles then, residential patterns within an area were significant in determining its 'crime career'. Areas with high numbers of children and young teenagers, for example, would be more likely to suffer from graffiti and criminal damage. The authors concluded that housing allocation policies should seek to find a suitable mix of residents within a particular area which would mitigate against the sustaining of anti-social and criminal activity in an area. Consideration of future demographic trends, they stated, should also be a key factor for consideration. This argument was later used to support the 'gentrification' of areas, but gentrification did not come without problems, some of which are discussed in the following sections of this chapter.

These insights into the links between housing and crime were further developed by the UK-based criminologist Tim Hope, who analysed a number of years of data from the British Crime Survey, a victimisation survey. In 1996 he published research demonstrating that crime was concentrated in a very few areas and that these areas suffered disproportionately from both personal and property crime. These were poor areas in which residents lacked economic resources, where (low quality) rental housing predominated, where a high proportion of young people (those under 25) resided and where there was a higher than average number of single-parent households. In these areas, Hope suggested, there lived a higher than average number of people who were vulnerable to crime, and these groups suffered disproportionately from victimisation. His figures were quite shocking. Hope divided his sample into ten groups (deciles) based on their levels of victimisation. The data demonstrated that those in the highest decile of victimisation suffered eleven times more offences against the person and four times the numbers of burglaries than those in the lowest decile. It was clear that crime was not distributed evenly across the population and that the unequal distribution of crime had to be taken seriously. Regeneration of neighbourhoods was closely allied with crime prevention and in the UK initiatives such as Safer Cities and Crime Concern were developed to combat concerns about the rising rate of crime and the fear that cities and town centres were unsafe places in which to do business (Crawford 1998:50–58).

Research such as that published by Rex, Moore, Bottoms, Wiles and Hope reinforced a trend for intervention in 'housing markets' designed to reduce social tensions and the number of criminal offences in disadvantaged areas. As a result of their work, housing policy became a key strategy in the armoury of crime prevention (see Chapter One for a discussion of social and community crime prevention theory and practice), along with the attempts at socially engineering neighbourhoods to find a suitable and stable mix of residents. In some countries, such as Canada, this intervention reached into policy-making at a national level, and housing providers were required to consider the social mix of their estates to ensure that social exclusion did not become enshrined and institutionalised within any area (Foley and Evans 1993a and 1993b). This intervention also saw the demolition, using public funds, of some of the most unpopular estates through which the brutal modernist architecture of concrete high-rises and 'streets in the sky' was replaced by more traditional family housing with gardens and 'picket fences', often supplied through the private sector but with public-sector support and approval.

For housing to continue to play a major role in regeneration and renewal, it must remain a significant issue for national and local government. However, since the 1980s and accelerating in the 1990s, the provision of housing has largely been left in the hands of the private sector, and in many countries owner-occupation has been promoted as the ideal form of housing tenure. In the Anglo-American context, publically-provided housing has been associated with multiple social problems and perceived as a failed social experiment. The move away from public-sector provision towards owner-occupation is driven by the idea that publically-provided accommodation leads to over-reliance on the state and a culture of dependence, while private ownership promotes self-reliance and responsibility. The charge that public-sector intervention in the supply of housing has failed was largely due, however, to housing policy which increasingly saw public housing as a solution of last resort, leading to a concentration of the poorest families in a few residential areas. This concentration of the poor in publically-provided estates is not inevitable. In Singapore, where the majority of residents live in housing provided through the public sector, it is argued that an income mix is ensured in each housing block and the qualifying income for public housing is frequently raised to ensure that most of the population is not debarred from access (Zhu Xiao Di et al 2009).

Urban gentrification logic and its problems

As the logic of the market became more closely embedded into the policy and practice of regeneration, the idea of 'housing markets' resurfaced. Rather than calling for the planning and building of more public-sector housing, regeneration organisations have sought to intervene in 'housing markets' in order to improve the quality and availability of housing stock. This intervention has entailed policy-makers operating at the neighbourhood level to facilitate private- and voluntary-sector activity in regenerating the supply of housing. In England in the early years of the twenty-first century, this approach was dubbed Housing Market Renewal. It was brought in as policy under a Labour administration and was clearly driven by market logic. Whole areas of housing which were deemed substandard, unsuitable or in low demand were demolished street by street, with the promise that they would be replaced by new-built stock which was of better quality, more attractive to potential residents and could be sold on the private market. Neighbourhoods were targeted for Housing Market Renewal if they were considered to have 'tipped' into a spiral of decline, which in the UK was defined as an area with a preponderance of rented housing, owner-occupiers living in low-quality stock, a uniformity in type and size of property, too many flats or terraced housing, an aging population and high unemployment (Webb 2010).

By the time Housing Market Renewal (HMR) became a popular option for local authorities, the rhetoric justifying policy intervention had turned away from regeneration towards the gentrification of neighbourhoods. 'Gentrification' suggests that areas need to attract a different type of resident rather than an approach which engages existing residents in a wholescale revitalisation of their area and lives. As a result, HMR involves the compulsory purchase of properties from their existing residents, the demolition of some of these properties and their replacement with 'desirable' dwellings which could be sold on the open market and attract a new type of local resident with money, aspiration and the personal resources to make a difference to the area. HMR involves disruption to the lives of existing residents and has also been criticised for destroying established communities as residential patterns are redesigned and residents find that they cannot afford to return or that there are no spaces left for them in the new neighbourhood configuration. Webb has argued that HMR policy is particularly blinkered in its focus and can only see the exchange value of property and the renewal of markets as significant, placing all other needs into obscurity. He further argues that 'factors which do not readily appear in statistical form and any factors which are not indicated as relevant by a market-based outlook' are essentially considered as an irrelevance (Webb 2010:320). Unsurprisingly, HMR has galvanised community action by residents who have campaigned vociferously against the destruction of their properties and way of life and have argued that the powerful forces governing their lives have ignored their own needs, perceiving them as problems to be swept aside rather than resources to be engaged in social and economic renewal.

Minton (2009) has also critiqued HMR. Her overall thesis in *Ground Control* is concerned with the corporatization of cities. She traces corporatization in Britain to Thatcher's Urban Development Corporations (UDCs) which were used as vehicles to secure the privatization of public space in cities. This, Minton argues, was achieved by circumventing local democracy; UDCs made extensive use of compulsory purchase powers and operated outside the normal planning rules and with little scrutiny of their activities. Minton also identifies another trend which she considered equally seditious and which she refers to as 'corporate capture' – aided and abetted by the neo-liberal state-of housing land that is privately owned and occupied by working-class people. Minton points out that this latter aspect of corporatization has been made possible by planning legislation which made it easier than ever to secure the compulsory purchase of housing. Minton describes how cities such as Liverpool have made extensive use of these strengthened compulsory purchase powers to remove working-class people from parts of the urban landscape. This has invited large-scale resistance, but, as Minton observes in Liverpool, urban elites have arrogantly ignored this resistance. Far from giving urban elites pause for thought, protestors' legal victories against the compulsory purchase of homes in Liverpool merely resulted in the issue of new compulsory purchase orders – on the same day that original compulsory purchase orders were quashed by the courts. The counter-response to resistance has been dubbed 'regeneration by attrition'. One resident, and a key opponent of HMR in Liverpool, Elizabeth Pascoe, in Minton's book, describes how this happens: 'When we got the second compulsory purchase notification, about a hundred people left. Then people did give in. They could see it was going to go on and on. About thirty of us have died, whether they stayed or gave in, because it has been very traumatic' (p. 88).

Communities and regeneration

While the state retained a central role in postwar renewal and regeneration, the inclusion of local organisations and residents in their planning was quite limited. From the 1960s, however, the role of the state in determining the present and future prospects of its population was beginning to be questioned. Social movements of global significance, built from the grassroots, organised within civil society to challenge a number of dominant values, and the ideals of participatory democracy and self-organisation gained some prominence (Castells 1983). Demonstrations of 'people power' across the world demanding civil rights for formerly oppressed groups contributed to reshaping social attitudes and wrested a range of human rights issues from the hands of reluctant states (Harman 1988). While some of this activity was organised from within the labour and student movements, it also came from an organisation at the community level which appeared unprecedented. The civil rights movement in the US, for example, was largely led by black community churches. Community action was also seen as an opportunity to build radical, grassroots alternatives to unpopular state-controlled policies, and such initiatives were largely built by progressive secular forces too. Many on the left were wary of state power, which had led the US into war in Vietnam, had enforced policies of racial segregation and had passed discriminatory legislation. In the self-styled communist states of the USSR and Eastern Europe, the first murmurs of dissent were also felt as the role of Stalinism in subjugating the people of the communist bloc was beginning to emerge. 'People power' was proclaimed as a new force in society, and unsurprisingly the enthusiasm and excitement of these movements played into radical models for community development, which it was believed could resist the growing powers of both state and capital. The involvement of the community in its own redevelopment has become something of a political mantra since the 1960s, but the shape of this involvement has taken many turns.

Community development in disorganised communities – community control and collective efficacy

In the 1970s, a decade influenced by the radicalism of the 1960s but also coping with the effects of sharp economic decline in many areas, community development encompassed a progressive approach looking to correct the problems created by an overbearing state and an economic system unable to prevent inequalities and severe social problems, including increasing rates of recorded crime. The community development model which emerged in this period was based on neighbourhoods which appeared to be excluded and marginalised from 'normal' patterns of growth and sustainability. Community development projects were subsequently proposed in areas of substandard housing, high crime and poor economic status with lack of work and other opportunities. It was suggested that the communities most affected by economic and social problems would include within them the knowledge and expertise to halt and reverse their decline. Projects were consequently developed which aimed to harness the capacity of an area's residents to organise as political subjects, thus 'empowering' them as a group and allowing their voices to be recognised, heard and acted upon. Sometimes the catalysts for change were community activists themselves initiating change from below such as tenant-controlled housing, community businesses, running local community centres or food co-ops. At other times, community development was supported and financed from above but focused on helping to develop community-based organisation.

The extent to which these developments have been rooted in community activism and self-help is a moot point. In 1969, Sherry Arnstein developed a 'ladder of participation' which was designed to distinguish projects in which participation was real and the interested community was in control of the scheme from those in which participation was claimed but was mere tokenism. The ladder consisted of eight rungs, labelled Citizen Control at the top and Manipulation on the bottom rung. The higher up the ladder, and the more elements introduced at the higher rungs, then the closer the project was to what Arnstein called citizen power. In the middle of the ladder at rungs 3 to 5, the community might be consulted or individuals might be placed on an advisory committee, but their views might be little heeded. By rungs 6 and upwards, the power to make decisions begins to be passed to the community and away from the powerful elites who are usually in control of decision making. The ladder can be used to test the claims of different projects which purport to be truly controlled by the community.

The community development model is anchored in social disorganisation theory and suggests that marginalised neighbourhoods are characterised by a failure to adapt to changing economic and social conditions. It nevertheless proposes that self-organisation is possible in these areas and should be encouraged in order to restore trust and civility between neighbours. In 1997 Sampson, Raudenbush and Earls introduced the idea of *collective efficacy* to explain why some neighbourhoods appeared to be more ordered and controlled than others. They proposed that some of the effects of difficult socioeconomic conditions can be offset by the willingness and ability of a community to self-regulate. Collective efficacy, they argued, can be said to exist where there are 'conditions of mutual trust and solidarity among neighbors' (Sampson et al 1997:919). It is most likely to be found, they maintained, where home ownership is high (residents have therefore financially invested in their area) and where a high proportion of residents have lived in the area for some time (residents have socially invested in the neighbourhood). It is least likely to be found in areas of concentrated poverty and where there have been high rates of migration into an area. Where collective efficacy was high, they argued, crime and violence are likely to be lower. Sampson et al were clear that their work should not be used to ignore structural inequalities (which, they stated, have a hugely negative effect on collective efficacy). Nevertheless, this model of community development can, and did, slip into denigration of struggling areas and their residents, and it feeds into arguments suggesting that poor areas are damned by a 'culture of poverty' (Lewis 1968).

Community development and capital deficit – economic and social capital meets communitarianism

In this second model of community development, the focus shifts from the problems of the particular community and its dysfunctionality and places the community into its wider economic context. From this perspective, the neighbourhood is struggling due to its isolation from significant economic networks, and 'financial and human capital are needed to re-activate dormant markets and create new wealth' (Wolf-Powers 2014:206). Residents are considered less as community activists and more as 'entrepreneurial subjects' (Lemke 2001:54 in Wolf-Powers 2014). Regeneration practices within this model are organised to improve the economic success of an area, to ensure that the area is connected to wider markets through better transport and telematics, to attract businesses through grants and tax breaks and to refurbish public spaces to a higher standard, removing signs of disorder, installing better lighting and giving the appearance of safety and security. Its social regeneration arm feeds money into improving local schools and revitalising local employment opportunities. In the last decade of the twentieth century, much of this work was passed into the hands of the private sector (see Anna Minton's *Ground Control* for a description of this turn in the UK). The privatisation of regeneration saw what Minton (2009) has termed the 'corporatisation' of public spaces. An increasing number of shopping centres, business districts and some regeneration zones were given over to private ownership, removing them from the oversight of public planning authorities. Areas of housing earmarked for 'gentrification' are increasingly built by private developers as 'gated communities', attracting premium prices and offering safety and security to their residents, but little of this will 'trickle' down to the surrounding streets. Large tracts of city land in some areas are now owned by these large corporations, and their future will be planned for profit-making by the boards of organisations which are not democratically accountable.

In the 1990s, the concept of *social capital* also emerged as an 'organising theme' in community development (De Filippis 2001:781). The concept was first brought to the attention of community development theorists by James Coleman in 1988 and developed on a more philosophical level by Pierre Bourdieu in 1986, but it was Robert Putnam's utilisation of the concept in *Bowling Alone* (2000) which popularised the term. While definitions vary as to what is meant by the term 'social capital', it is generally used to refer to the advantages conferred on an individual as a consequence of the social environment in which he or she has been raised and the importance of the systems of knowledge, behaviour, appearance and social networks which can be accessed as a consequence, giving the person or community with social capital distinct advantages over others. While Coleman and Bourdieu saw social capital as something which could be built up and possessed collectively, for Putnam a community's 'social capital' is the aggregate of individual social capital which is held in any area. In *Bowling Alone* Putnam argues that social capital in America is in steep decline; that membership of community organisations is no longer central to social life; and that individuals and entire communities lack access to the forms of social capital which could help them to succeed. For Putnam this deficit needs to be addressed, so that healthy social relationships and civic values can be restored, rejuvenating co-operation and participation in democratic structures. Later, Putnam added the concept of 'bridging capital' to develop his analysis further in his effort to promote the importance of the vertical links to sources of economic and political power which lie outside the locality. While Bourdieu's analysis of social capital described and critiqued its various elements, Putnam elevated the possession of social capital to the status of a 'public good' (De Filippis 2001). In addition to the focus on building economic and social capital, Putnam's work also raised the issue of civic connectedness. Earlier theorists had advised that a community strengthen its horizontal (local relationships between residents) and vertical (connecting local institutions to centralised power structures) networks (Hope 1995) in order to put pressure on the locally powerful to bring about necessary change. In contrast, the concept of 'civic capital' assigned the individual and the community the responsibility to bring about change through their own activity and interventions. So community activists were encouraged to stand for positions locally and to enter onto the operating boards and policy-making teams of local organisations in order to make a difference. In this way, Putnam thought that they could tap into wider networks which would afford them access to different forms of capital and break them from the isolation holding them back.

Elements of Putnam's work accorded with the philosophy of *communitarianism* as it was espoused by Amitai Etzioni in his much-cited *The Spirit of Community* (1993). In this book Etzioni rejected the self-centred individualism which he believed had characterised the liberalism of the preceding decade and called for an orientation towards a sense of community belonging. He advocated a turn towards mutuality and respect, starting within and between families and moving out to schools, education and the wider society. Etzioni has been dubbed a 'moral authoritarian' (Hughes 1998), but his argument that individual rights could not exist without social responsibilities and that individuals build allegiance with others in reciprocal relationships has been enthusiastically taken up by a number of governments on all sides of the political spectrum. As will be discussed in more detail in Chapter Seven, communitarianism has underpinned a great deal of policy intervention in the intervening years, not least in the construction of 'the active citizen' explored more fully in Chapter Seven. It must be remarked that the active, democratically engaged and responsible citizenship promoted by communitarian thinkers stands in stark contrast to the simultaneous corporatisation of city spaces and their futures discussed earlier – though these two, seemingly incompatible approaches have often had the same champions.

Regeneration – a critique

Castells wrote in *The City and the Grassroots*:

> [T]he search for spatial meaningfulness and cultural identity, the demands for social goods and services, and the drift toward local autonomy, have triggered in the last decade a series of urban protest movements that, in very different contexts, called for urban reform and envisioned an alternative city. The squatter communities in Germany, Holland, and Denmark; the youth movement in Zurich; the neighbourhood associations in Spain; the massive uprisings over public services in Italy; the tenants struggles in Frances [sic]; the revolt of inner cities in England; the growing urban mobilization in the metropolises of newly industrialised countries, such as Caracas, Rio de Janeiro, Sao Paulo, and Mexico; the self-reliant squatter settlements of the third world, from Lima to Manila; the widespread new neighbourhood movement arising in American cities from the ashes of urban revolts of the 1960s, across a much broader social spectrum; the environmentalist movement throughout the world. In spite of their obvious diversity, all these movements have proposed a new relationship between space and society.
>
> (1983:xv)

This search for urban reform continues in the many social movements today which have sought to find meaning and purpose in today's urban spaces and economic formations. Over the last decades, these have been joined by the demand for control over the countryside, the right to ownership of land, anti-corporatism and the demand to return privatised space to public ownership. However, notwithstanding some brief moments when community activism was encouraged, regeneration activity has remained largely top-down and designed without the full involvement of the communities it was meant to advantage.

Regeneration policies have largely kept to a specific script. They are not critical of the dominant organisation of economy, production and property, but they seek to ensure that struggling communities adapt to the prevailing conditions of economic decline and social exclusion. In addition, they have not succeeded in eliminating poverty, inequalities and lack of opportunities to thrive, which are constructed outside the confines of neighbourhood. Too often the lack of success in turning marginalised neighbourhoods around has been explained by reference to a deficit in the individuals and communities which have been damaged by decades of poverty, worklessness and despair (Power and Tunstall 1997). As Power and Tunstall observe, the attempts to involve residents in what is seen as necessary change have not succeeded in protecting them from victimisation, disorder and unrest. Too often the focus has been on the physical fabric of place rather than on changing the structural conditions which have led to a neighbourhood's decline.

In addition, the language of the market has been imposed on regeneration agendas. Areas have had to compete with one another for scarce resources; engagement in economic success is considered paramount; the public sector has been downscaled; and essential services have been left in the hands of private operators. Rather than giving a voice to those who are excluded from the marketplace for reasons of poverty, ill-health, discrimination and so forth, the excluded have been demonised as worthless and a drain on society. When the rights of the excluded – to housing, funds for living, education and health – are raised, we are told that there is no 'entitlement' to these necessary resources but that they must be earned – utilising the very market logic which has excluded them in the first place. It is little surprise that under these circumstances people are likely to choose 'exit' rather than 'engagement'. As Wolf-Powers (2014) remarks, regeneration has followed the dominant ideas regarding the welfare state as inflexible, out-of-touch and a creator of dependency cultures, while the market is said to be dynamic, responsive and motivational, underlying the argument that regeneration policy over the last fifty years has been complicit in exclusionary practices rather than combatting them.

Some concluding comments and questions

The rebuilding of community and neighbourhood which began after the Second World War was based on a reinstatement of the physical fabric of a damaged Europe. In many areas, the social relations of neighbourhood were as devastated as the built environment, but in a frenzy of postwar reconstruction there was little heed paid to sustaining the community relations which had survived. The following decades therefore witnessed further uprooting of individuals and families as they were rehoused in newly built estates. Still the mood was one of optimism, and in this period national governments were keen to reestablish some sort of order in a world which had been turned upside-down. The promise of work, housing and government which would help to take care of the sick and elderly was seen as a reward for years of fighting and the privations of war. Once the economic boom of the 1950s and 1960s petered out, however, a harsher environment was ushered in. Economic slump and the shock tactics of neo-liberal economics which have been implemented as a consequence have had a devastating effect on many people's lives. The demands of global markets have shaped lives at a national and a local level, but the regeneration or rebuilding of shattered neighbourhoods and communities holds out the promise that local restructuring can make the difference that is needed. Communities have been co-opted into this regeneration practice and held responsible for its ultimate success or failure. It is important to consider:

1. To what extent can global problems be solved at a local level?
2. What part can local communities play in this process?

Further reading

Castells's work on social movements *The City and the Grassroots* (1983) and Harvey's *Spaces of Hope* (2000) are a useful starting point for understanding how communities can engage in struggles to fight their exclusion and for re-connecting residents to wider economic and social opportunities. They stand in stark contrast to the top-down attempts at regeneration which have been implemented through national and local government policies. Minton's *Ground Control* (2009) supplies a devastating critique of market ideologies and their effects on community.

References

Arnstein, S. R. (1969) 'A Ladder of Citizen Participation' *Journal of the American Institute of Planners* 35(4) pp. 216–24.

Bayona-i-Carrasco, J., and Gil-Alonso, F. (2013) 'Is Foreign Immigration the Solution to Rural Depopulation? The Case of Catalonia (1996–2009)' *Sociologia Ruralis* 53(1) pp. 26–51.

Bell, D. (1960) *The End of Ideology: On the Exhaustion of Political Ideas in the Fifties* Cambridge, MA: Harvard University Press.

Bottoms, A. E., and Wiles, P. (1986) 'Housing Tenure and Residential Community Crime Careers' in Reiss, A. J., and Tonry, M. (eds), *Communities and Crime* Chicago: University of Chicago Press.

Bourdieu, P. (1986) 'The Forms of Capital' in Richardson, J. (ed), *Handbook of Theory and Research for the Sociology of Education* pp. 241–58. Westport, CT: Greenwood Press.

Buhnik, S. (2010) 'From Shrinking Cities to Toshi no Shukushō: Identifying Patterns of Urban Shrinkage in the Osaka Metropolitan Area' *Berkeley Planning Journal* 23 pp. 132–55.

Castells, M. (1983) *The City and the Grassroots: A Cross-Cultural Theory of Urban Social Movements* London: Arnold.

Cochrane, A. (1999) 'Building Urban Utopias' in Pile et al (eds), *Unruly Cities? Order/Disorder* London: Routledge.

Coleman, J. (1988) 'Social Capital in the Creation of Human Capital' *American Journal of Sociology* Supplement 94: S95–S120.

Crawford, A. (1998) *Crime Prevention and Community Safety* Harlow, UK: Longman.

Crowther, C. (2000) *Policing Urban Poverty* Basingstoke, UK: Macmillan Press.

De Filippis, J. (2001) 'The Myth of Social Capital in Community Development' *Housing Policy Debate* 12(4) pp. 781–806.

Edgar, B., and Taylor, J. (2000) 'Housing', in Roberts, P., and Sykes, H. (eds), *Urban Regeneration: A Handbook* (pp. 153–175) London: Sage.

Etzioni, A. (1993) *The Spirit of Community: Rights, Responsibilities and the Communitarian Agenda* New York: Crown Publishers.

Fainstein, S., and Campbell, S. (eds) (2006) *Readings in Urban Theory* London: Blackwells.

Ferrell, J. (2001) *Tearing Down the Streets* Basingstoke, UK: Palgrave.

Foley, B., and Evans, K. (1993a) 'Housing Co-operatives, Education and Tenant Participation' *CCEPS Occasional Papers* University of Liverpool.

Foley, B., and Evans, K. (1993b) 'Housing Co-operatives in Canada' *CCEPS Occasional*.

Hancock, L. (2001) *Community, Crime and Disorder: Safety and Regeneration in Urban Neighbourhoods* Basingstoke, UK: Palgrave.

Harman, C. (1988) *The Fire Last Time* London: Bookmarks.

Harvey, D. (2000) *Spaces of Hope* Edinburgh: Edinburgh University Press.

Hope, T. (1996) 'Communities, Crime and Inequality in England and Wales' in Bennett, T. (ed), *Preventing Crime and Disorder: Targeting Strategies and Responsibilities* Cambridge: Institute of Criminology.

Hope, T. (1995) 'Building a Safer Society: Strategic Approaches to Crime Prevention' *Crime and Justice* 19 pp. 21–89.

Howard, E. (1946) *Garden Cities of To-Morrow* London: Faber and Faber.

Hughes, G. (1998) *Understanding Crime Prevention* Buckingham, UK: Open University Press.

Lacey, N., and Zedner, L. (1995) 'Discourses of Community in Criminal Justice' *Journal of Law and Society* 2(3) pp. 301–25.

Lewis, O. (1968) *La vida: A Puerto Rican Family in the Culture of Poverty* London: Panther.

Lupton, R. (2013) *A Tale of Two Cities? London's Economic Success Does Not Seem to Have Translated into Lower Rates of Poverty or Inequality* http://blogs.lse.ac.uk/politicsandpolicy/a-tale-of-two-cities/ [Accessed 07.07.14].

Minton, A. (2009) *Ground Control: Fear and Happiness in the Twenty-First-Century City* London: Penguin.

Norris, C., and Armstrong, G. (1999) *The Maximum Surveillance Society: The Rise of Closed Circuit Television* Oxford, UK: Berg.

OECD (2014) *World Migration in Figures* http://www.oecd.org/els/mig/World-Migration-in-Figures.pdf [Accessed 07.07.14].

Power, A., and Tunstall, R. (1997) *Dangerous Disorder: Riots and Violent Disorders in 12 Areas of Britain 1991–92* York, UK: YPS.

Putnam, R. D. (2000) *Bowling Alone. The Collapse and Revival of American Community* New York: Simon and Schuster.

Rex, J., and Moore, R. (1967) *Race, Community and Conflict* Oxford, UK: Oxford University Press.

Roberts, P., and Sykes, H. (eds) (1999) *Urban Regeneration: A Handbook* London: Sage.

Rubin, B.A. (2012) 'Shifting Social Contracts and the Sociological Imagination' *Social Forces* 91(2) pp. 327–46.

Sasaki, M. (2010) 'Urban Regeneration through Cultural Creativity and Social Inclusion: Rethinking Creative City Theory through a Japanese Case Study' *Cities* 27 pp. 53–59.

Sampson, R. J., Raudenbush, S. W., and Earls, F. (1997) 'Neighborhoods and Violent Crime: A Multilevel Study of Collective Efficacy' *Science* 277 pp. 918–24.

Taylor, I., Evans, K., and Fraser, P. (1996) *A Tale of Two Cities. Global Change, Local Feeling and Everyday Life in the North of England, A Study of Manchester and Sheffield* London: Routledge.

The Migration Observatory (2014) *London Census Profile* http://www.migrationobservatory.ox.ac.uk/briefings/london-census-profile [Accessed 07.07.14].

Webb, D. (2010) 'Rethinking the Role of Markets in Urban Renewal: The Housing Market Renewal Initiative in England' *Housing, Theory and Society* 27(4) pp. 313–31.

Wolf-Powers, L. (2014) 'Understanding Community Development in a "Theory of Action" Framework: Norms, Markets, Justice' *Planning Theory and Practice* 15(2) pp. 202–19.

Zhu Xiao Di, Lan Deng, and Hao Hu (2009) 'Three Models of Public Housing in the 20th Century: Cases in the U.S., China and Singapore' in Hammond, E.P. and Noyes, A.D. (eds), *Housing: Socioeconomic, Availability, and Development Issues* New York: Nova Science Publishers.

5
FRACTURED COMMUNITIES

This chapter explores the differences within and between what are loosely termed 'communities'. Policy documents largely use the term uncritically and without reference to the ways a community might be experienced very differently by its various members. We have already seen that in the place-based community certain social groups are likely to possess a different sense of place than others. Some, as we saw in Chapter Four, are more likely be victimised than others, and we will see in Chapter Six that other groups are more likely to be monitored and surveilled by the authorities and attract more police attention. Women also appear to experience and perceive their environment differently than men, responding to different environmental cues, experiencing a vulnerability to fear which is not shared by men and avoiding certain places or activities within the residential neighbourhood which would not present similar problems to male residents. The chapter begins, however with a consideration of the differences between and within cities which give their neighbourhoods a distinct character. It then goes on to discuss the different fractures which exist within what can be considered place-based communities and the difficulties these have posed in the construction and maintenance of cohesive communities in the present day.

Divisions of labour and the stratification of place

Industrial cities and towns did not explode into existence fully formed but came into being in a more gradual (and largely unplanned) manner. The first industrial cities were built around rural settlements with already established customs, traditions and productive forces. They were formed around the natural and social attributes of already existing places. Manchester, England, often heralded as the first industrial city, was built around a textile industry which was already centuries old.

The industry took advantage of the damp climate of the place itself, which was particularly beneficial to the spinning of cotton and wool fibres and also the rearing of sheep (Taylor et al 1996). The city of Chicago in the US developed into such a significant city in large part because of its unique geography and its importance in the provision of lumber to the settlers of the Midwest:

> Chicago did not just lie on the edge of two different geographies – one of prairies and one of forests – it made them overlap: partly by transferring commodities – food and wood – between them; and, partly, by converting both the forests into lumber and the prairies into grain-producing farms and pig-rearing ranges. Chicago, therefore both lived off the land, and created a new geography by integrating the markets for wood and food across the American mid-west.
>
> (Pile in Massey et al 1999:30)

Both of these iconic industrial cities, then, developed from the rural trades which characterised them in their pre-industrial forms. Such cities were therefore steeped in and formed from the practices and ways of life which were laid down in their pre-industrial history. Industry transformed, modernised and industrialised these practices, it is true, but the living city is a product of its history as well as of its present and this would have been even more the case in the late nineteenth and early twentieth centuries when their pre-industrial history would have endured in the living memories of their older inhabitants. The history of cities like Manchester and Chicago is still present today in their symbolic representations and built environments. Older cities also retain a certain 'structure of feeling' (explored in Chapter Three) related to their social histories as well as a local pride and knowledge of the people who made the city and in doing so influenced its particular trajectory and current form – expressed perhaps consciously or unconsciously as those 'who made the city what it is today' (Taylor et al 1996). As a result, industrial cities were and are not homogeneous places, though obviously retaining much in common, not least in their size, the extent of the built environment and the experience of living alongside others in a way which rural settlements could not compare. Entire cities gain a reputation associated with both their past and present; there are cities of culture, of music and arts, of employment opportunities, of technological or intellectual growth and there are towns and cities associated with crime, poverty, slums and deindustrialisation. They retain diversity within their boundaries too – neighbourhoods which are suburban, 'sink' and settled , and although these categories are not fixed, specific places gain a reputation which is likely to endure into their future and which may attract or repel future residents or help to retain and sustain existing inhabitants.

At the point of industrialisation, the working class was newly formed, but it did not represent one monolithic entity. It was immediately fragmented by the division of labour and the growth of specialist work practices. Whole communities and neighbourhoods were formed around large workplaces which could employ thousands of people, and some towns and cities were built around one particular industry. In the developing world, these patterns of growth and settlement can still be seen today. In traditional societies based around small-scale agricultural production, the population will share similar work patterns as their lives revolve around the seasonal requirements of the production of food. Increasingly, the neighbourhoods formed from the needs of industrial production, however, demanded further specialisation of roles to provide services, shops, finance and housing so that in the city close neighbours might lead very different lives as skilled or unskilled manual labourers, shop owners, white-collar workers, pensioners and so forth. So within 'communities of place' lie stratifications and occupational classifications which can act as points of division.

Discourses of dysfunctionality and difference

Within the city great swathes of land are used to house the working classes. Robert Park remarked as an example that the East End of London housed two million labourers, but within these areas, he argued, were additional fractures forged along distinctions of class and race. Vocational and cultural specialisation was thereby entrenched across the city, creating different 'types' to study such as 'the shopgirl, the policeman, the peddler, the cabman, the nightwatchman, the clairvoyant, the vaudeville performer, the quack doctor, the bartender, the ward boss, the strikebreaker (Park in Sennett 1969:103). In Park's eyes, certain neighbourhoods were also built around moral frameworks. He considered that sections of the working class living outside of normative frameworks. and therefore not considered as 'respectable', sought out like-minded city residents to share common cultures and 'vices'. These sub-cultural adaptations, he argued, were then normalised and handed down to future generations of residents who could only work with the hand they were given and had to make the most out of the circumstances in which they found themselves. Park's views therefore coincide with contemporary characterisations of 'problem areas', peopled with a dysfunctional 'underclass' and, in the words of David Cameron in 2008, two years prior to his election as Prime Minister of the UK:

> Children whose toys are dad's discarded drink bottles; whose role models are criminals, liars and layabouts; whose innocence is lost before their first milk tooth. What chance for these children? Raised without manners, morals or a decent education, they're caught up in the same destructive chain as their parents.
>
> (Cameron 2008, quoted in Mooney 2010:1)

While Park viewed these neighbourhoods as interesting and worthy of sociologists' attention and understanding, the discourse of dysfunctionality which he and others attached to differences in the contemporary world serves to construct a damning and punitive discourse around the decision to be different. More recently, the journalist Owen Jones has spoken of the vilification of the 'chav' in Britain, a section of the white working class popularly considered as stupid, brutish and seduced by the trappings of wealth even as they are largely unable to afford them. As Jones also observes, however, the 'nouveau riche' from this group, for example, the extremely highly paid professional footballers and their wives who nevertheless hail from a working-class background, do not escape the label (Jones 2011).

Mooney and Hancock (2010:14) understand 'contemporary valorisations of "the poor" ' as 'problem population' [as] a series of anti-welfare narratives and ideologies which are working not only to construct people in poverty as "other", but which operate in different ways to harden public attitudes to poverty and to those experiencing it, as well as paving the way for much tougher and punitive welfare policies'.

The fictions of community

Individuals form their own social identities through comparison with others. In order to understand their own place in the world people collectively and individually categorise the people around them. This act of categorisation and classification can reproduce structural inequalities as particular groups are variously considered 'rough/respectable, undeserving/deserving and unreliable/reliable' (Rogaly and Taylor 2009:9). Depending on how the particular group to which you are attached is categorised, life can either be constrained or opportunities opened up so that this categorisation has real, material consequences. The categories which are created to identify groups may be enduring in their popular construction, but they are rarely completely fixed or uncontested. Instead their boundaries, the meanings attached to membership of the group and their acceptability to others will fluctuate and change under different conditions. Sometimes the categorisation can be based on occupation, with certain sectors of employment perceived as more respectable than others. This is not always based on the division between 'professional' or middle-class status and the working class, but there are gradations internal to social 'classes'. In the early industrial period, certain skilled occupations in industries such as textiles and engineering conferred an elevated status within the working class. Those who held these positions were dubbed an 'aristocracy of labour' and were thought to possess more culture and intelligence than the rest of their class (Hobsbawm 1994).

So the idea that living as close neighbours will automatically lead to a shared community feeling has been revealed to be inaccurate, yet the fiction of place-based community, especially within working-class areas, continues to be related. Communities can exclude as much or even more than they are inclusive. As Rogaly and Taylor remark, in the making of social space 'the personal and spatial often become inextricably entwined' (2009:18). Whole areas can become subject to stigmatizing tropes, or one particular street may become subject to the same. In the same way, different social groups can be demonized within a working-class neighbourhood. So the problem of distinction and differentiation is not just found between different classes or in labelling particular areas as 'affluent', 'nice' or 'problematic' but within areas which might seem to the external viewer as homogeneous places. In the deindustrialised spaces of the late twentieth and early twenty-first centuries 'spatial ordering' is less likely to be based on the stratification of social types by reference to the type of employment but might exist in relation to the status of being in paid employment or without work.

As the following case study reveals, in the neighbourhoods without work a division of labour may be equally contingent on a different set of social roles which can arise as a result of adapting to a lack of employment opportunities that may have persisted now for more than one generation. This study shows the complexity of social relationships which can exist in a small area of less than 7,000 residents, and it also demonstrates the problems of overgeneralisation and categorisation of the urban poor and unemployed.

CASE STUDY – COMMUNITY AND FRAGMENTATION IN 'OLDTOWN'

Oldtown (a pseudonym given to a residential area in a city in the north of England) historically housed a great number of the city's industrial workforce and dock labour. It is predominantly a council-owned estate, part of which, known locally as the Oldtown Triangle, is situated in the heart of the estate and includes much of the area's lowest standard of housing. The area underwent a number of transformations in the second half of the twentieth century. In the 1960s and 1970s, its back-to-back terraces were largely demolished and replaced with system-built high- and low-rise housing stock. From the early 1980s, the local council controversially embarked on a policy which sold off much of its worst housing to private developers, who transformed these hard-to-let estates on the periphery of the ward into owner-occupied "yuppy" flats. At the same time, some residents of the Triangle area set about to improve their own housing through setting up a housing co-operative. By 1990, the defunct and derelict dock area became a prestigious docklands development attracting inward investment, cultural attractions and expensive housing units. In the 1990s, the remaining council stock was improved by Estates Action funding, which promoted a policy of mixed residential tenure. By 1991, however, only 38 per cent of the adults living in the area were in some form of employment and just over 10 per cent were classed as permanently sick. Youth unemployment was high, with around one-third of the economically active young males between 16 and 19 without paid employment. Oldtown was a profoundly unequal area with pockets of real affluence on its periphery but with a central core within which intergenerational unemployment and poverty had remained stubbornly high since the closure of the docks in the early 1980s.

Perhaps as a result of the area's strong working-class demographic, Oldtown was always seen as a 'rough' area. In the heyday of its dockland economy sea-farers from all over the world – with their hard-drinking image – frequented its pubs, and prostitution was common on the main route past the dock area. After the docks closed, the area soon gained a reputation for crime and disorder. In 1983, a local paper reported the central estate to be full of 'marauding teenagers bent on destruction'. The paper put the demise of the area down to the council's housing of 'problem families' in the area, using it as a 'general dumping ground'. Whatever the truth of these allegations, the area became further isolated and depressed throughout the 1980s as unemployment worsened and local services were closed down. Those amenities which remained served as a public arena in which 'grasses' are named and shamed through in graffiti (Evans, Fraser and Walklate, 1995). With little reason for most city residents to enter the area, its reputation as a problem neighbourhood was easily sustained. This reputation was further underscored with the reporting of a "riot" in 1992 in which a carpet warehouse was razed to the ground and gunshots were fired at a police vehicle.

Within the impoverished areas of Oldtown, however, the term 'community' was used by local residents to describe the area, with the support given by close family and friends living nearby cast in a very positive light. Links to school, church, com-munity and family worked to keep people in the area. As one resident explained:

'For me it's the things I belong to, the library, what happens at the library, the school, what happens at the school, the church that I belong to. All the things that I like and all the things that make up my life are all in this small area. ... If I moved out of the area that would all be gone and I'd have to start somewhere else'.

Within the Triangle, especially, there were strong familial and community ties, with over one-half of the residents stating that most of their family and friends lived locally. This area was also host to a criminal gang called 'The Firm' which was said to be responsible for any crime on the estate. It was commonly said that The Firm was organised enough to ensure that 'locals do not rob off their own' and that instead they would target areas which lay outside their own estate. However, living on the estate and classed by The Firm as 'outsiders' were the wealthier newcomers to the area and others who were perceived as not fit-ting in with the cultural norms of the established estate residents. Those who were 'included' in the eyes of The Firm enjoyed a certain protection from victi-misation. The local 'Mr Big' would even indulge in small acts of philanthropy – 'taxing' local criminals if convinced that someone had become a victim of crime who should not have been so targeted, or, in one case, giving money to a local family whose belongings had been destroyed in a house fire. Local people acknowledged that the existence of this gang and its moral code conferred a certain degree of safety and security, if they played by the gang's rules. How-ever, far from winning over the hearts and minds of the majority of the estate,

(Continued)

even those who acknowledged that they benefited from the gang's 'code of honour' expressed a sense of unease that this was the case, and others worked, surreptitiously, with local authorities to try to undermine The Firm locally.

Adapted from Evans (2003)

Gendered places

A large body of work suggests that the experience of community and place is heavily gendered. Historically, it has been said that women have played a key role in sustaining family and kinship networks and have therefore been seen as active in the private rather than the public sphere, which has remained heavily dominated by men. However, the public/private dichotomy has been questioned by feminist theorists who have argued for a more nuanced understanding of place and politics which acknowledges the role that women have played in many aspects of social life (Howell and Mulligan 2004). Nevertheless, as a result of their exclusion from full participation in the public sphere in the past and also in the present, women have often been central to organising outside of this male-dominated realm. The female sex, however, has often been central to building and sustaining community relations, which could be said to lie somewhere between the private and public sphere, incorporating elements of both while not clearly in either camp. The significance of community should not be explored without consideration of the part women have played in both the creation and maintenance of community relationships and community activism.

Research has suggested that women perceive and respond to their local environment differently from men and that the locality in which they are situated can be more important to those women who raise children, maintain the family home and spend long periods of their lives based in their residential neighbourhood using its facilities and experiencing its problems on a day-to-day-basis (Rollero et al 2014). Research into the differences in men and women's health has even suggested that the local environment has a greater impact on women's physical and mental health than it does on men's health (Stafford et al 2005 in Rollero et al 2014). It is also commonly believed, and backed up by much research in this area, that women are more likely to forge relationships with others which are interdependent and communal whereas men are more likely to act independently and to act in their own self-interest (Rollero et al 2014). If this is indeed the case, then it is also highly likely that 'community' will have different meanings for men and women and that its presence or absence may hold a different significance for women.

In her book *The Sphinx and the City* published in 1991, Elizabeth Wilson, documents women's ambiguous relationship with the urban. She charts the history of women's engagement with the built and social spaces encountered in the city. Wilson argues that, although cities are dominated by masculine architectural forms, they are lived in and enjoyed by women as well as men. She suggests that women have found a freedom in the city which was absent in traditional, pastoral communities which were heavily patriarchal and oppressive. The relative obscurity afforded to women in densely occupied urban space, Wilson posits, meant that they could act in ways which had previously been prohibited to them. Many used the opportunities provided to push the boundaries of what it meant to be female, taking on active roles outside the home and pushing for necessary reforms in society which would open up their lives to further opportunities. Wilson's research reveals that:

> [w]omen had traditionally always been involved in struggles over housing; they led rent strikes, organised childcare and were also involved in the provision of outings and entertainment and help in times of sickness or special poverty. In the movements of the 1960s and 1970s women were once again prominent.
>
> (1991:118)

Wilson argues that public services and facilities such as transport and decent housing had always had a particular relevance for women trapped in poverty within urban neighbourhoods. She reports on the inner cities of North America, for example, as almost feminised spaces occupied, in 1977, by 115 women to every 100 men, with single-parent families (mainly headed by women) more commonly situated within these areas, a higher proportion of the older age group as female (157 women over 65 to every 100 men of the same age) and with women more likely to enter the workforce (but also more likely to be without work and on benefits). As a result of their involvement in community activism, Wilson argues, women (together with lesbian and gay activists) gained a voice previously denied them and an opportunity to experience respite from patriarchal social formations. My own research into community activism in the housing co-operative movements of the UK and Canada in the 1980s, as well as in community crime prevention and urban regeneration in the 1990s and beyond in the UK, has also shown that these sites have been dominated by the activism of women (Foley and Evans 1993; Walklate and Evans 1999; Globalisation and Social Exclusion Unit 2000).

The study of women's activism and community involvement testifies to both the strengths and vulnerabilities which characterise their lives. The issues with which women have been strongly engaged in activist roles show women to be disproportionately affected by poverty (Carlen 1988), intimate partner violence (Dobash and Dobash 2004) and fear of crime (Stanko 1987), amongst other issues pertinent to the social life of cities. Within the realm of community crime prevention, it is not surprising that women have played a significant role. It has been argued, too, that crime itself is a masculine activity. Naffine has remarked that:

> [m]en are vastly more criminal than women. Though the vast majority of women and men do not enter the official criminal statistics, those individuals who do become known as criminals are usually men.
>
> (2003:10)

It is also commonly accepted that when women and girls do commit crime their relationship to offending is more tangential to their lives, they commit fewer crimes, their criminal careers are shorter and their rates of recidivism are lower than those of men (Worrall 1990). There also appears to be a stark contrast between men and women's attitude to crime and victimisation. The UK-based feminist author and journalist Beatrix Campbell uncovered these differing attitudes in her research into communities torn apart by joy-riding, violence and anti-police rioting in the early 1990s in the UK. In the book *Goliath*, which explores these events, Campbell describes the violence and destruction inflicted by men on their communities. She argues that the destructive behaviour exhibited by these men was a consequence of their lack of engagement with the world of work which had previously been so significant in building social perceptions of what it is to be male. Campbell contends that as their masculinity and the power which that masculinity bestows were taken away from men through loss of waged labour, some appropriated alternative arenas in which to perform their masculinity. In Campbell's account, this involved appropriating public space as the arena in which gendered power was enforced. Young men used a very public involvement in crime and celebrated the identity of 'offender' in their quest to distinguish themselves from traditionally powerless groups (such as women), to assert their masculinity and to maintain dominance over others. Campbell's interviews and observations led her to make the very bold claim that:

> [c]rime and coercion are sustained by men. Solidarity and self-help are sustained by women. It is as stark as that.
>
> (1993:319)

Although Campbell's conclusion may overstate the contrast in gendered experiences, it remains likely that the problem of crime may indeed fracture communities along gendered lines.

The fear of crime certainly has a gendered dimension. Surveys on fear of crime repeatedly demonstrate that women articulate higher levels of fear than those men report. Various explanations have been offered to explain this disparity in reported fear. They are too numerous to explain here, but it is worth remembering that crime itself is gendered and that men are vastly more criminal than women (Naffine 2003). Moreover, when women are victimised, it tends to be at the hands of men. Women experience higher levels of crime in both their private and public lives, being more vulnerable to domestic violence, sexual assault and rape and lower level, but still troubling, forms of sexual harassment. The experience of crime and victimisation is therefore different for women. Crime concerns women on an everyday basis; they learn to adapt to its constant presence, and they consequently have a different relationship to crime than do men (Stanko 1990). Not surprisingly, women are often found to play a significant role in campaigns and projects which aim to prevent crime and to minimise the harm crime can cause.

CASE STUDY: WOMEN WAGING PEACE: WOMEN'S ACTIVISM IN CAPE TOWN

After the formal ending of apartheid in South Africa, the newly elected government led by the African National Congress (ANC) was left to tackle the
social problems left behind after decades of enforced segregation of the black
South African population. The election of the ANC in 1994 transformed the
role of activism in the country. This role had previously focused almost wholly
on the political struggle against apartheid, but it now shifted to building civil
society organisations which could take on issues embedded in the poverty
and discrimination suffered by black South Africans for decades. South African
women have played a major role in constructing a new landscape of community organisation 'conceptualising and developing innovative methods of
meeting people's needs' (Keegan 2004:34), bringing the problem of domestic
violence to the attention of the authorities; demanding that the victims be
taken seriously and supported when they report their victimisation; and creating community vegetable gardens and soup kitchens to feed the poorest
people in their communities. From 2000 onwards, the work of women activists organising in their community on a voluntary basis has been celebrated
annually in the Women Waging Peace awards which highlight 'the work that
women do in their communities to combat domestic and community violence
and the neglect or abuse of children, people with disabilities and the aged'
(Keegan 2004:35). The women who have been nominated for the award have
created organisations which fill a gap in service provision. Their projects have
involved sheltering the victims of domestic violence, mediating in violent conflicts, negotiating ceasefires between gangs and providing legal advice, coun-
selling and support to victims of violent crime. Their work has also included
setting up schemes to divert young people from crime and from gang involvement, running after-school programmes and supporting families struggling
with the care of their children.

Keegan's research on the award nominees has concluded that the women
who have been successful in attaining the recognition of the award possess
certain characteristics in common:

- They can no longer tolerate regularly witnessing problems which are not
  being addressed.
- They act locally, often in tandem with other women from their area.
- They overcome a significant lack of financial resources initially to build the
  organisation.
- They often have no formal training, and as a result of their activism they
  generate new forms of knowledge and new practices.

(Continued)

- Their organisations can rely on the continued activism of a few people and may not attract further funding. As a result, they are difficult to sustain despite their meeting a clear need.

It is clear that women's solutions to the problems they encounter on a day-to-day basis in South Africa face a number of hurdles. They are meeting complex needs where government and third-sector non-governmental organisations have not shown an active presence. The solutions which these women create are often rooted in their neighbourhood and community structures and are informed by local situated knowledge. As a result of their experiences and knowledge, they are able to find local solutions to local problems, but all too often they lack the institutional support and financial backing which would sustain and grow their organisations. The problems faced by these activists may be local in their manifestation but reflect entrenched structural inequalities which are felt across the nation.

Adapted from Keegan (2004)

The segregated city

The city is a place of diversity and difference, fractured into different spaces and creating places for the rich which are distinct from those manufactured for the poor. The boundaries between these spaces are both real and symbolic, and they limit the ways in which we experience and 'know' the different communities which inhabit areas that outsiders rarely visit (Lefebvre 1968). Separating groups into these distinct spaces is a function of the ways urban environments were initially created and sustained by the planning of cities which created zones of different form and function. It is also a consequence of the natural and complex movement of people into and out of neighbourhoods, sometimes as a matter of choice and other times out of necessity. The modern city, according to Sennett (1990), created 'internal' walls rather than permeable borders (Sennett in Massey et al 1999:312) in order to establish order from the chaos of the 'shock city', but in doing so it has re-created old orders and prejudices. Peter Marcuse differentiates between segregation which forces people into ghettos based upon hierarchies of wealth, status and power – which he considers 'is objectionable and should be countered by public policy measures' (2005:15) – and the voluntary congregation of people into what he terms 'enclaves'.

As we have seen in earlier chapters, the sheer diversity encountered within industrialising cities has been considered a problem in itself, and repeated attempts have been made to flatten out this diversity and to create homogeneous neighbourhoods where, it is suggested, social relationships will flourish between like-minded people. This zoning and installing of people in their 'right places' has resulted in severely discriminatory practices which have served to exclude whole groups of people from parts of the city and to divide communities from each other. In countries such as the US, South Africa and Nazi Germany, racial segregation was enshrined in law. Exclusion can also be woven into the very fabric of the city. In the colonial cities of the British Empire, for example, Europeans were housed away from the centres of established population so as to protect them from disease and cultural transmission from the host population. Exclusion can also result from discrimination – either individual or institutional. Migrants moving to England in the 1950s and 1960s might well have been met by signs in the windows of rented accommodation making it very clear that black and Irish people were not considered suitable tenants. The providers of public housing and private housing and finances (in a process dubbed 'redlining') have operated openly discriminatory policies which have excluded minority groups from the 'nicer areas' in the UK and US (Evans 1987; Garner 2007). Segregation has been overt and boldly displayed, but it has also been applied in much more subtle and underhanded ways which Garner has argued should be seen as 'collective segregationist action' (2007:16).

The vocabulary we use to describe the process of exclusion, Marcuse argues, should help to distinguish and clarify the various forces which contribute to form-ing spaces of exclusion and inclusion so that we can see them for what they are and respond accordingly. The separation of a social group in space, he argues, could be a consequence of:

- Hierarchies – through which areas differentiated by status reflect and reinforce relationships of power, exploitation and domination. Racism, he argues, is also based on a hierarchical ordering of racialised groups and stands as a specific form of discrimination which can result in an enforced (whether legally or socially) segregation of populations.
- Market forces – which segregate the poor from the rich in class ghettos through financial means such as the price of housing or the operation of the private sector in 'zoning' areas for particular types of development. The most extreme of these forces is the building of walled enclaves, the 'gated communi-ties' which physically and financially exclude others.
- Social exclusion – which maintains segregation by limiting the opportunities for those in the ghetto to gain access to those resources which would enable them to leave and to prosper elsewhere.
- Planning – which may create zones or 'quarters' with specific functions. Some-times these also involve the building of walls to exclude or contain 'undesir-ables', for example, the ghettos the Nazis used to separate Jews from non-Jews in cities such as Warsaw.
- Clustering – in which those who identify with a particular social group live in close proximity in order to protect and enhance their economic, social, politi-cal and/or cultural development (Marcuse 2005).

Whether clustering is ever entirely 'voluntary' is a moot point. The forces which segregate are more powerful than those which allow for voluntary 'clustering'. Of course, some individuals can choose to live in neighbourhoods where they feel most comfortable and avoid those places where they do not feel they fit in. With the available resources, they can choose to live near places of worship, preferred schools and community facilities, but those without resources create their own places of relevance to their way of life in the neighbourhoods in which they live.

CASE STUDY – THE NORTHERN MILL TOWNS OF ENGLAND

The old mill towns of the Northwest of England expanded on the back of the British Empire's domination of the cotton and wool industries in Victorian times, with parallel developments in the engineering and coal mining sectors. In the nineteenth and early twentieth centuries, these were boom towns which depended on a skilled labour force. They were centres of capital and also of a strong labour tradition. Towards the middle of the twentieth century, however, the economic base of the area began to shift. In the first instance, increased mechanisation in textile production meant many of the jobs in this sector became semiskilled or manual. They proved less attractive to the indigenous population, who could find better wages working in other industries. Migration from the Caribbean and then South-East Asia, mainly from Pakistan, helped to plug a growing shortage of labour. But the 1970s saw the collapse of the textile industry in Britain, with factories closing and many of the newly arrived population finding themselves out of work. Any cursory look at the economic demographics of these towns shows them to have been low-wage economies for some decades. They contain some of the poorest wards in England, house prices are often extremely low, and their town centres are dilapidated and do not attract many of the usual high street chains or high spending shoppers. In 2001 there were more than 4,000 empty homes in Burnley, for example, and some two-bedroomed terraced properties were being sold for as little as £4,000, if they could be sold at all. Many people would abandon their houses because they were too difficult to sell or too costly to repair.

The populations of these towns are very diverse, Burnley's ethnic minority population, mainly Pakistani and Bangladeshis, make up 6 per cent of the resident population. Just over 11 per cent of Oldham's population are Asian – 14,000 are of Pakistani, 9,000 of Bangladeshi and 1,600 of Indian origin. In Bradford, black and Asian residents make up 20 per cent of the population. In all these towns, people of Asian origin are concentrated in a few inner-city wards. These are generally the poorest and most rundown areas of the town.

Daneshouse in Burnley, for example, is in the poorest 1 per cent of all wards in England, and Bank Hall is in the poorest 2 per cent. Asian populations are concentrated in poorly maintained, private-sector homes. Only 2.25 per cent of council housing and 8.5 per cent of other social housing is let to people of Pakistani and Bangladeshi origin in Bradford, despite the fact that they make up nearly one-fifth of the population.

The children of Asian parents attend struggling schools with low rates of academic achievement. Family income levels are poor, and many rely on self-employment in taxi work, small retail businesses or restaurants. Asians worship in their local areas, often in mosques which they have struggled to build out of money coming from their own community. In many ways, this population is self-sufficient, and their lives have been described as "separate" and even "seg-regated" (Cantle 2001). Such areas have been dubbed 'ghettos'. Glodwick, for example, has some of the worst housing in Oldham. In one of its schools, 98 per cent of pupils are Bangladeshi in origin. People are living separated lives and do not know anything about other areas; they are deprived of contact with people unlike themselves.

It is often said that black and Asian populations in Britain chose self-segregation. This myth has been perpetuated by people who, for whatever reason, have chosen to ignore the history of Asian and Caribbean settlement into the country. Those commentators who have carefully and intelligently documented the arrival of black and Asian people as migrant workers and refugees have underlined the particular discrimination in housing, schooling and employment which they faced in the 1950s and 1960s in particular. Those who use the idea of self-segregation to explain the divisions which exist in these towns today should remember that many businesses in these areas sim-ply did not recruit Asian workers. Some mill owners segregated shifts, giving the less popular night work or less skilled jobs to Asian workers. Black and Asian people have found their employment opportunities severely restricted. They have had to generate their own sources of employment and run their own businesses. Under these circumstances, it might have been expected that the local council would step in to set a good example. Yet in 2001, less than 2 per cent of Oldham council's workforce was Asian, and Burnley employed less than half of 1 per cent non-whites. There has been systematic discrimination against people of Asian and Caribbean origin in housing for decades, in both the public and private sectors. As late as 1990, an internal report on the housing allocations of Oldham council revealed that discrimination against people of Asian heritage was still wide-scale. This report was leaked to the Commission for Racial Equality (CRE) which investigated further and ruled that Oldham was unlawfully discriminating against its Asian population, denying them access to decent public housing, keeping them on waiting lists for longer than was necessary and keeping Asians out of particular housing estates altogether.

(*Continued*)

Furthermore, the report stated that segregation did not happen out of choice but as a result of discrimination and racism. The CRE worked with Oldham to develop a five-year plan to put things right. The plan was lost. In 1990, the CRE exposed a number of Oldham estate agents who were "redlining" or limiting the number of areas to which they would offer housing to Asians. Similar patterns of ethnic segregation can be found throughout the smaller towns and cities of the previously industrial north of England.

From author's own research

It is all too easy to see clustering as voluntarily achieved when the different forces which shape social and spatial segregation work in subliminal and subtle ways over time to produce the spaces subsequently considered normal and natural. The separation of social groups has continued apace in the twenty-first century, so that David Harvey bemoans the loss of the right to the city for many groups. He has written of the consequences and impact of urban spatial divisions that make it much harder to maintain feelings of attachment, belonging and community:

In the past three decades, the neoliberal turn has restored class power to rich elites. … The results are indelibly etched on the spatial forms of our cities,[and …] in the developing world in particular, the city is splitting into different separated parts, with the apparent formation of many 'microstates'.

(2008:32)

Lefebvre (1968) first wrote of the right to the city following the urban social activism which rocked Paris at the end of the 1960s. He believed that the right to the city should include the right of citizens to be central to its decision making, planning and distribution of financial resources, yet he recorded a city in which the unskilled and the workless were moved to the banlieues, outside the environs of the city itself and 'decentred' from the opportunities the city of Paris had to offer. This 'decentring' of the poor has also been apparent in US cities which have emptied out their centres of housing and moved their mainly African American populations to peripheral estates where they remain isolated and socially excluded.

Robert Park considered community a protective factor in the lives of those who as a result of racism, class division and other forms of discrimination found themselves confined to living in segregated neighbourhoods. Using the racialised language of the time, he stated:

Every great city has its racial colonies, like the Chinatowns of San Francisco and New York, the Little Sicily of Chicago, and various other less pronounced types. In addition to these, most cities have their segregated vice districts, like that which until recently existed in Chicago, their rendezvous for criminals of various sorts. Every large city has its occupational suburbs, like the stock-yards in Chicago, and its residential enclaves, like Brookline in Boston, the so-called "Gold Coast" in Chicago, Greenwich Village in New York, each of which has the size and character of a complete separate town, village or city, except that its population is a selected one ... they are composed of persons of the same race, or of persons of different races, but of the same social class.

(Park in Sennett 1969:99)

Park was interested in the different spaces in which common interests are formed – either through residential association or professional experience. He was also interested in the ways a city's neighbourhoods are further shaped by loyalties, sentimental attachments and prejudices which may become entrenched and inhibit further mobility and migration around and between cities. As certain groups become more specialized, and therefore isolated, he stated, they run the risk of becoming pathological places or pathologised by those who live elsewhere and do not enter their streets and shared spaces. This perspective has led to the idea of the 'problem community', the community which exists outside the pale and may represent a 'no-go' area for the respectable classes. Park saw cities as constantly evolving and adapting to changing conditions, communities constantly built and destroyed as the people living within them moved upwards and onwards or lost opportunities, but he had little notion as to how exclusion and the removal of the right of certain groups to inhabit city spaces would constrain individual choices to such a clear extent. In Park's words, segregation was almost benign and chosen rather than damaging and coerced. He wrote that this:

make[s] the city a mosaic of little worlds which touch but do not interpenetrate. This makes it possible for individuals to pass quickly and easily from one moral milieu to another, and encourages the fascinating but dangerous experiment of living at the same time in several different contiguous, but otherwise widely separated, worlds.

(Park et al 1925:126)

This unproblematised version of the segregated city is devoid of a structural analysis which might throw a very different light on the portrait of the city which Park outlines.

The racialisation of difference

The marginalisation and decentralisation of the urban poor have had disproportionate effects on racialized minorities. The many groups which make up the black and minority ethnic populations of various cities and towns have suffered social and economic inequalities, which all too often placed them in the poorest parts of the city. However, in addition, to their poverty, they also had the added burden of racial discrimination which limited their opportunities even further and kept them trapped in low-income employment and degraded neighbourhoods (see Taeuber and Taeuber 1964 for a discussion of how residential segregation limited the socioeconomic advancement of African Americans). In the post-crash 1970s, while the white population could leave the inner cities and find work and housing in the suburbs or within 'respectable' public housing, this option was not available to black and minority ethnic (BME) populations left behind to deal with the results of economic crisis. Statistical evidence therefore shows that a higher number of BME and migrant populations are found in areas of 'social disorganisation' (Sampson and Groves 1989; Sampson and Wilson in Cullen and Agnew 2003:114). Their 'clustering', however, has been blamed for a lack of social networks across the neighbourhoods in which they live (as white populations are presumed not to network with communities of colour), loss of social control and high levels of crime (see Varady 2008 as an example of such arguments). Varady acknowledges the structural forces shaping residential segregation and immobility, yet still considers these as secondary to the 'choice' to live nearer friends, family and peers. Indeed, Varady even suggests that migrant communities from India and Pakistan arriving in England in the 1960s showed a preference for moving into 'low quality, privately rented, housing' (Varady 2008:49), whereas research has shown that, as a result of their own relative poverty and the discrimination they faced at the hands of individuals and public authorities, this was generally the only accommodation available to them (Evans 1987). The current segregation of minority groups which continues to bar them from full engagement in employment and housing markets is then considered to be a consequence of these earlier 'choices' rather than the continued discrimination institutionalised within the working of the markets themselves. Varady is particularly concerned about the 'clustering' of Muslims across Europe. The situation of people who share the Islamic faith is revisited in Chapter Six when the concept of 'suspect communities' is raised and further explored.

Solomos (2003) has argued that, until the 1970s, the study of BME communities was focused on the 'problem' of race relations rather than on the exploration and understanding of racism, its structural elements and its roots in inequalities of power. The US civil rights movement and the radical and revolutionary politics which emerged in the 1960s, however, brought these issues squarely to the fore. This movement emerged in the segregated communities of African America and became global in its reach and significance, taking inspiration from and in turn inspiring, similar struggles all over the world (Slate 2012). A different story began to materialise, which developed a more political understanding of segregation as the movement for civil rights combined with neo-Marxist accounts of the emergence and subsequent impact of racism and discrimination and challenged the idea that black and minority cultures were to blame for a lack of social and residential mobility. Important in the recounting of this story was the global history of racism, imperialism, slavery and the part these played in maintaining capitalist production and economic inequalities (Miles 1982).

Robert Miles (1982) in *Racism and Migrant Labour* set out to apply a Marxist framework to the study of racial discrimination. His starting point was that 'race' as a category is a social construct which has no basis in scientific fact but which is nevertheless a divisive tool utilised on a daily basis. 'Race' serves the system of capitalist production, Miles argues, by masking exploitative economic relationships. Capitalism needs a steady stream of labour to hand, so global migration is important, especially in times of economic growth. However, it is also important that this labour can be procured as cheaply as possible. Labour which is established, which has gained employment rights and which is organised is more expensive to maintain than newly-arrived, unorganised labour which may not even enjoy rights of citizenship which it can utilise as a lever to win better pay and conditions. Of course, when given citizenship rights, newly arrived labour becomes established, settled and organised itself. However, the ideology of race serves to divide the working class internally and places barriers to full integration. Racism therefore plays an important part in suppressing wages and employment rights.

Miles shows how employers have used racism in extremely overt ways in the past to divide the working class. Following Marx, he uses the example of the migration of Irish labour into the UK in the nineteenth century to demonstrate how racial stereotypes of the lazy and feckless Irish were used to segregate workforces and to justify lower wages. In addition, the employment of the Irish on lower wages undercut the wages of the indigenous labour force, thus raising fears that migrant labour would be hired in preference and that migration would thereby destroy the lives of the British working class. These arguments have surfaced with depressing regularity and have caused internal divisions not only within workplaces but also within the residential communities where much migrant labour moved into, thereby doing much to perpetuate racist ideologies. It is not enough that these arguments have been largely disproved and that unity between workers – migrant and indigenous – can combat such crude divisive attempts to restore, and indeed strengthen, wages and rights which might otherwise be lost. Later studies have focused on the growth and maintenance of these racist ideologies and on the political structures and imperatives which sustain them (Solomos 2003).

Racism has been a particularly divisive force in society, but it has also been a tool for unity and collective action. Despite Miles's claims that race has no scientific basis and therefore does not exist, the popular use of race and racial categorisations continues to persist and to negatively affect the lives of those who are racialised by this discourse. In the UK, the Centre for Contemporary Cultural Studies – the Birmingham School – led by Stuart Hall took up the challenge posed by Miles. They demonstrated that the social construction of race has material consequences and that meaningful identities are based on this construction. They also revealed a history of resistance to racism which was hardly recorded in popular culture or in institutional memories but in which minority groups identified as 'black', 'Jewish', Asian' and so on have grouped together under a common umbrella of 'black consciousness' and as a collective force which could defend all against racism and organise to bring about change. In the 1970s, the identification 'black' was a radical act for some and could incorporate any minority group excluded from the majority culture identified with white domination and supremacy (Garner 2007). The black identity was 'reforged into a political movement of opposition' (Solomos 2003:28) in many countries around the globe where it permitted a wide variety of national and cultural origins.

In the 1990s, postmodernist and poststructuralist thought had a significant influence on the study of race and racism, challenging what was considered to be simplistic and homogeneous conceptualisations. Rather than talk of *racism*, the multiple nature and extent of *racisms* were explored together with the different historical, cultural and philosophical roots of racist ideologies. It was acknowledged that racism could take on different forms and affect groups in different ways. Racism can attach negative connotations to skin colour and physical differences but also to religious and cultural distinctions. It was proposed that each group therefore experiences racism differently, depending on the particular racist ideology attached to them. Thus, as Modood explains how this differentiation might work in the US:

> cultural racisms […] build on 'colour' a set of antagonistic or demeaning stereotypes based on alleged or real cultural traits. The ways in which racism works with Latinos, for example, both in terms of representation but also in terms of treatment – perhaps they are more likely to be hired than a black jobseeker but are more vulnerable in terms of immigration policing and the possibility of being deported – will be different to how it is for African-Americans. Similarly, American-Asians may be admired in distinctive ways (e.g., for their academic and occupational achievements) but may also be racialized as 'nerds' and 'geeks', not to mention as foreign and un-american.
> (2013:41)

By the end of the twentieth century, the concept of cultural difference and the politics of identity rather than of class had driven a wedge between the different groups connected under this common understanding of race and racism. The politics of race identity emerged first within community-based pressure groups which sought to rightly challenge the racial categorisations and discriminatory practices forced on them from above by the state. This history shows that identities are fluid, forged for particular purposes which work at the level of individual and community for ends that are personal or political. Kundnani (2007) argues, nevertheless, that this shift in thinking about racial discourses had profound effects on unity across minority groups. The shared experience of racism, colonisation, slavery, segregation and resistance had previously acted as a unifying force which the identity politics of the 1980s broke down to some extent. As Kundnani states, this was not inevitable. As he explained:

> The danger … was that in throwing out false universalisms, an inward look-ing, reductive and conservative notion of identity would take hold. The important idea that our culture or ethnicity was a central aspect of who we were did not imply the mistaken idea that our ability to transcend that culture in identifying with others was fatally limited – but it was sometimes assumed to. This was especially the case when culture came to have an anthropological meaning; a distinctive way of life in which a people was rooted, organically, holistically and traditionally.
>
> (2007:49)

Culture thus differentiated and distinguished groups from one another. Although it could be read as a defence of the right for minorities to *not* assimilate into white culture, it could also be used as an argument that these groups were somehow dif-ferent from each other and from their 'host' communities. Both of these positions have gained ground over the last two decades and have resulted in a very different political landscape on which 'race' is now discussed.

The end of multiculturalism?

The idea of progressive multiculturalism had predominated in the 1970s as dif-ferent groups established their right as minorities to coexist alongside domi-nant groups without abandoning their own histories and cultures. This idea of multiculturalism contained within it the knowledge that most nations were not monocultural and that histories of colonialism and slavery as well as the needs of modern capitalism had resulted in both forced and elective migration. This migration had brought heterogeneity and a mixing of peoples and culture across the globe for many centuries. The philosophy of multiculturalism declared that all migrant groups had a right to participation in the countries in which they were settled, regardless of their rates of assimilation. Some countries gave more rights than others; Germany continued, for example, to deny full citizenship and the rights which accompanied citizenship to the *gastarbeiters*, 'guest workers', pre-dominantly from Turkey and residing in Germany, who despite their somewhat precarious status, were essential to the functioning and growth of the German economy. Neither was multiculturalism a new phenomenon; many ancient cities were trading centres and host to multiple religions and cultures. But following the Second World War, the concept took on a new meaning and served as an antidote to the ideas of racial supremacy, ethnic cleansing and genocide which had found space to flourish and become a normalised frame of reference in much of Europe (Neitzel and Welzer 2012).

The growth of the ideas of modern multiculturalism meant that nation-states had to rethink their responses to the needs of a diverse population. It required that they explore ways to foster a collective national identity, whilst recognising cultural diversity. A balance had to be struck between demanding loyalty from all citizens to the national state and its legislative codes whilst recognising different religious and cultural practices and group identities. Countries such as the Netherlands were once perceived as the 'pioneers of multiculturalism' (Modood 2013:12). The Dutch government believed it could win loyalty by facilitating difference and legislating against discrimination in employment, housing and education. The benefits of affirmative action and the recognition of difference within state-funded education and cultural output were hotly debated, but for a brief period in the 1970s and early 1980s it seemed that multiculturalism was here to stay. The mid-1980s and the 1990s, however, witnessed the development of a backlash against progressive multiculturalism which accelerated after 2001. As the global political heat built up in countries such as Afghanistan and Iraq, this backlash became distinctly anti-Muslim in flavour.

Multiculturalism first came under attack from a 'new right' (Kundnani 2007:42) which claimed that accommodation to difference and diversity had gone too far. The new right emphasised the importance of national identity and the powerful nation-state on the global stage, whilst claiming that domestically the state had become too powerful and should withdraw from interference in public life. Celebration of difference and the protection of minorities from discriminatory practices were seen as the actions of an overbearing state which, through interference at the level of community relations was more likely to sow division than to promote harmonious coexistence. Rolling back the welfare arm of the state which the new right advocated necessitated stepping back from involvement in the private lives of citizens, and progressive multiculturalism was recast as a forcing of 'politically correct' ideas which were an affront to freedom of thought and action. The new right's insistence on national unity meant that cultural differentiation was considered divisive and assimilation the only way forward to attain the goal of a socially cohesive society. Whilst the activism of the 1960s and 1970s had done much to dispel crude racist stereotypes linking superiority and intelligence to skin colour, the *cultural racism* which emerged in this period was more subtly fashioned and insidious and has grown in its extent. People who might not consider themselves 'racist' as far as the old stereotypes are concerned nevertheless felt that it was appropriate and acceptable to pass judgement and to question the values and tenets of minority cultures. The 'new racism', concerned with social cohesion rather than racial superiority, has had a significant effect on immigration policies, with national governments protecting their borders and tightening access to visas. Not all borders are treated equally. For example, the Schengen Agreement in Europe has removed border restrictions across member states, and the Central America Border Control Agreement in 2006 allowed free movement across El Salvador, Guatemala, Honduras and Nicaragua, but these are considered nations which enjoy a certain similarity of culture. At the same time, borders have been strengthened against in-migration by those considered to be more 'alien', and an anti-immigration rhetoric has grown in strength across Europe and the US in particular. This rhetoric has been extended to refugees, those seeking political asylum and escaping extreme danger, who have increasingly been cast as 'bogus' claimants and denied basic rights to welfare, housing and medical aid as a consequence.

The attack on multiculturalism has not been confined to the politics of the new right. Multiculturalism has also been criticised from the political centre and the left. For the radical left, multiculturalism was also divisive and served to erect barriers between people in the working class who could have shown unity in action against racism and had demonstrated the power of such unity on many occasions. From the political centre came the argument that multiculturalism had not worked and had segregated communities more successfully than had racism. From this perspective, multiculturalism was perceived as a threat to democracy and freedom, with minority groups using the progressive force of multiculturalism to erect barriers and build enclaves from which the majority population was excluded. From this viewpoint, exclusion had not been done to minorities, but rather they had imposed it on themselves to promote their own interests. The solution posited was for minorities to ally more with their 'host' nation than with their cultural heritage. Even Trevor Phillips, the Chair of the Commission for Racial Equality in Britain, an organisation built around multicultural principles, argued that these principles should now be abandoned by new and established migrants for the sake of the future social order. This argument built up a head of steam as it was used, in particular, to explain the segregation of Muslim minorities across Europe. A series of suicide bombings perpetrated by men espousing anti-Western Islamist philosophies and nationals of countries such as the UK and the Netherlands, which had prided themselves on leading the multicultural charge, sealed its fate. It is unsurprising that this change in political direction towards minority cultures has had a profound effect on community relations in these countries. It appears that intolerance towards cultural difference may have risen in recent years. There has been a rise in far-right, anti-immigration groups in many areas, some of which are fascist or proto-fascist in their beliefs and are not averse to using violence against those perceived to be 'different' in any way and consequently are considered a threat. These consequences will be further explored in the following chapter.

Some concluding comments and questions

The social and physical divisions which exist inside contemporary society have a complicated history which needs to be understood before judgements can be made on the value or otherwise of segregation and difference. This chapter has shown that there are multiple perspectives within the city and that not all social groups experience their neighbourhoods and social environments in the same ways. It suggests, too, that there are ways in which communities of attachment and belonging do play a part in the experience of the city. Complex networks of inclusion and exclusion shape our experiences and have to be acknowledged and understood if any positive changes are to be made to improve access to the city and the right to the city for all. It is important to consider:

1.   To what extent are cities fractured by choice rather than coercion, and what are the different elements which would support these different positions?
2.   Who has a right to the city, and what does this mean in practice?

Further reading

Elizabeth Wilson's *The Sphinx in the City* (1991) is an important starting point for understanding the city from the perspective of the women and children who inhabit more than half of city spaces. Their experiences are often underexplored, and this book is a useful reminder to us all of the dangers of androcentric and masculinist assumptions concerning city and community. N. Finney and L. Simpson, 'Sleepwalking to Segregation?' *Challenging Myths About Race and Migration* (2009), is a journal article which explains the ideas behind the shift from multiculturalism to the current push to assimilation and the foregrounding of national pride.

References

Cameron, D. (2008, December 8) *Daily Mail Newspaper.*

Campbell, B. (1993) *Goliath: Britain's Dangerous Places* London: Virago.

Cantle, T. (2001) *The Cantle Report – Community Cohesion: A Report of the Independent Review Team* London: Home Office.

Carlen, P. (1988) *Women, Crime and Poverty* Milton Keynes: Open University Press.

Cullen, F. T., and Agnew, R. (2003) *Criminological Theory: Past to Present, Essential Readings* (2nd ed.) Los Angeles: Roxbury.

Dobash, R. P., and Dobash, R. E. (2004) 'Women's Violence to Men in Intimate Relationships: Working on the Puzzle' *British Journal of Criminology* 44 pp. 324–49.

Evans, K. (2003) 'Out of Control – Community Responses to Crime' in Boran, A. (ed), *Crime: Fear or Fascination?* Chester: Academic Press.

Evans, K. (1987) *Ghetto-Building: Racism and Housing Policy Since the Second World War* Faculty of Economic and Social Studies Working Paper No 11, University of Manchester.

Finney, N., and Simpson, L. (2009) *Sleepwalking to Segregation? Challenging Myths About Race and Migration* Bristol, UK: Policy Press.

Foley, B., and Evans, K. (1993) 'Housing Co-operatives, Education and Tenant Participation' *CCEPS Occasional Papers*, University of Liverpool Centre for Continuing Education.

Garner, S. (2007) *Whiteness: An Introduction* London: Routledge.

Globalisation and Social Exclusion Unit (2000) *Dingle Pride: An Evaluation* The Globalisation and Social Exclusion Unit: Liverpool.

Harvey, D. (2008) 'The Right to the City' *New Left Review* 53 pp. 23–40.

Hobsbawm, E. J. (1994) *The Age of Extremes: 1914–1991* London: Weidenfield and Nicholson.

Howell, D., and Mulligan, J. (2004) *Gender and Civil Society* London: Routledge.

Jones, O. (2011) *Chavs. The Demonization of the Working Class* London: Verso Books.

Keegan, M. (2004) 'Women Waging Peace: Reflections on Women's Activism in Cape Town' *Agenda: Empowering Women for Gender Equity* 60 pp. 33–37.

Kundnani, A. (2007) *The End of Tolerance* London: Pluto Press.

Lefebvre, H. (1993) *Writings on the City* Oxford, UK: Blackwell.

Lefebvre, H. (1968) *Le Droit à la Ville* Paris: Anthropos.

Marcuse, P. (2005) 'Enclaves Yes, Ghettos, No' in Varady, D. P. (ed), *Desegregating the City. Ghettos, Enclaves, and Inequality* New York: State University of New York Press.

Massey, D., Allen, J., and Pile, S. (eds) (1999) *City Worlds* London: Routledge.

Miles, R. (1982) *Racism and Migrant Labour* London: Routledge and Kegan Paul.

Modood, T. (2013) *Multiculturalism* London: Wiley.

Mooney, G. (2010) 'The Disadvantaged Working Class as "Problem" Population: The "Broken Society" and Class Misrecognition' *Concept* 1(3) winter.

Mooney, G., and Hancock, L. (2010) 'Poverty Porn and the Broken Society' *Variant* winter pp. 14–17.

Naffine, N. (2003) 'The Man Question of Crime, Criminology and the Law' *Criminal Justice Matters* 53(1) pp. 10–11.

Neitzel, S., and Welzer, H. (2012) *Soldaten: On Fighting, Killing and Dying: The Secret Second World War Tapes of German POWs* New York: Random House.

Park, R. E., Burgess, E. W., and McKenzie, R. D. (1925) *The City* Chicago: University of Chicago Press.

Rogaly, B., and Taylor, B. (2009) *Moving Histories of Class and Community Identity, Place and Belonging in Contemporary England* Basingstok, UK: Palgrave Macmillan.

Rollero, C., Gattino, S., and De Piccoli, N. (2014) 'A Gender Lens on Quality of Life: The Role of Sense of Community, Perceived Social Support, Self-Reported Health and Income' *Social Indicators Research* 116 pp. 887–98.

Sampson, R. J., and Groves, W. B. (1989) 'Community Structure and Crime: Testing Social Disorganization Theory' *American Journal of Sociology* 94 pp. 774–802.

Sampson, R. J., Raudenbush, S. W., and Earls, F. (1997) 'Neighborhoods and Violent Crime: A Multilevel Study of Collective Efficacy' *Science* 277 pp. 918–24.

Sennett, R. (ed) (1969) *Classic Essays on the Culture of Cities* New York: Appleton-Century-Crofts.

Slate, N. (2012) *Colored Cosmopolitanism: The Shared Struggle for Freedom in the United States and India* Cambridge, MA: Harvard University Press.

Solomos, J. (2003) *Race and Racism in Britain* Basingstoke, UK: Palgrave Macmillan.

Stanko, E. (1990) *Everyday Violence. How Men and Women Experience Sexual and Physical Danger* London: Pandora.

Taeuber, C., and Taeuber, I. B. (1964) In Kalra, V. S., and Kapoor, N. (2009) 'Interrogating Segregation, Integration and the Community Cohesion Agenda' *Journal of Ethnic and Migration Studies* 35(9) pp. 1397–1415.

Taylor, I., Evans, K., and Fraser, P. (1996) *A Tale of Two Cities. Global Change, Local Feeling and Everyday Life in the North of England, A Study of Manchester and Sheffield* London: Routledge.

Varady, D. P. (2008) 'Muslim Residential Clustering and Political Radicalism' *Housing Studies* 23(1) pp. 45–66.

Walklate, S., and Evans, K. (1999) *Zero Tolerance or Community Tolerance? Managing Crime in High Crime Areas* Aldershot, UK: Ashgate.

Wilson, E. (1991) *The Sphinx in the City. Urban Life, the Control of Disorder, and Women* Los Angeles: University of California Press.

Worrall, A. (1990) *Offending Women: Female Lawbreakers and the Criminal Justice System* London: Routledge and Kegan Paul.

6
SUSPECT AND PROFILED COMMUNITIES

In 1993, Paddy Hillyard introduced the idea of 'suspect communities' into British criminology. Hillyard had conducted research into the Irish people's experience of anti-terrorism legislation which was introduced into UK legislation in 1974 and subsequently subject to a number of amendments. The Act was drawn up in some haste following the bombing of two Birmingham pubs in which 21 people died and 182 were injured. It was introduced as a temporary measure, conferring powers on the police which were said to be unprecedented in peacetime and which could have a profound impact on the rights of those suspected of terrorist activity. For this reason, the then Home Secretary, Roy Jenkins, proposed that the law would need to be renewed on an annual basis as Parliament saw fit. The legislation was eventually replaced by the Terrorism Act 2000, which removed the requirement for annual renewal. Under the Prevention of Terrorism Act of 1974, certain organisations were proscribed (made illegal) in law, so that membership of these organisations became an arrestable offence. It was also an offence to solicit financial support, display any sign of public support or attend a meeting supporting or addressed by a member of any of the proscribed groups. The Act also provided for the authorities to issue an exclusion order to prevent certain individuals from entering mainland Britain. In addition, the police were given powers to detain any individual for up to 48 hours (which could be extended up to an additional five days with the Home Secretary's approval) if the police had 'reasonable suspicion' that the individual had committed an offence under the Act. The Provisional Irish Republican Army (IRA) was held responsible for the Birmingham bombings, although its leadership denied any knowledge of the attack and later declared that it was an error of judgement which was made by lower ranking IRA officers without their approval (Mullin 1990). Whatever part of the chain of responsibility had led to the bombings, they sparked off a wave of revulsion fuelling popular anti-Irish sentiment in some areas and leading to a number of violent attacks on Irish people.

Hillyard's main concern was the way in which the state responded to enactment of the legislation and the consequent powers conferred on different organs of the state machinery. He argued that the discretion the legislation awarded to the police, immigration officials and customs officers was being used to detain and interrogate people who were not guilty of any offence, often at the point of their entry into mainland Britain. The data revealed that 86 per cent of the 7,052 people detained under the legislation from 1974 to 1991 were released without charge. The people Hillyard interviewed who had been detained or arrested under the Act told of interrogation techniques which were designed to place extreme pressure on those detained and which also brought family and friends under suspicion. Irish people recounted ad hoc stops and searches, often at border points, which appeared to be based on little more than the whim of the official. Hillyard concluded that the Irish in Britain were being treated by the state as a 'suspect community' which could be stopped and interrogated at will in the interests of some 'common good' but that this also strayed into treatment that more generally should have been considered unacceptable but was seemingly delivered with some impunity. At the time, Hillyard suggested that people of Irish descent were being singled out, subjected to harsher surveillance and policing than the general population and that once in custody they were treated poorly and without care – certainly less favourably than those detained under different circumstances. Since Hillyard's introduction of the concept of 'suspect communities', however the term has been seen to have significance to other groups who have come under the attention of the state.

Using Hillyard's basis, Pantazis and Pemberton take a wider definition of a suspect community as:

> a sub-group of the population that is singled out for state attention as being 'problematic'. Specifically in terms of policing, individuals may be targeted, not necessarily as a result of suspected wrong doing, but simply because of their presumed membership to that sub-group.
>
> (2008:649)

It is not necessary for the individuals deemed part of the suspect community to t see themselves as a part of that group, but identifying them as such by the state, or by those organisations the state gives powers to discriminate is sufficient. As Hillyard rightly reveals, categorisation of a group as 'suspect' and the subsequent treatment of members of that group are 'institutionalised' within the organs of the state. The remainder of this chapter considers how Hillyard's ideas have been utilised more recently and suggests that the concept of 'suspect community' has been used to understand the response to a range of groups considered to be a threat to the wider social order.

The Muslim diaspora as a 'suspect community'

Pantazis and Pemberton have applied the concept of 'suspect community' to the treatment of Muslims in the UK where, they argue after 2001, 'the legislative framework, which developed in response to the perceived new threat of terrorism, identifies Muslims as the predominant target of the state's attention' (2008:649–50). This 'new' threat was conceptualised as a different and more dangerous form of terrorism perpetrated by emerging groups motivated by the ideals of religious extremism and ethnic separatism rather than a clear political goal. Their use of tactics such as suicide bombing was also perceived to signal a clear departure from the methods of previous terrorist groups. The 'new terrorism' was said to pose a threat globally rather than just locally or nationally. The emergence of a new type of terrorism has been questioned by a number of academics (Burnett and Whyte 2005), but it has retained popular and political appeal so that the idea that we are living in unprecedented times has again been used to justify legislative responses with far-reaching consequences. In the US, the Congress passed anti-terrorist legislation in some haste after September 11, 2001, and the subsequent discovery of anthrax spores sent through the US postal system. By the end of October, the then President, George W. Bush had signed the Patriot Act which allowed for an enhanced and unprecedented level of surveillance of the population, legalizing electronic 'snooping' into the private communications of all its citizens, roving wiretaps, access to business, library and financial records and the searching of property without consent. The Act also allowed the rapid expansion of the Immigration and Naturalization Service (INS) and a widening of its remit allowing for indefinite detention of immigrants, tighter visa controls, fingerprinting of all non-US citizens at the border and so on. The Act came under intense criticism in particular for curtailing the civil liberties of US citizens, but it was overwhelmingly carried nevertheless and has been little amended and also made permanent since. As a consequence, it has been argued that a 'securitisation agenda' has dominated UK and US government policies since 2001. These governments have granted broad discretionary powers of search and arrest to a wider range of government officials than ever before and have also overseen a shift to the use of preemptive detention for those suspected of involvement in terrorist activity (Pantazis and Pemberton 2013:359).

Partly as a result of the circumstances in which anti-terrorist legislation was rushed through various national legislatures after September 11, the 'new terrorism' has been linked in the popular imagination to the threat of radical Muslims using extreme Islamist ideologies to engage in a holy war, or jihad, against the West. This link has been further strengthened as a result of the so-called war on terror promulgated primarily by the US and UK on Afghanistan and Iraq. The destabilisation of the Middle East and predominantly Muslim countries of Asia and the north of Africa as a consequence of enhanced military, political and economic intervention in these areas since 2001 has contributed to a popular perception of Muslims as a problematic community and even as a security threat. It is estimated that over 15 million Muslims are living across Europe (Modood 2013:4), and they have 'borne the brunt' of the securitisation agenda promulgated by national governments (Pantazis and Pemberton 2013:368). They have been subject to heightened surveillance, increased use of search and detain powers, a raised and largely negative media profile and a political discourse which has questioned their commitment to democracy and civil liberties. The increased suspicion raised concerning the activities and (what are considered to constitute) the shared belief systems of those following the Muslim faith has also spilled into the public consciousness. so that the suspicion is felt by Muslims as emanating not just from the state but also from society more generally (Shirazi and Mishra 2010).

The growth of anti-Islamic rhetoric and of organisations which have coalesced around a concern about, or absolute hatred of, the Muslim religion has been noticeable in the first years of the twenty-first century. The growth of these ideas has been characterised as a rising tide of *Islamophobia*. Whether this term adequately represents the threat which Muslims feel to their acceptance as full citizens and their everyday well-being is a moot point, but the term has been used as a useful shorthand. Although some of these Islamophobic organisations have a history which began prior to 2001, they were generally considered minority and marginal, whereas post-2001 they have been able to capitalise on an emerging consensus that paints Islam as a threat to Western values and ways of life, and have gained membership and a louder political voice as a consequence. There has been a reaction to these agendas from the Muslim community itself – which Pantazis and Pemberton have perceived as resistance from below (Pantazis and Pemberton 2013). This 'resistance' has taken various forms, one being that it has solidified the identity of 'Muslim' for many following this religion. Islam, although one religion, is as varied in practice as any other religion; not all those who are born into the faith are observant, and those who do observe the faith do so to different degrees, attend mosques whose imams will vary in their teaching style and emphases, may be allied to different sects within Islam and practice in a way which is influenced by their cultural and national heritage. It is therefore true to say that there is no unified Muslim community; rather, it is made up of myriad overlapping networks built around mosque, family, neighbourhood, sect affiliation, national origin and individual preference. However, there are also points which promote unity across the Muslim diaspora, notably the Islamic concept of 'umma' which binds all Muslims together as a global community and the Western concept of Islamophobia which stereotypes all Muslims as the same and denigrates their way of life and beliefs equally.

Shirazi and Mishra (2010) and Frost (2008) have recorded the ways in which an external threat can be responded to by forming a protective barrier around a collective, group identity. Northern Irish Catholics, Frost argues, coalesced around such a collective identity in response to being singled out as 'suspect' in the 1970s. This subjective identity was inherently political in its nature as the interests of Irish republicans, who were more likely to follow the Catholic religion, stood in opposition to the interests of the British state. The securitisation agenda is also informed by the needs of certain arms of the state and the political parties which make up government. Thus similarly, to coalesce around a Muslim identity in the West in the twenty-first century can also be seen as a political or symbolic choice. Certainly in Shirazi and Mishra's research, the deepening of ties to Islam and the adoption of more traditional Islamic dress outside of the private sphere of the mosque and in the public sphere of the streets have been interpreted across Europe as an active choice inspired by a political stance to resist pressures to assimilate (see the discussion on assimilation in Chapter Five). In France, the state has responded by banning the wearing of the face-veil, either the *niqab* or *burqa*, in public space and the headscarf, *the hijab*, in state-run, secular and semi-public spaces such as schools and government offices. These bans have been justified as the pushing forward of anti-oppressive measures by a secular government determined to maintain the separation of church and state. In an atmosphere of hostility towards Islam's belief system, however, many members of the Muslim faith have interpreted these new rules as another form of anti-Muslim discrimination which limits the choices of Muslim women who wear these pieces of clothing and prevents their movement through public spaces (Frost 2008).

Understanding the politics of hate

Singling out Muslims for attention from the institutions of the state has been mirrored by Islamophobia from below. Frost (2008) prefers to utilise the term 'race hate' to explain the rising tide of attacks on Muslims and their way of life. She argues that this race hatred is not simply a carbon copy of the state's agenda but that the rise in far right groups with an anti-Muslim agenda and the rise in recorded hate crime against Muslims have their own particular provenance and trajectory, which is founded in loss of white privilege and marginalisation of previously dominant groups. She explains that the context in which Muslims are currently situated:

> serves to reinforce the class fracture apparent within the working class forged by the ideology of difference and "white privilege" … those not marginalised or defined as "Other" may choose to identify with the state [to] reinforce their "belonging" and their "natural right of access to scarce rights and resources"
>
> (Frost 2008:554)

Frost uses the cited studies in the US and the UK (Perry:2003; DeKeseredy and Schwarz:2005) to suggest that the economic restructuring of the 1970s led to a crisis in masculinity as sectors which provided traditional male employment were swept aside and were replaced by industries which were more likely to employ women. These changes affected the balance of the nuclear family and disrupted patriarchal social ordering. While DeKeseredy and Schwarz relate the loss of the patriarchal control felt by some males to an increased violence against their female partners as they attempt to wrest back some of that power they have lost, Perry further argues that the social and economic marginalisation of white working-class males similarly led to a growth in racist and homophobic violence. In each example, men, who felt disempowered used their masculinity and the privilege it affords them in a world which continues to be ordered along racialised and patriarchal lines to dominate and control those who have always been subdued and considered inferior. In this instance racialized minorities have been targeted.

Economic restructuring since the 1970s has had other significant effects which have reached further into the lives of both men and women. There has been a 'critical reversal' (Hellier and Chusseau 2012) in the fortunes of the global superpowers since the Second World War. After two decades in which traditional patterns of economic growth were sustained, there has been a surge in the growth of many countries of the global South (formerly referred to as 'developing nations') at the same time as the fortunes of the North (formerly the 'developed nations') have suffered a series of economic collapse and uncertainty. Hellier argues that industrialisation led to two centuries of 'great divergence' in which the North dominated and colonised the South and consequently benefited from significantly higher growth rates, but that this has been followed by a 'great convergence' as the global South has freed itself from colonisation and has developed economic power and strength in its own right. The economies of the BRIC countries (Brazil, Russia, India and China) have asserted themselves onto the global stage in spectacular fashion, and their growth rates have outpaced those of many traditionally dominant economies. It has become clear in recent decades that the power of countries such as the UK, France, Portugal and Spain, which were leading colonial forces in the world, has waned substantially, and they no longer hold a central position in world politics. Their populations, schooled in the ideologies of supremacy and power which sought to justify their place on the world stage, have had to acknowledge that they will play second fiddle to the newly emerging economies. The rise in affiliation to organisations which still preach national superiority and white supremacy must also be understood against this backdrop as an attempt to hold on to the power which has been removed from these populations on the world stage.

Yet another factor must be considered in order to understand the populist move to assert the politics of difference. As inequalities of income *between* countries have been eroded in the 'great convergence', there has been no concomitant reduction in inequalities *within* countries. In fact many have seen the opposite – a rising gulf between the rich and poor inside many national populations. In fact, Hellier (2012:1) reports that '[f]ollowing several decades of reduction, income inequality has increased in almost all advanced countries, sometimes dramatically, over the last 30 years'. The causes of this increasing inequality are varied. In the North, unskilled manual workers have lost employment opportunities as production has moved to the South; the labour market has changed in many ways, which has left people in different sectors struggling to find work; wage rates have stalled in many countries and even gone backwards in the case of the US and more recently in the UK;

intergenerational mobility has also reversed itself, so that the current generation of workers is likely to be worse off than their parents; basic necessities such as food, fuel and housing have been subject to disproportionately high inflation (and it is these which make up a high proportion of the expenditure of low-income families); policies on taxation have favoured those with the most resources; many places have seen 'temporary or permanent under-education traps' (situations in which a population remains unskilled from generation to generation) (Hellier 2012:2); and welfare payments to the poor have been limited and have ceased altogether for some who are no longer deemed eligible (Hellier and Chusseau 2012). These factors have had even more of an impact since the global economic crisis of 2008.

In the South growing inequalities have slightly different causal factors. For the South, as different countries have expanded at different rates and been subject to a variety of political influences, the picture is more mixed; some emerging East Asian economies experienced a decrease in inequality during the 1970s and 1980s, but this was followed by growing inequalities in the 1990s and 2000s. Whereas inequality increased in the majority of Latin American countries and in China during the 1990s, the years after 2000 have seen a decrease in inequality and India has experienced growing inequalities for the entire period (Hellier and Chusseau 2012). Where inequalities have increased in the South, a great deal of the increase in inequality can be understood by reference to the rapid economic growth in those countries, which has benefited a proportion of the population and led to an increase in their spending power and quality of life but has left a large proportion of the population untouched and continuing to live in poverty and squalor. In these countries, the general rise in profits has been kept in the accounts of private individuals and corporations rather than collected by the state to improve the nation's infrastructure and public services. In Latin America and China, where inequalities have appeared to be eroded over the last ten years, there has been a greater willingness to allow the state to intervene to attempt to improve standards for the population as a whole.

Powerful arguments have been made to support the contention that unequal societies face a number of social problems not shared by their more equal counterparts. In 2009, British epidemiologists Richard Wilkinson and Kate Pickett published *The Spirit Level. Why More Equal Societies Almost Always Do Better*. The authors gathered information from across the globe on income inequalities and social issues. They concluded that in the most unequal societies the population suffered more stress and mental illnesses and were more likely to take drugs, to have obesity problems and to have higher rates of recorded crime. More unequal societies also reported lower levels of trust and fewer networks of mutual support and were less likely to live happily with others they considered different. Wilkinson and Pickett's work has been criticised for offering too simplistic a view of social relationships across multiple cultures. All the same, it does highlight some of the issues which can arise when populations are fractured and separated from each other through disparities in wealth in times when standards of living are falling more generally.

As we will see in subsequent sections of this chapter, it is important to understand the ways in which disparities of wealth can set up physical and social barriers. It was reported in August 2014, for example, that it is now a usual practice for blocks of flats in London that were supposed to be built as mixed social housing to be constructed with two entrances. One of the entrances opens into a plush reception area for the wealthier occupiers who can afford to buy into the accommodation block, and the other, far less salubrious, entrance opens around the back for the less well-off tenants (Osborne 2014). Such disparities of treatment can become more easily embedded and normalised in systems that are structurally unequal. If it becomes acceptable to plan and build difference into the physical and social environment, then this suggests a fertile ground for the politics and practice of difference to thrive. In addition, however, the ways in which increasing inequalities are felt by different groups can have an effect on social cohesion. Those who benefit from increased income and wealth might develop a sense of entitlement to their lifestyle and believe that they enjoy what they have because of their own or familial merit rather than as a consequence of structural inequality and accident of birth. Conversely, those who find themselves without similar opportunities to thrive can internalise their identity as 'urban outcasts' (Wacquant 2008), as they are routinely 'decivilised' and demonised by external forces (Clement 2010). As a result, it is argued that they may subsequently be more likely to be involved in committing crimes against others, often against people like themselves whom they consider equally worthless and vulnerable. As Clement states, the lives of those who live on the margins of society can appear meaningless to themselves just as they are criticised and denigrated by others:

> [O]n the sink estates of the city, young people in the age of transition from child to adulthood see their future life chances profoundly undermined by the present lack of opportunities for development educationally, psychologically and vocationally .... [and ...]their sense of territorial stigma is real
>
> (2010:442)

So the wider context in which the politics of hate have been able to flourish demonstrates that there are much deeper roots to difference than those represented by white, male privilege. This politics has a class dimension which is joined by racial categorisations and patriarchal constructions of gender which combine to separate and distinguish certain groups as worthy and others as worthless.

Within communities affected by the politics of difference, the structural reality of separation and the emotional response to marginalisation can combine in strange and toxic ways. As Perry concedes:

> [B]oth the threat and use of violence by white perpetrators enhance their authority in the eyes of the communities of both victim and the offender. Violence is empowering for its users: physical dominion implies a corresponding cultural mastery.
>
> (2003:155)

Within neighbourhoods which might be considered as 'communities' from the outside, the reality is that the discourse of 'suspect communities' and of hierarchies of power and influence may well serve as ordering practices internally. Frost (2008) quotes research by Bowling and Phillips which suggests that under certain conditions racist views and violent behaviour of individuals can be reinforced within their communities and that, especially in times of austerity and welfare cuts, BME groups can serve as scapegoat, especially where they are in the minority in an area. Frost, by example, catalogues a rise in race hate crimes in the UK where the official figures show that people with an African or Caribbean heritage are eleven times, those with an Arab or Egyptian heritage are twelve times and those with an Indian, Pakistani or Bangladeshi heritage are thirteen times more likely to be a victim of racial crime than are those classed as white European (Frost 2008:551).

Suspect communities and the construction of the ghetto

In Chapter Five we looked at ways in which the city is divided into different spaces, zones and enclaves. One particular type of 'enclave' has raised more concern than any other – the 'ghetto'. In the popular imagination today, 'ghettos' are 'no-go areas' peopled by the poor and desperate considered dangerous to outsiders, bedevilled by drug use and dominated by criminal, violent gangs Yet the ghetto has a very different history. The first ghettos were spaces within a city which were set aside to separate the Jewish population from the rest of a city's residents. This separation was often legally and physically enforced, and ghettos could be found throughout the Ottoman and Holy Roman empires. Walled Jewish ghettos with gates which were often closed and patrolled at night were typical throughout Europe in the Middle Ages, but by the nineteenth century the practice of containing and surveilling people belonging to the Jewish faith had largely died out – and not to be instigated again until the Third Reich gained power during the years leading up to and including the Second World War. Ghettos were therefore the places which contained probably the first ever 'suspect community' and to terrible effect. The total segregation of the Jewish population helped to construct this community in the popular imagination as a pollutant, as a defiled population and as a dangerous community to be feared. The containment of Europe's Jews in the 1930s and 1940s also helped the Nazis to launch and almost succeed in the 'final solution' to exterminate the Jewish population of Europe in what we now know as 'The Holocaust'. After the Second World War, very few Jewish people returned to their former homes, and the ghettos were filled by refugees from the fighting and those who had been made homeless by the wholesale destruction of property. The modern use of the term 'ghetto' cannot escape this particular, sorry history. Today 'the ghetto' is commonly used to refer to urban areas which have been settled by other minority groups which have also been subject to widespread social prejudice and discrimination.

While the Chicago School and those subsequently influenced by their approach have considered the 'ghetto' in terms of its 'human ecology', more recent writing on the ghetto considers as key to understanding its contemporary significance, its symbolic nature and the material inequalities of power which led to its construction as a place of danger in the popular imagination. The notion of 'the ghetto' in modern times has distinct parallels with the Jewish ghettos in that they continue to 'define, confine and control problem categories' (Wacquant 2011:27) within the population. In the US 'the ghetto' is associated with areas settled by African Americans, whose lives and histories have also been subject to a structural violence and who have been treated as a subhuman population without civil and individual rights, exposed to enforced segregation and deeply violent discrimination which went to the very heart of society.

The great migration

The twentieth century saw the relocation of millions of African Americans from the rural South to the rapidly industrialising cities of the North and West. Cities such as Chicago, Detroit, and New York sucked in labour from across the US and also from abroad. The movement of African Americans into these cities, however, was fuelled not only by the availability of employment but also as a consequence of the relative freedom which these cities offered away from the segregationist laws common in the South. Outside of the South, African Americans could also play a more meaningful role in public life. Laws enacted in the South had barred African Americans and some poor whites from the right to vote or stand for public office, so a move to the cities of the North represented a significant benefit to the African American population of the US. Many African Americans eagerly took up the opportunities afforded them in the North, so that:

> African Americans began to build a new place for themselves in public life, actively confronting economic, political and social challenges and creating a new black urban culture that would exert enormous influence in the decades to come.

> (History US 2014)

As we have seen in previous chapters, however, the newly industrializing US cities presented their own challenges. Racial discrimination, though not enshrined in law in the same way as it was in the South, still limited opportunities for African Americans; work was often hard to come by and when it was found it was poorly paid; and additionally housing was scarce and often overcrowded. The northern cities did not always welcome the migrants from the South with open hearts and minds. and so, tensions, which sometimes spilled over into 'race riots' were an everyday issue. From these beginnings, however, African Americans built neighbourhoods replete with culture, art and political activism which have radically changed the cultural and social landscape of the US and which have had a significant influence on the country's cultural output on a global scale, bringing billions of dollars into the US economy. This story is not one of *social disorganisation* as told by the Chicago School. On the contrary, the overcrowded rooming houses, dilapidated housing and precarious economies of the inner cities were settled and improved physically, socially and economically by migrants who brought families, schools, businesses and leisure opportunities into these neighbourhoods. The writings of the Chicago School, however, are largely devoid of such an historical overview and an understanding of the trajectory in which the areas which they were studying were heading and where they had come from. In its stead there is a distorting focus on life as it is played out in the streets by those who continue to be marginalized even as, behind doors which were closed to the Chicago ethnographers, families and individuals were shaping a different kind of life for themselves. Of course, poverty, marginalization and crime were not eliminated in the self-improvement of these areas and were still there to be observed, but this was not the entire picture.

The portraits of city life painted by Chicago's ethnographers afforded a 'snapshot' of life in the city which, once printed and widely published, have all too often been read as eternal and immutable truths. This adds to a negative and pessimistic view of African American and black culture more generally, a view which has not served the community well. Furthermore, by the end of the twentieth century, the socially cohesive and supportive neighbourhoods built by African American migration had deteriorated dramatically following sharp economic decline. The 'hollowing out' of the US city, a process by which industry and commerce relocated from city centres to the less crowded and more affluent suburbs where land was cheaper, left those with the resources to do so little option but to move out to follow the jobs. As a result, the black middle classes largely moved out to better jobs and housing in the suburbs. Those left behind now had to cope with the collapse of industries in which many African Americans had been employed and with the withdrawal of state support and inner-city investment programmes. Many US cities were left to deal with impoverished and degraded inner-city environments which were a shadow of their former communities. They were still largely occupied by an African American population but as, Wacquant argues, a population that was far poorer individually and collectively. He explains how once solid communities had now become degraded and atomised:

> [T]he hyperghetto of the late century has weathered such organizational depletion that it contains neither an extended division of labour nor the spectrum of black classes, nor functioning duplicates of the central institutions of the broader urban society. The organizational infrastructure – the black press and church, the black lodges and social clubs, the black businesses and professional services, and the illegal street lottery known by the

name of 'numbers game' – that gave the ghetto of the 1950s its communal character and strength, and made it an instrument of collective solidarity and mobilization, has become impoverished and withered away, and along with it the networks of reciprocity and co-operation that used to crisscross the city.

(2008:61)

Mainstream criminology has largely sought to understand the collapse of these areas as a problem, once again, of social disorganization. It appears that criminology has a short memory. The years which saw a relatively successful transformation of these areas has been written out of the narrative in political, public and academic discourse, replaced by a discourse of difference, strangeness and fear of the 'other'. The development of the 'fear of crime' debate in the 1980s aided the construction of the 'urban ghetto' as a place of danger and a cause for concern and fear.

The problematisation of crime and crime fear

In the years of expansion and relative political calm after the Second World War, it was possible to believe that countries such as the US were becoming increasingly equal, democratic spaces which allowed all citizens an opportunity to attain 'the American Dream'. However, this idealized notion of a nation working together for all hid the reality of continuing discrimination and limits placed on the growth and development of black America. The impressive postwar economic growth of the US economy did not filter down to all its citizens, and many African Americans were left without work and adequate housing. The persistence of poverty in African American neighbourhoods can partly be explained, Wacquant (2008) argues, by their continued social segregation which he considers was uniquely imposed on African Americans as a consequence of centuries-old racialized notions of black culture and capabilities still circulating from the years of legalised slavery. Yet the postwar decades also included the years of 'the war on poverty' and state intervention, which boasted that poverty would be eradicated in the US by the mid-1970s. Beginning in 1965, President Lyndon B. Johnson pushed through programmes which his predecessors had touted as necessary but had never implemented. According to Lee, Johnson's:

> Great Society agenda was in many aspects anti-welfarist, yet it involved the greatest expansion of the American State in the post-war period: increased aid to public education, an area hitherto off limits to federal involvement; an attack on disease via the expansion of medical knowledge and increased Medicare; programmes of urban renewal; beautification; conservation; the redevelopment of depressed regions; a widescale 'fight' or 'war' against poverty; control and prevention of crime and delinquency; and the removal of obstacles to the right to vote.

(2007:62)

During this period, crime and poverty were closely linked, with the eradication of poverty considered essential to the reduction of crime. The political landscape shifted fundamentally, however, during the Reagan administration (1981–89) when the goals of welfare were abandoned and the pulling back of the state was clearly institutionalized in government policy for the next three decades. Reagan reduced funding for social and welfare programmes and advocated for 'small government'. At the same time, support for the 'fight against crime' moved to the political centre-stage and consumed a growing proportion of the state's resources.

In the intervening years since Johnson announced his war on poverty and Reagan ushered in a war on crime, the problem of crime had taken on a new political significance. The use of victim surveys had demonstrated that crime and the fear of crime were on the increase and that the political right was gaining the upper hand. These were the years in which the myth of 'black criminality' gained media and political attention (Gilroy 1982). Despite Johnson's stated intention to eradicate poverty, the problem of crime rose sharply in the 1970s (Wilson 1987) and the poorest neighbourhoods suffered in all respects. Wilson writes that the continued migration of African Americans from the South to the North in this period of economic downturn exacerbated the problems of the inner cities by replacing the black middle class with a younger population looking for work, which was increasingly difficult to find. The 1960s and 1970s also saw the African American 'ghettos' rocked by urban unrest. The movement for civil rights had instilled a new confidence in black America, and the residents of the ghetto were more prepared to demand their rights and stand up against discrimination and the effects of stigmatisation. In an ironic twist, the very years in which the US appeared to wake up to the need to put right the consequences of years of segregation and discriminatory practices, to allow that black America had been 'truly disadvantaged' (Wilson 1987) by legal and social frameworks which had kept African Americans at the bottom of the social hierarchies of power and privilege, the economic downturn hit at its hardest and condemned any affirmative action to failure. In the minds of the conservative right, however, affirmative action, welfare interventions and the maintenance of state-funded support networks were considered the problem. A new rhetoric and consensus of individual responsibility and blame replaced the more progressive politics of state responsibility and welfarism. 'The ghetto' (and in particular the black ghetto), its culture and its individual residents, have since been held up as peculiar spaces, unattached to and unlike 'normal', mainstream society and the generator of a whole host of society's ills.

The globalisation of 'the ghetto'

The previous section has concentrated on the US experience and story to the exclusion of all others. This is not to imply that an account of what has transpired in the US over the course of the twentieth century has been replicated elsewhere.

Each country and region of the world has its own particular social history which has differentiated and segregated certain parts of their population under different historical and political circumstances. Nevertheless, the twentieth century was dominated by America economically, politically and culturally to the extent that many of the ideas and practices forged in that crucible have been applied elsewhere. The myth of black criminality and dysfunctional black culture which was constructed in the heart of the US certainly had widespread impact on both sides of the Atlantic. Hall et al's *Policing the Crisis* (1978), Cowell et al's *Policing the Riots* (1982) and Lea and Young's *What Is to Be Done About Law and Order* (1984) have all become classic texts in the UK; these works have reported on and battled with the stigmatisation of black British neighbourhoods. More recently, the situation of the French *banlieues* has also been recorded and analysed (Wacquant 2008; Waddington et al 2009). These areas, as well as the Asian American enclaves which are also found in many US cities, were certainly spaces of 'structurally imposed, racialized class inequity, of involuntary containment to [sic] racialized poverty and blight' (Chang 2010:2). As such, they attracted the label of 'the ghetto' and raised 'anxious public and political discussion' (Taylor et al 1996:198). As such, they were stigmatised and singled out for particularly authoritarian policing styles (see Chapter Seven for a fuller account).

After the experiences of the Second World War and the growth of multiculturalism (explored in Chapter Five), however, with a few notable exceptions (see, for example, Ron [2003] on Serbia and Israel and also Christopher [2005] on ghettos within South Africa), ethnic ghettos, which were institutionalised in the practices and legal frameworks of nations, were considered unethical and unacceptable to the larger population. If the US attempted to segregate and ghettoise its African American population and blame 'black culture' for its own demise, it has not universally succeeded. Indeed, the latest research suggests that in the US 'more disadvantaged neighborhoods were significantly more likely to become integrated than less disadvantaged communities' (Karafin 2010: 4066). In addition, many 'black' urban neighbourhoods do not resemble the 'hyperghettos' of Chicago, which Wacquant describes but are run by politicians from minority backgrounds (but not necessarily to any better effect than their white counterparts) in which black, Latino, Asian and other 'minority' groups exhibit a certain pride and confidence. Wacquant's ethnically segregated 'hyperghettos' may well be the exception rather than the rule. This convergence is even more stark in the European context. As Slater has written of the British experience:

> Britain's often ethnically diverse marginal neighborhoods display no signs of the exclusionary closure that historically and geographically characterizes ghettoization. … St. Paul's in Bristol, a dangerous "Black ghetto" to many [is…] a … multi-ethnic … place with a remarkable array of state-funded or subsidized institutions to assist the working class.
>
> (2010:164)

So while the concept of the 'black ghetto' does not translate to the European context (and increasingly less so in the US), it is still used to vilify and denigrate certain areas and their residents. Research does show, however, that there has been a convergence of poorer populations in cities over the last few decades. What *does* translate across the Atlantic, is the increasing marginalisation, segregation and stigmatisation of the urban poor, whatever their ethnic background, and the myth of the black ghetto is also perpetuated.

Whatever the reality of marginalisation, fear of 'the ethnic ghetto' continues to loom large. It is generated not only by racial stereotypes which associate black culture with criminality and danger, but also by reaction to the very real resistance to discrimination and marginalisation which from time to time has exploded onto the streets. Those who are treated as second-class citizens and worse have rightly protested against this treatment and have shown great courage by standing up against the dominant racialized hierarchies of power within which they are forced to operate. For many of the urban poor, as Chang (2010:46) observes, 'race is the 'modality' in which class is 'lived', the medium through which class relations are experienced, the form in which it is appropriated and 'fought through'. As Gilroy (1982b) has argued, the 'frontline' of the anticolonial struggle within Britain could be found in the 1970s in:

> such areas as Railton Road in Brixton or Saint Paul's in Bristol [which] represent the toehold of colonial people fighting back against imperialism. The frontline is a colony *within* [italics in original] the host country. The culture that has grown up there is the vanguard of Afro-Caribbean culture – it is the culture of survival which every now and then breaks out into the open as resistance.
>
> (Lea and Young 1984:119)

In the US the fight for minority rights has been played out on the streets as well as in the political arena. As Mumford has suggested, however, civil disobedience and unrest have too often been reported as a function of the breakdown of race relations rather than as a protest against antidemocratic practices, political corruption and social and political exclusion (Mumford 2007). In reality, however, the struggles of minority groups have challenged political hierarchies and contributed to their construction as problem communities which need to be controlled and dominated (Slater 2010).

The decade around the turn of the twentieth century in particular witnessed a political and media panic about ghettoization. This panic followed an increasing number of incidents of urban unrest which involved minority groups in violent clashes with predominantly white, organised xenophobic groups. In 1991 and 1992, for example, Hoyerswerda and then Rostock in Germany saw sustained and vicious attacks on hostels where migrant workers were housed, while local people (ethnic Germans) looked on and cheered (Eisenhammer 1992). On the British mainland, the intimidation of British Asians by far right groups in Oldham, Bradford and Burnley in 2001 led to successive nights of confrontation with the police in all three towns (Frost 2008). In Germany and the UK, the minority groups under attack complained that the police were insufficiently motivated to protect them, raising concerns that the xenophobic claims of the extreme right that immigrants were polluting the national culture were tacitly accepted as justified by the state. While these examples predate the 'war on terror' instigated in 2001, ample evidence demonstrates that anti-immigration and anti-Muslim campaigning has increased in the ensuing period. The official reaction to the growing presence of anti-immigrant organisations, however, rather than condemnation of their extremist views has been to accommodate to their arguments, to concede to the idea of immigration, and Islam, as a social problem, and to enforce tougher entry requirements for migrants and limiting visas to some nationalities. In Europe, the internal borders of the European Union have remained open, while restrictions have been placed on migrants from further afield. The US has seen a rising tide of anti-immigration legislation with only seven states (Alaska, Connecticut, Delaware, New Hampshire, Ohio, Wisconsin, and Wyoming) failing to pass anti-immigration laws in 2010 and 2011 (Gordon and Raja 2012). The problem has been cast as one of 'community cohesion' rather than that of the rise of racist ideologies and the threat this poses to minority cultures and religions.

CASE STUDY – COMMUNITY COHESION IN THE UK

Civil disturbances in Bradford, Burnley and Oldham in 2001 were followed by a number of local enquiries which blamed the separation and segregation of diverse communities as key to understanding the events. The then Home Secretary, David Blunkett, responded by setting up a Ministerial Group on Public Order and Community Cohesion, led by Ted Cantle, '... to seek the views of local residents and community leaders in the affected towns and in other parts of England on the issues which need to be addressed to bring about social cohesion and also to identify good practice in the handling of these issues at local level' (Cantle 2001:2). The ensuing 'Cantle Report' offered the view that different religious and ethnic communities in the affected towns were leading 'parallel lives'. It reported that:

> Separate educational arrangements, community and voluntary bodies, employment, places of worship, language, social and cultural networks, means that many communities operate on the basis of a series of parallel

(Continued)

lives. These lives often do not seem to touch at any point, let alone over-lap and promote any meaningful interchanges.

(Cantle 2001:9)

This theme of communities living 'parallel lives' dominated the national debate after publication of the Cantle report. Cantle argued that building 'community cohesion' and bringing disparate communities to the same table to work together on common difficulties was the answer to the problems of cultures at variance with each other' (Burnett 2004). In the ensuing debate, another discourse gained ascendancy – that building commonalities in cul-ture and values, a common identification with the nation-state and a shared concept of 'Britishness' were solutions to divided lives. Those who insisted on a lifestyle which was not deemed 'British' enough were held responsible for their isolation. Cantle's report also concluded that all people wishing to take up British citizenship should take an oath of allegiance to Britain, that there should be a discussion of the rights and responsibilities conferred by 'citizenship' and that what it means to be 'British' should be more clearly delineated. Blunkett took this approach a step further – not only focusing on new migrants to Britain but also calling for all British people of Asian heritage to integrate, adopt British 'norms of acceptability' and marry other British Asians rather than anyone from their country of origin (Werbner 2005:746). Unsurprisingly, Blunkett's comments were met with much outrage. Migrants to Britain and particular minority ethnic communities were singled out for specific attention and their own 'internal cohesiveness and cultural distinc-tiveness' (Werbner 2005:746) constructed as a problematic rather than as a positive force, while the part played by white separatists and extremists in attempting to divide communities and neighbourhoods was largely over-looked. All economic and political explanations were set aside as problems at the neighbourhood level and were placed firmly at the feet of a clash of cultures rather than:

> economic deprivation or racism, or the sense of threat to community provoked by the presence of racist organisation in the towns where the riots took place, but a lack of community cohesiveness and leadership were thus blamed.
>
> (Werbner 2005:748)

At the neighbourhood level, this culminated in a largely superficial set of solu-tions to locally-experienced problems which emphasised the importance of dialogue between segregated communities. Meanwhile, the material circum-stances which had led to segregation were left unaddressed and the role of extremist politics in setting alight underlying tensions remained underplayed.

> The marriage of local and international concerns with suspect 'cultures' led to a powerful and persuasive focus on the most culturally distinct groups, rather than the more amorphous and unorganised indigenous white population. 'Britishness' was held up as culturally and morally superior to all other ways of being and, as the fundamentals of Islam were questioned and attacked on a global scale, so this translated easily down to the local level.
>
> From author's own research

Kalra and Kapoor (2009) have argued that the re-packaging of segregation as 'parallel lives' and of integration as 'community cohesion' allowed the discourse to shift away from a discussion of material inequalities and political exclusion and to focus instead on cultural differences and what were seen as conflicting value systems. As they also go on to point out, the discourse of 'integration' which has dominated since 2001 demands a cultural integration into a dominant (white) value system and an (unstated but clear) assumption that this is somehow superior to black, Muslim or any other minority culture. It also assumes that segregation is always negative, whereas, as Brice (2007) and others have demonstrated, there can be benefits to living close to family and support networks based, for example, around places of worship and community centres. What exactly constitutes the 'white value system' to which minority groups should assimilate is poorly defined, but its definition is less important than its use as a tool for separating what is seen as good, pure and wholesome from the troublesome and the problematic. This separation was thrown into very real and stark relief in England in 2011 when the media-savvy historian David Starkey attributed the country-wide riots of August 2011, in which as many (if not more) white men and women as any other group participated, to the white population 'having become black' in their behaviour, characteristics and values (Rhodes 2013:50). Recently, a number of academics have taken up the topic of *whiteness* in order to explore the privileges which being categorised as 'white' confers on the individual and how this separation demotes every other group which cannot claim a white identity (Garner 2007).

The poor as a suspect community

Earlier chapters have described the formation of the working class and the urban poor at the beginning of the industrial period. From its inception, working-class people were considered dangerous and destructive elements within society. Working-class cultures were thought to be strange and unsettling, and when organised collectively, as 'dangerous' to the social order. The non-working poor were variously classified as 'the residuum', 'the lumpenproletariat' or 'social scum' (Evans et al 1996). This group was beleaguered from both sides – from the side of capital non-workers have no use and are merely a drain on the resources of society; from the left they are non-unionised, without a collective allegiance and consequently likely to act in self-centred, individualistic ways which could be destructive of community and antithetical to the interests of labour more generally. During the nineteenth century, the separation of the deserving from the undeserving poor rested on as assessing whether individuals were poor through no fault of their own, and therefore were entitled to social support to get back on their feet; or whether they did not have the means to support themselves through idleness or possessed a poverty of moral values and were therefore in need of religious guidance and a punitive response designed to shock them back onto their feet and into the workplace. After industrialisation, any person who chose not to settle into the life of permanent work and who continued in an itinerant lifestyle which had previously been an accepted way to find employment – following the work as a casual labourer to different places for seasonal employment – was looked upon with some mistrust and lack of understanding of their choices. To be itinerant was recast as 'vagrancy' in both Europe and North America The practice was roundly condemned and could be subject to criminalisation, fines and imprisonment. Indeed, travellers have continued to be a group shunned by society and cast as 'outsiders' across Europe, and attitudes toward the rough sleeper (street homeless) have changed little in the intervening century. These outsiders, whether travelling people or whether the settled and unemployed, have been considered beyond the pale, linked with criminality and considered anti-social elements. By contrast, those who stuck with the world of work and were gainfully employed making their job a permanent feature of their lives were considered 'respectable' and pillars of society.

After the First World War, attitudes toward the poor in society began to change but very slowly. The liberal consensus of the nineteenth century, in which the state was non-interventionist and placed responsibility firmly on the individual to find a way to ensure that their needs were met, began to be replaced, albeit slowly, by the idea that the purpose of government was to provide some form of social insurance. This idea gained some momentum as the Great Depression of the late 1920s and early 1930s led to financial collapse and mass unemployment among formerly 'respectable' working and middle classes. This wide-scale underemployment and unemployment did not really end until the start of the Second World War and the militarisation of the economies of the nations which took part. The fighting and the need for constant replacement of soldiers and munitions provided work for many more people, so that unemployment was practically eradicated at this time. After the war ended, the working class had a clear memory of how state intervention had seemed at first unable but then, under conditions of war, eminently capable of solving the problem of worklessness. Therefore, the working class demanded that state intervention continue to play this role. This consensus broke down in the 1970s as the conservative right gained political and popular ground, pushing a return to the liberal values of the nineteenth century (Crowther 2000).

The 1980s was the decade in which the concept of 'the underclass' gained political ascendancy, but it was in the 1990s that the underclass became clearly linked to criminality. Crowther (2000) gives the example of Newt Gingrich's speech to the House of Representatives in the US in November 1995 as a significant moment in the triumph of this discourse. Crowther recalls that in this address Gingrich explicitly equates the murder of a woman and her children to the problem of the growth of the welfare state. For Gingrich, the link was the use of illegal drugs, and he claimed that 'we end up with the final culmination of a drug-addicted under-class with no sense of humanity, no sense of civilisation and no sense of the rules of life in which human beings respect each other'(Gingrich 1995 cited in Crowther 2000:51). Although the 'problem' of welfare dependency had been a recurring trope of the neo-liberal politics of Reagan and Thatcher, the 1990s saw this looming even larger in political rhetoric, and it has continued to feature as a particular fear in the many attempts made since to pull back on government expenditure – so much so that Jones and Novak (2009) have argued that we have seen a return to nineteenth-century differentiation and stigmatisation of the poor.

Certain problematic 'characters' have resurfaced in the imagination of the con-servative right – the single mother on benefits, the man who has fathered children without offering continued financial support, the 'bogus asylum seeker' pretending to be in fear of his life but really moving countries to look for work and the family which has been without work for generations are but a few which are brought out regularly to make their points. As Skeggs (2004) and van Swaaningen (2005) have argued, these are 'handy figures' used to identify 'a social problem' which requires a punitive response. This response does not end with the treatment of these bogey-men and women, however, and the measures employed to discipline the 'problem' are then enacted on the general population. The conflation of criminality with welfare dependency has created a toxic welfare system in the US and the UK which treats all those on benefits as potential scroungers who must jump through many bureaucratic hoops before being considered eligible for support. They may well be 'sanctioned' and denied benefits if they do not conform to stringent requirements. Hancock and Mooney (2012) have also identified the public 'naming and shaming' of the poor in political rhetoric, which is reflected in media stories on television and in the newspapers. In these discourses, Hancock and Mooney contend, pov-erty is strongly associated with criminality and anti-social lifestyles. In addition, those who are dependent on welfare are considered as 'scroungers' who are actively 'milking' a generous system at the expense of 'hard working tax-payers'. Fear of the workless criminal is joined by a condemnation of the poor, which has created a toxic environment in which working-class communities become a primary object for police and state attention. It is the subject of policing to which we turn in the following chapter.

Some concluding comments and questions

This chapter started with a discussion of Hillyard's concept of 'suspect communities' and has considered ways in which, not only the state, but also popular discourse has coalesced around suspicion of certain minority groups, their cultures and ways of life. As a consequence, these groups are targeted for unwelcome attention and are considered as responsible for their own isolation and the stereotypes which abound concerning their values and lifestyles. This suspicion, rather than culminating in myriad 'communities' living side by side, has created tensions at both the national and local level. It is important to consider the following:

1. What functions does the concept of Islamophobia perform in society today?
2. Can the concept of 'suspect community' be further extended to understand the state's treatment of the poor?

Further reading

The work of Pantazis and Pemberton, 'From the 'Old' to the 'New' Suspect Community' (2008), updates Hillyard's initial concept of 'suspect communities' to include the experience of Muslim communities post-2001. Hancock. and Mooney's 'Welfare Ghettos' and the 'Broken Society' (2012) makes an important argument concerning the creation of a particular ideological onslaught on poorer communities, which, while centred around social housing estates in the UK today, can be more widely applied.

References

Brice, M.A.K. (2007) 'Sleepwalking to Segregation or Wide-Awake Separation: Investigating Distribution of White English Muslims and the Factors Affecting Their Choices of Location' *Global Built Environment Review* 6(2) pp. 18–27.

Burnett, J., and Whyte, D. (2005) 'Embedded Expertise and the New Terrorism' *Journal of Crime, Conflict and Media Culture* 1 pp.1–18.

Cantle, T. (2001) *The Cantle Report – Community Cohesion: A Report of the Independent Review Team* London: Home Office.

Chang, Y. (2010) *Writing the Ghetto: Class, Authorship, and the Asian American Ethnic Enclave* Piscataway, NJ: Rutgers University Press.

Christopher, A. J. (2005) 'Does South Africa Have Ghettos?' *Journal of Economic and Social Geography* 96(3) pp. 241–52.

Clement, M. (2010) 'Teenagers Under the Knife: A Decivilising Process' *Journal of Youth Studies* 13(4) pp. 439–51.

Cowell, D., Jones, T., and Young, J. (eds) (1982) *Policing the Riots* London: Junction Books.

Crowther, C. (2000) *Policing Urban Poverty* Basingstoke, UK: Macmillan Press.

DeKeseredy, W. S., and Schwarz, M. D. (2005) 'Masculinities and Interpersonal Violence' in Kimmel, M. S., Hearn, J., and Connell, R. W. (eds) *Handbook of Studies on Men and Masculinities* Thousand Oaks, CA: Sage.

Eisenhammer, J. (1992) 'Mistakes Admitted in Effort to End Rostock Riots' *The Independent* August 28.

Evans, K., Fraser, P., and Walklate, S. (1996) Whom Can You Trust? The Politics of "Grassing" on an Inner-City Housing Estate *Sociological Review* 44(3) pp. 361–80.

Frost, D. (2008) 'Islamophobia: Examining the Causal Links between the State and "Race Hate" from "Below"' *International Journal of Sociology and Social Policy* 28(11) pp. 546–63.

Garner, S. (2007) *Whiteness: An Introduction* London: Routledge.

Gilroy, P. (1982a) 'The Myth of Black Criminality' in Spalek, B. (ed), *Ethnicity and Crime: A Reader* Milton Keynes: Open University Press.

Gilroy, P. (1982b) *The Empire Strikes Back. Race and Racism in 70s Britain* London: Routledge.

Gordon, I., and Raja, T. (2012) '164 Anti-Immigration Laws Passed Since 2010? A MoJo Analysis' *Mother Jones* March/April Issue http://www.motherjones.com/politics/2012/03/anti-immigration-law-database [Accessed 12.12.12].

Hall, S., Critcher, C., Jefferson, T., Clarke, J., and Roberts, B. (1978) *Policing the Crisis. Mugging, the State and Law and Order* London: Macmillan.

Hancock, L., and Mooney, G. (2012) '"Welfare Ghettos" and the "Broken Society": Territorial Stigmatisation in the Contemporary UK Housing' *Theory and Society* 1 pp. 1–19.

Hellier, J. (2012) 'Introduction and Overview' in Hellier, J., and Chusseau, N. (eds), *Growing Income Inequalities Economic Analyses* (pp. 1–10) Basingstoke, UK: Palgrave MacMillan.

Hellier, J., and Chusseau, N. (eds) (2012) *Growing Income Inequalities Economic Analyses* Basingstoke, UK: Palgrave MacMillan.

Hillyard, P. (1993) *Suspect Community: People's Experiences of the Prevention of Terrorism Acts in Britain* London: Pluto Press.

History US (2014) *The Great Migration* http://www.history.com/topics/black-history/great-migration [Accessed 14/04/14].

Jones, C., and Novak, T. (2009) 'Power, Politics and the Welfare State' in Coleman, R., Sim, J., Tombs, S., and Whyte, D. (eds), *State, Power, Crime* London: Sage.

Kalra, V. S., and Kapoor, N. (2009) 'Interrogating Segregation, Integration and the Community Cohesion Agenda' *Journal of Ethnic and Migration Studies* 35(9) pp. 1397–415.

Karafin, D. L. (2010) *Racial and Ethnic Integration in U.S. Metropolitan Neighborhoods: Patterns, Complexities and Consequences* Dissertation Abstracts International Section A: Humanities and Social Sciences, 70(10-A) p. 4066.

Lea, J., and Young, J. (1984) *What Is to Be Done About Law and Order?* London: Penguin Books.

Lee, M. (2007) *Inventing Fear of Crime* Cullompton, Devon, UK: Willan Publishing.

Modood, T. (2013) *Multiculturalism* London: Wiley.

Mullin, C. (1990) *Error of Judgment. The Truth About the Birmingham Bombings* Dublin, UK: Poolbeg Press.

Mumford, K. (2007) *Newark: A History of Race, Rights, and Riots in America* New York: New York University Press.

Osborne, H. (2014) 'Poor Doors: The Segregation of London's Inner-City Flat Dwellers' *The Guardian* 25 July 2014 http://www.theguardian.com/society/2014/jul/25/poor-doors-segregation-london-flats [Accessed 25.07.14].

Pantazis, C., and Pemberton, S. (2013) 'Resisting the Advance of the Security State: The Impact of Frameworks of Resistance on the UK'S Securitisation Agenda' *International Journal of Law Crime and Justice* 41(4) pp. 358–74.

Pantazis, C., and Pemberton, S. (2008) 'From the "Old" to the "New" Suspect Community: Examining the Impacts of Recent UK Counter-Terrorist Legislation' *British Journal of Criminology* 49(5) pp. 646–66.

Perry, B. (2003) 'Accounting for Hate Crime' in Schwarz, M. D., and Hatty, S. E. (eds) *Controversies in Critical Criminology* Cincinnati, OH: Anderson Publishing.

Rhodes, J. (2013) 'Remaking Whiteness in the "Postracial" UK' in Kalra, V. S., Kapoor, N., and Rhodes, J. (eds), *The State of Race* Basingstoke, UK: Palgrave Macmillan.

Ron, J. (2003) *Frontiers and Ghettos: State Violence in Serbia and Israel* Berkeley: University of California Press.

Shirazi, F., and Mishra, S. (2010) 'Young Muslim Women on the Face Veil: A Tool of Resistance in Europe but Rejected in the United States' *International Journal of Cultural Studies* 13(1) pp. 43–62.

Skeggs, B (2004) *Class, Self, Culture* London: Routledge.

Slater, T. (2010) 'Ghetto Blasting: On Loïc Wacquant's Urban Outcasts' *Urban Geography* 31(2) pp.162–68.

Taylor, I., Evans, K., and Fraser, P. (1996) *A Tale of Two Cities. Global Change, Local Feeling and Everyday Life in the North of England, A Study of Manchester and Sheffield* London: Routledge.

Van Swaaningen, R. (2005) 'Public Safety and the Management of Fear' *Theoretical Criminology* 9(3) pp. 289–305.

Wacquant, L. (2011) 'A Janus-Faced Institution of Ethnoracial Closure: A Sociological Specification of the Ghetto' in Hutchison, Ray, and Haynes, Bruce (eds), *The Ghetto: Contemporary Global Issues and Controversies* (pp. 1–31) Boulder, CO: Westview.

Wacquant, L. (2008) *Urban Outcasts* London: Polity Press.

Waddington, D., Jobard, F., and King, M. (eds) (2009) *Rioting in the UK and France. A Comparative Analysis* Cullompton, Devon, UK: Willan Publishing.

Werbner, P. (2005) 'The Translocation of Culture: "Community Cohesion" and the Force of Multiculturalism in History' *The Sociological Review* 53 pp.745–68.

Wilkinson, R., and Pickett, K. (2009) *The Spirit Level. Why More Equal Societies Almost Always Do Better* London: Allen Lane.

Wilson, W. J. (1987) *The Truly Disadvantaged: The Inner City, the Underclass, and Public Policy* Chicago: University of Chicago Press.

7
POLICING COMMUNITIES

The policing of communities – their monitoring, regulation and control – is carried out at a number of different levels and by various organisations. This chapter looks at the ways in which the state interacts with communities but also at more recent insights into governance which have created the expectation that communities will monitor, regulate and control themselves.

Policing with a capital 'P'

Prior to the Industrial Revolution, investigation and prosecution of crime were private functions, carried out by individuals, organisations employing guards and groups within a community who might form prosecution associations to patrol an area or investigate a particular crime or series of crimes (Allen and Barzel 2011). The Metropolitan Police Act (1829) established the 'Police' as a public service to patrol and prevent crime on the streets of London – then the largest city in Europe. It took just under three decades before the policing model established on the streets of London at that time later became a national force, but this model of public policing has since been exported to many other areas of the world. As Brogden and others have noted, reaction to a uniformed presence on the streets of London was initially mixed:

> Working class response to the police institution during the first century varied over time, by region, by strata. In general, by the end of that period the relations that had developed were not so much ones of consent but rather a grudging acceptance, a tentative approval, that could be withdrawn instantly in the context of industrial conflict. … For the lower classes, the participants of the street economy … attitudes to the police institution remained essentially unchanged.
>
> (1982:244)

In certain areas, as Brogden notes, attitudes to the Police were distinctly ambivalent. Their presence formalised a set of law enforcement practices which were previously informally carried out by the community itself. As a consequence of removing responsibility for the maintenance of order from the community, policing was no longer embedded in local social relations and became a standardised and top-down tool of community management (Sharpe 2001:135). In addition, although the Metropolitan Police were nominally constituted as a physical presence to deter and prevent the commission of crime at a time when crime rates appeared to be rising significantly in the capital, this was also a period of revolutionary upheaval across the continent. The old ways of ruling and of popular capitulation to the whims of the aristocracy and monarchy were being tested and resisted by the emerging bourgeois and working classes (Sharpe 2001:142). New forms of collective organisation, some resisting industrialisation and others seeking to build associations of the industrialised working-class to improve conditions of work and pay rates, were also making their presence felt. It was clear that the Police would also be charged with controlling the collective resistance of workers. From their inception, therefore, the Police were charged with a dual role: (1) to prevent crime and victimisation – one part of their responsibility which would gain them popular support; and (2) as a uniformed and professional arm of the state, to maintain order on the streets and protect the national interest as defined by government and politicians. This second role did not endear the organisation to those who were organising the working classes to bring about social change in their own interests.

Meanwhile, as the Police balanced these two functions, concern about 'dangerous areas' pulled them into potential conflict with another group – the urban poor classified by the science of the day as pathologically deviant and the source of myriad social problems. The Police subsequently focused their activities on this group and the areas in which they would be found.

Lea (2002:36–41) explains how the poor came to be regarded as a problem population. He cites changing perceptions of crime and criminality in the nineteenth century as lying behind much of the demonization of working-class communities. First, the move from feudalism to industrialisation required new forms of property ownership and the protection of private property by law. Property became not solely a thing to be used, but something which could be exchanged in order to generate profit. In the first volume of *Capital*, Karl Marx explains that the generation of profit which lies at the heart of the capitalist project requires that the exchange-value of objects supercedes their use-value. Under capitalism it is the legitimate owner of the property who is entitled to extract its exchange-value, and it became necessary at this point to transform the existing social order to incorporate this fundamental shift in perception. It had been customary for people to glean; to gather fallen wood from forests; to graze animals on land which was held in common; to pick through crops which had been harvested, for miners to pick through slag-heaps for coal that they could burn; for workers to take home and trade in the scraps left over from the production process; and for those who worked in the docks to claim a portion of the cargo they unloaded. These traditional ways for the poor to increase their chances of survival were criminalised during the eighteenth century, but in the eyes of the poor this shifting definition of crime impoverished them further and met 'active resistance' (Lea 2002:37). In addition, certain activities which were always considered illegal, such as poaching and smuggling, but which were sometimes condoned as they gave the poor access to food and financial resources when times were hard were also criminalised. These activities, now crimes, could be considered legitimate and their perpetrators as 'Robin Hood' figures, stealing from the rich to give to the poor. A culture of silence, of opposition to 'grassing' and to giving information over to the authorities which might incriminate another person, developed as a result.

The working class was controlled in other ways: Many street-based activities which were common in working-class neighbourhoods were also criminalised. Industrialists needed a compliant workforce that would fit into the regulated lifestyle of work needed to keep the wheels of industry turning and to overturn traditional practices which put work and leisure on a more equal footing. The needs of industrial capitalism set up an antagonistic relationship between working-class communities and the law, and in some areas today some of these old practices and community codes are still in evidence. It is doubtful, however, whether their provenance is widely understood (see, for example, Evans et al [1996] and their discussion of the former dockside community of Oldtown).

Who can be trusted?

Towards the end of the nineteenth and the beginning of the twentieth centuries, industrial society settled into a different rhythm, and the street-based culture of the nineteenth century was replaced by one which was more centred on home and family. The revolutionary fervour of earlier decades was calmed by the creation of reformist organisations working on behalf of the working class to improve economic and social conditions. It is in this period, Lea argues, that 'crime control comes to assume its modern form'(2002:41). The control of crime evolved into a normalised and professionalised practice and therefore became based on more information and specialised knowledge. During this period of stability, Lea contends, the working class as an entire social group was no longer assumed to be a criminal class, but instead the focus of crime control shifted to the poorest sections of society, 'the residuum' who continued to be without steady employment. It also turned towards the regulation of young people who were yet to enter the world of work. It is clear at this point that policing had developed two significant elements. The first of these elements is that the Police focus on those groups they consider to be 'troublesome', these being the groups which are monitored, surveilled and most closely regulated. The second key element is that the Police need the support of the 'respectable' groups in society, those who have accommodated to the police presence. This is the group which will report crime and which can furnish the Police with the information they need to effectively detect and solve the crime which is committed. The decision as to which groups are to be considered 'suspicious' and which groups are to be trusted becomes an important part of the Police function, and of course their decisions are influenced by the political, social and economic mores of the day.

The first half of the twentieth century was beset by two world wars, economic and financial instability and, in some countries, significant social unrest, but the patterns of policing established in the late nineteenth century endured. By the middle of the twentieth century, postwar economic growth in the economically developed nations meant that employment patterns stabilised and the availability of employment expanded to the extent that everyday life for the majority was no longer focused on mere survival, and instead work could furnish the family and individual with the means to enjoy leisure time and plan for the future. Cohen (1979) argued that a new moral economy of place and space developed which shifted attitudes to crime and criminality. Crime was no longer considered a necessary adaptation to a brutal existence, but as it was perceived that legitimate alternatives were clearly available, it was considered more of a lifestyle choice for the minority or a way of life that some fell into as a result of personal or economic difficulties. Either way this lifestyle could be reversed with the right punishment and/or support. This was the era, then, of consensus policing. As Banton suggests in his 1964 publication *The Policeman in the Community,* the police and society more generally, held shared values about right and wrong, punishment and rehabilitation.

Banton's view that there existed a shared consensus between Police and the general public did not fit all situations and all societies. His own work compared the *consensus model of policing* in the UK with the harsher and violent policing he observed in the US, which he characterised as a *conflict model of policing.* The different models of policing Banton outlined were predicated on the co-presence of a particular set of social conditions and popular attitudes. Consensus policing depends on the community, considering the Police as a socially useful force in society; under these conditions, the community will share information with the Police. Their detection rates are therefore higher than they would otherwise be; and the Police will in turn trust the community and put effort into developing good relations with them. Under the conflict model, however, the Police are considered as socially or politically repressive by the policed community, which might at times show open hostility to the Police. In these areas, there may be some support for people who are targeted for police attention, and individuals are less likely to come forward with information which would help find those who have committed crimes. Under these circumstances, police find it difficult to carry out their job effectively, and they are likely to use covert surveillance or more overt and forceful tactics such as house-raids or stop and search to gain the information they require. These policing tactics are likely to create more hostility and suspicion between the Police and those who are subject to this policing style. Relationships of trust are missing from this second scenario. The issue of organisational culture within the Police is also significant here. Reiner (2010) and others have located this culture as being embedded in police officers who possess a sense of mission in their work, but it includes a cynicism and suspicion of others which is considered necessary to get the job done. This cynical and suspicious attitude towards others can set up a cultural divide between the Police and those whom they police. Police occupational culture is, in addition, said to be masculinist, racially-prejudiced and suffused with a conservative and pessimistic outlook, as well as a sense that the Police are isolated from society more generally. As a result, police officers develop a strong solidarity with their peers, which means that they are less likely to speak out against their fellow officers.

Policing for crime prevention and maintenance of order has always involved suspicion and stereotyping (Christian 1983:115). The Police themselves will admit that with finite resources it is simply not practical to police all social groups in exactly the same way. However, the stereotyping of populations is more than merely a practical measure to target resources more efficiently. It is also a consequence of political decision making, of the exercise of the power of the state over certain groups which are considered as undermining the accepted order and of the state's concern to protect its interests (Bunyan 1977). The stereotyping which the Police will use in the normal course of their work also reflects the accepted values and hegemonic ideologies of the day and of the particular culture in which the Police are operating. After all, police officers do not exist in a social vacuum. They are drawn from society, live within society and carry with them into their work all the values they draw on in their everyday lives. Stereotyping by the Police can come both from organisational demands which are institutionalised into common practices, and it can be more personally exercised by the police officer in the course of their contact with the public. Each police officer is bound and regulated in their duties by a chain of command which requires them to police to common goals and to particular standards, but they are also able to exercise a great deal of discretion in their work when out on patrol and at this point are unsupervised, raising concerns about over-, under- and selective enforcement of the law and the feeling that the Police as an organisation may be unaccountable to their public (Burke 2013).

It is important for the state that its systems of criminal justice are considered as effective and legitimate. The increase in crime and victimisation which was recorded over much of the industrially developed world in the second half of the twentieth century was a challenge for which states had to find new ways to meet. Questions were raised about the competence of national criminal justice systems to meet this challenge, which led to a rethinking of the practice of policing and preventing crime. As a result, two distinct approaches have been developed. They have gained prominence alongside each other, although seemingly are mutually incompatible. They are the increasing turn to community-focused policing built around a consensus-led approach and at the same time the incorporation of increasingly sophisticated technology to surveil and control populations, which has pushed policing closer to a military-style conflict model.

Policing with the community

By the 1980s, the idea that the Police should move closer to and work *in partnership with* the community was established as an innovative practice which would achieve better results in the prevention of crime. The shift to policing *with* the community was tried in many jurisdictions across the globe and in each case involved setting up new structures of local organisation which could bring relevant local organisation, local residents and the Police together. It is not possible to explore every operational outcome of policing with the community which has been attempted, but the following sections look at some of the more iconic policing practices which emerged as a consequence.

Community 'Watch' schemes

One particular practice, the setting up of Neighbourhood Watch (NW) groups, was adopted in the US and quite quickly afterwards in the UK in the 1980s. It has become an enduring staple of community policing, with the 'success' of NW schemes evaluated by their rapid proliferation rather than their effectiveness as a crime prevention tool (Fyfe 1995). Finegan (2013), for example, has estimated that 40 per cent of the US population lives in communities covered by NW schemes. Perhaps their true 'success', however, can be gauged by their ideological role in transferring responsibility for a core policing function away from the organisations of the state and towards individual members of the community. This shift in responsibility has not come without its own problems and dangers. In the UK, NW was designed as crime deterrence, to publically involve communities in the surveillance of their areas and to signal, through the use of NW window stickers (later more permanent street signs were used), that particular areas were being 'monitored' even in the absence of the uniformed Police. NW has been perceived as a largely benign public policy tool which can nevertheless have unfortunate consequences.

In the early 1990s the UK government pushed citizen involvement in policing onto another level, using the perceived success of NW to call for citizens to act as 'the eyes and ears' of the Police in 'Streetwatch' schemes. This citizen engagement in the policing role takes the concept of NW but incorporates what Sharp et al (2008) refer to as 'civilian policing'. This has led to a number of unfortunate incidences of vigilantism in which citizens have operated outside the boundaries of legitimate action and have become involved in sometimes violent action akin to retributive justice. In the US there have also been fears that NW activism has been interpreted as more akin to citizen enforcement; consequently, the idea of NW has been open to more critical scrutiny. In the US, after all, members of NW may have guns, and although the guidelines stress that NW activity should involve no contact with suspected 'intruders' and merely a phone call to the police, the deaths of a number of people at the hands of NW patrollers are testament to the fact that this guideline is not always adhered to. Finegan (2013:106) argues that NW schemes 'allow members of the public to skirt procedural protections guaranteed to criminal suspects and lead to the diminution of civil liberties,' which may be especially the case for civilian policing of 'suspect groups' and in particular those who can be visibly perceived as hailing from BME groups. Sharp et al (2008) linked the rise in civilian policing schemes in the UK in the 1990s with the general public's concern about rising crime levels and the apparent failure of the Police to make an impact on crime levels locally. Research in other countries has similarly linked a rise in vigilantism to a general sentiment that the state has lost its authority and cannot keep the peace (Smith 2004).

Community policing

Histories of policing note that the practice of formal policing changed dramatically in the twentieth century. Before the invention of the motor car, policing involved uniformed officers patrolling the streets on foot or bicycle. Officers knew the community which they policed and often lived within it. However, modern technologies moved the policing role away from intimate contact with the streets and the public, placing it further away from the role of the neighbourhood officer. To reverse this trend, as crime rates rose and communities demanded more protection, the role of community policing was established, which involved getting the police officer out of the car and on to the streets once more. This 'preventative patrolling' was established in order to maintain a reassuring uniformed presence on the streets and to develop a more proactive role for officers, who would be encouraged to attend local events, connect with community organisations and get to know and be known by local residents. It was hoped that this new policing style would build up trust between the Police and the community as well as ensure that policing was more informed by local priorities and concerns (Shapland 2008). Community policing was built on a number of key principles: a shift from the centre to the periphery with unit commanders giving up some control to the officers on the street; a move from reactive to responsive policing whereby closer contact with the community would help them to articulate areas of concern; acknowledgement that the police do not have the monopoly on knowledge and expertise within an area; a shift in perception of the community to that of a 'customer' with demands which must be seen to be satisfied; and use of the community as co-producer of policing plans and objectives. In return, the community was asked to play its part by offering information, advice and actively work alongside the Police to shape their priorities, to look for solutions to local problems, and to participate fully in local initiatives which followed as a result.

Community policing widened the police officers' range of activities. They could move out of the relatively narrow confines of situational crime prevention to include social crime prevention in their repertoire. Some community police officers embraced this opportunity and used their local contacts to get involved in school-based activities, youth programmes and regeneration initiatives. In the UK after the Police Reform Act of 2002, community policing in England and Wales was boosted by the inclusion of Police Community Support Officers (PCSOs), civilian officers in Police-style uniforms who were recruited to complement and support the public-facing work of the Police. PCSOs, though lacking many of the powers granted to the regular Police, took over many of the roles of community police officers such as supervising street patrols, issuing fixed penalty notices for minor offences such as littering and enforcing local by-laws, for example, preventing the consumption of alcohol on the streets, alongside a raft of other measures designed to keep the peace of the streets. Community policing was adopted as an innovative practice in the UK and the US, but it has continued in reality to be policing from above, notwithstanding the Police's mandate to forge a closer connection to sources of community information.

Problem-oriented policing

Although community policing reassured local residents and deterred potential offenders by putting resources into a uniformed presence on the streets, in reality it had little impact on preventing crime or increasing feelings of community safety. This was known as early as 1974 when the Kansas City Preventive Patrol Experiment first evaluated street patrols and found them to be an ineffective policing tool which displaced crime elsewhere. Notwithstanding this knowledge, popular 'common-sense logic' demanded that street patrols continue to be supported (Braga and Weisburd 2010). As community policing was rolled out further, it was closely tied in the late 1980s to another policing innovation – that of 'problem-oriented policing' (POP), also known as local problem solving which, it was argued, would ensure community policing was more effective (Bullock and Tilley 2009). POP was devised by two US-based criminologists who were well known for their research on policing and who received large amounts of government support for their work. Sherman and Weisburd highlighted the concentration of crime in certain areas, and within these areas the higher concentration of crime at particular addresses which they named 'crime hotspots'. Sherman's research in Minneapolis, Minnesota, revealed that the vast majority of addresses in the city appeared to be free of criminal victimisation, whereas 50 per cent of calls to the police were linked to 3.5 per cent of the city's addresses (Sherman and Weisburd 1995). It made more sense, they argued, for the Police to focus their attention on these places, to deal with the issues which contributed to the high numbers of crimes, and by doing so to solve crime without displacing it onto other areas. In later studies, Sherman and Weisburd concluded that general, randomised patrols had little effect on crime but targeted patrolling of discrete addresses led to significantly improved results. The POP approach was also used to focus policing on problems of anti-social behaviour or non-crime disorders using contact with the community to identify and prioritise local problems, to bring together data from different sources to try to understand the problems which arose and then to draw in a range of agencies which could help devise and implement a solution.

Finally, the Police were required to constantly update their data and evaluate the effectiveness of their intervention and then to report back to all interested parties. In the abstract, POP was intended as a policing style which would see a cross-fertilisation of information sources, using community lay knowledge to help the Police and expert Police knowledge would be fed back into the community. This sharing of information was made more easily available when computer software programmes were developed which could translate this information into easily-read, visual maps. In the UK, since the Crime and Disorder Act of 1998 established Community Safety Partnerships across England and Wales, these maps are now readily available to all on publically available Internet sites. They allow residents to check where 'hotspots' of crime occur and to use this information in various ways – for example, to check rates of recorded crime in an area before committing to buying a property.

Policing with the community – some problems

Policing in partnership with the community is double-edged. On the one hand, it is informed by the recognition that if trusting relationships can be built between the Police and members of a policed community, the Police will be able to tap into sources of local knowledge to gather important intelligence. On the other hand, as Shapland observes (2008:15), community policing has also been used as 'an attempt to shift responsibility' for the prevention and detection of crime onto civilians. This 'responsibilization' strategy, discussed below, demands that individual citizens and communities begin to police themselves, to take more precautionary measures, to 'arm' themselves with the tools they need to prevent themselves from becoming subject to victimisation and to neutralise possible threats. It is not surprising that these measures can ramp up individual and collective fears and increase feelings of insecurity. In apparently insecure times, with 'suspect communities' increasing in number and range and with the state seemingly less able to deliver security on either a national or global scale, then this latter impetus for involving the community in policing work can lead to unwelcome and unhelpful intrusions from unregulated citizens and citizen groups, which can lead to heightened tension within and between communities. Reflecting on this policy shift in the Netherlands, Van Swaaningen asks:

> to what extent the governance of safety has become an issue of *us*, law-abiding citizens, *against them*, the homeless, drug users, street prostitutes, youth gangs and notably the (Muslim) ethnic minorities, and what the possible consequences are of this tendency.'
>
> (2008:101)

The development of focused, problem-oriented, 'hotspot'-driven policing demonstrates the development of a policing logic which is ever more concentrated on 'problem areas'. In effect, the 'community' becomes not just the place where policing occurs but also the subject of close and detailed scrutiny. Community police surveil and record local activities; they get to know local residents, organisations and the patterns of behaviour of local people known to be involved in committing crimes as well as those who work with the police to solve them. The community therefore becomes a unit of analysis as well as the site for the practice of policing, and as we demonstrated earlier, certain communities are more closely analysed than others. The police also collect data ('intelligence') on local families, networks and interaction between different groups and individuals. The disproportionate attention on discrete individuals, addresses and communities will then skew the crime statistics, leading to cumulative feedback loop of over-attention and over-policing.

As policing with the community and partnership and multi-agency policing gather more support and become further entrenched into policing strategies, the focus on particular problem communities and individuals continues to develop more momentum. In recent years, particular attention has been paid to the 'persistent and prolific offender' (PPO), who is more easily identified by the problem-oriented analysis of police data. As more information is passed around a range of agencies, the self-fulfilling prophecy is further set in motion whereby those perceived as in need of a range of interventions gain a shared reputation as 'troublesome'. These 'troubled' areas and individuals continue to be more closely monitored and their indiscretions highlighted. Hopkins and Wickson (2012) have estimated that after the Prolific and Other Priority Offender (PPO) programme was introduced into the work of Community Safety Partnerships in England and Wales in September 2004, the 10,000 individuals were referred to the programme in the first five years. There was little evidence, however, that the programme would have much impact on their levels of desistance from crime.

Police and community partnerships – local policing with a small 'p'

Hughes reminds us that 'by the last decades of the twentieth century nation-states have been increasingly unable to meet their core responsibility to provide citizens with security' (Hughes 2003:3). As a result of this failure, national governments have increasingly co-opted 'community' into the practice of crime prevention and control in order to fight crime on more than one front. As Crawford explains, 'global pressures are increasingly refracted through local meanings, identities and sensibilities' (Crawford 2002:215) and a politics of insecurity and fear has been utilised to change the nature of the contract between state and locality and to encourage the community to organise itself to tackle the problem of crime on its doorstep.

The community has been co-opted into crime control at the same time that there has been a general retreat from welfarism and a withdrawal of financial and political support for the very institutions of community which have been said to make a difference locally. Lister (2006) has argued that, rather than directly maintain communities, the state now expects communities to maintain themselves – albeit working alongside other institutions of governance and voluntary organisations. This requirement has had a raft of unfortunate consequences, as Jamieson states:

> [T]he USA and many European states have sought to abrogate their welfare responsibilities necessitating the introduction of a 'new institutional machinery for managing poverty' [which ...] make[s] access to welfare increasingly conditional on conduct ... In effect ... engender[ing] what has been characterized as a 'criminalisation of social policy.'
>
> (2012:450)

For many authors (Crawford 1997; Gilling 2001; Grover 2008; Muncie and Hughes 2002; Tufail 2014), the circumstances leading to the criminalisation of social policy have had the effect of normalising policing and security agendas so that, as Tufail demonstrates in his recent research on policing in the north of England, organisations which offer public services to the community are acting with and can end up behaving in the same ways as law enforcement officials. In one example which Tufail highlights, a local social landlord rewrote the tenancy agreement in partnership with the police, who weighted it heavily towards a crime control and law enforcement agenda. On another occasion, a group of neighbourhood workers and local residents persuaded a group of homeless people to go into a Police station on the promise of some food and housing advice, whereas in reality officers from the Border Agency were waiting to question them about their immigration status. Where policing and public service boundaries become so blurred, it appears from these examples that it is the public service ethos which can become the victim.

Strategies of 'responsibilization'

Over the last three decades, the Anglophone states have shifted more of the responsibility for controlling crime away from their own institutions and towards third-sector, private and community-based organisations instead. These non-state actors, though disparate in their construction, in their ability to act and in their motivations for involvement in the arena of crime, have been hailed as significant players with 'the notion of "community"... deployed as the central motif' (Crawford 1997:247), around which they and the general public are being mobilised to participate in crime prevention. Garland has dubbed this shift a *responsibilization strategy* which:

> involves the central government seeking to act upon crime not in a direct fashion through state agencies (police, courts, prisons, social work, etc.) but instead by acting indirectly, seeking to activate action on the part of non-state agencies and organizations.
>
> (1996:449)

For Garland the new technique of 'responsibilization' was formed as an adaptation to three decades of sustained, and what appeared to be unstoppable, increases in crime rates. The state, Garland argued, had to face the reality that it had reached the limits of its sovereign power and its inability to prevent, or make any major impact on, the problem of crime. It is this adaptation, he argued, that led the state to look for innovative solutions, finally settling on the recourse to partnership working and the practices of 'multi-agency approaches', 'activating communities', creating 'active citizens' and 'help for self-help'. Others, however, have seen a more ideological push behind this trend, which 'needs to be connected firmly to the spread of a neo-liberal political ideology which has sought to transform the modern state' (Crawford 1997:247) and to establish alternative ways of maintaining control of troublesome populations. The functions of disciplinary control have also been passed down to private-sector organisations. The surveillance and patrolling of semi-public areas such as shopping malls, the building and running of prisons and more recently detention and deportation of those deemed to be in the country illegally have been given over to the private sector to run as profit-generating activities. This shift has taken place, not merely to persuade non-governmental actors to behave more appropriately, but to expand disciplinary control into new areas of social life (Gilling 2007).

CASE STUDY – COMMUNITY SAFETY PARTNERSHIPS IN THE UK

In 1979 in the UK, a Conservative government, initially led by Margaret Thatcher, was elected to office. Over the next seventeen years, in which the Conservatives were reelected a further three times, they highlighted the problem of rising crime rates to solidify a discourse of 'law and order' and punitive sanctions for those committing crime. Whilst in reality their policies were not always as punishing and anti-progressive as the strident voices of the various Home Secretaries might have led many to believe, they engendered in the popular imagination a need to deal swiftly and directly with those who transgressed the penal code. At the same time, the government implemented an economic agenda in the early 1980s which initially saw a rise in unemployment from around one to nearly six million, threw many into poverty and oversaw the destruction of areas of industry which had sustained communities for many decades and longer. What became known at the time as 'Thatcherism', but what we now understand as the early throes of a neo-liberal economics, was also closely associated with a diminishing of the state's role in the provision of welfare and a safety net for its citizens. These policies met with some resistance on the industrial front but also from a number of local authorities which continued to be led by the main opposition group – the Labour Party. A number of these Labour-led authorities continued to set spending targets and priorities which directly contravened national government objectives, and they did so in direct defiance of the government. The Labour-led city of Sheffield, for example, gained the moniker 'The Socialist Republic of South Yorkshire' as it stubbornly promoted a public service ethos and spent funds on heavily subsidised transport for the unemployed and elderly (Taylor et al 1996:40). In the area of crime control, these authorities embraced the concept of 'community safety' rather than 'crime prevention'.

The approach of community safety saw the problem of crime from a structural vantage point. Squires (2006) explains:

> At a time when some commentators were detecting a worrying drift towards a more neo-classical, punitive and situational drift in law and order policies (Brake and Hale, 1992) and ... an emerging 'criminalisation' of social policy, community safety policy appeared to offer a more optimistic and progressive alternative. It has been seen as a direct descendant of the 'left realist' shift in academic criminology (Lea and Young, 1988; Matthews and Young, 1992), giving new emphasis to patterns of victimisation (Mawby and Walklate, 1994) in relatively deprived communities, whereby crime was understood as yet another burden compounding the poverty and social exclusion endured by some UK citizens).

Community safety went beyond crime prevention discourse and sought to construct an organisational framework within troubled communities which could ensure that voices from below were heard on all sorts of issues related to neighbourhood safety, such as providing safe transport or working with school truants, which were not problems of 'crime' per se but still considered relevant social concerns which affected rates of crime locally. These 'Community Safety Partnerships' typically included representatives from the Police, Social Services, Health Authorities, local schools and the Probation Service but were co-ordinated and led by a key local authority department which could ensure that the concerns raised were heard by key local politicians and

(Continued)

were acted upon where possible. Nationally, the community safety perspective was rejected despite the fact that a government-commissioned report, *Safer Communities: The Local Delivery of Crime Prevention through the Partnership Approach,* known as the Morgan Report, delivered in 1991, recommended a shift from crime prevention to community safety. Nevertheless, a number of local authorities implemented this approach, funding the work through successful bids to government-led regeneration initiatives and European funding.

In 1997, the seventeen-year period of Conservative-led government was overturned by a landslide Labour victory. In 1998, Labour's flagship Crime and Disorder Act created a statutory duty for Local Authorities and the Police to collaborate in setting crime reduction audits and strategies. As the 'responsible authorities', they collaborated in the development of Community Safety Partnerships (CSPs) or Crime and Disorder Reduction Partnerships (CDRPs). CDRP later became the preferred title, signalling a move away from the principles of community safety and a return to a focus on crime and social disorder as the key problems to address in local communities.

From author's own research

Although the drive for community engagement in the control of crime has been a generalised trend, it has not always played out in the same way. In France, for example, the Bonne-Maison Report of 1982 commissioned by the then Socialist President Francois Mitterrand, encouraged the creation of three tiers of governance, a national body overseeing regional crime prevention councils and local administrative structures to deliver the crime prevention strategy on the ground. The Report recommended an outlook informed by social crime prevention practices which would devolve authority and decision-making powers to the local level. Crawford (2002) found these structures to be responsive, proactive and concerned with fully integrating local unemployed people into professional structures in a manner that would develop their skills and expertise and provide permanent employment. Given the highly centralised nature of the French Police, they had little input into the formation and delivery of local policy and projects. Crawford identifies the role of the state as 'moral unifier' (2002:228), as a key reason as to why until recently, the politics of division in France took less of centre stage and the politics of welfarism were still in evidence at the end of the twentieth century.

Conflict and community

At the same time that states have built their armoury of policing strategies, they have not abandoned recourse to a more authoritarian policing style for communities and situations which in their eyes remain stubbornly problematic. The 'suspect' and 'problem' communities introduced in Chapter Six and the 'crime hotspots' described earlier in this chapter have been the subject of varied policing styles. It is possible for the residents of these places to be subject to both consensus and conflict policing at one and the same time. The presence of conflict policing, however, will tend to destroy the conditions under which consensus policing might otherwise have had some possibility of gaining ground.

Zero tolerance and the policing of the poor

'Zero tolerance' joined the policing lexicon in the early 1990s. Linked to Wilson and Kelling's broken windows thesis, application of the concept of zero tolerance to policing was seen as offering a solution to the problem of spiralling crime and disorder in US cities. Zero tolerance policing can be classified as a confrontational policing strategy, and its proponents often show contempt for people living on the margins of the economy. Consider this justification for the adoption of zero tolerance policing written by the New York Department Police Commissioner, William Bratton, who introduced this policing style into the city in the mid-1990s:

> When I first came to New York City from Boston in 1990 … I remember driving from La Guardia Airport down the highway into Manhattan. Graffiti, burned out cars and trash seemed to be everywhere. It looked like something out of a futuristic movie. Then as you entered Manhattan, you meet the unofficial greeter for the City of New York, the Squeegee pest. This guy had a dirty rag or squeegee and would wash your window with some dirty liquid and ask for or demand money. Proceeding down Fifth Avenue, the mile of designer stores and famous buildings, unlicensed street peddlers and beggars were everywhere. Then down into the subway where everyday over 200,000 fare evaders jumped over or under turnstiles and demanded that paying passengers hand over their tokens to them. Beggars were on every train. Every platform seemed to have a cardboard city where the homeless had taken up residence.
>
> (1997:35)

New York, along with many other US cities in the 1980s and 1990s, was in crisis. The rise in poverty, homelessness and precarious employment which Bratton noted was a consequence of years of underinvestment in the people and the infrastructure of the city. Policies of urban redevelopment and regeneration discussed in Chapter Four had not come into effect. Begging and homelessness were on the increase as expenditure on welfare decreased. Yet, rather than treat the ensuing social problems as economic and structural, Bratton sees them as a problem of crime and one for the police to target and clear up – and where these social issues were not crimes, then they were likely to be made so. Zero tolerance policing declared that society would no longer tolerate disorder and the signs of disorder. The street homeless, the beggars and the squeegee 'pests' were considered, not as people with needs which were not being addressed, but as signs of disorder. As Crawford maintains, the intention of zero tolerance policing is 'to clear away and thus hide ... the socially dispossessed', so that this policing strategy is 'more about policing the boundaries of increasingly fragmented social divisions within society' (1998:154). The proponents of zero tolerance policing nevertheless proclaimed it to be a great success. Crime rates fell dramatically, order appeared to be restored to the city's streets and subways, and the city attracted enough inward investment from private companies to redevelop major parts of Manhattan. It was not long before zero tolerance policing was picked up outside the US and used to justify the confrontational policing of disorder and the signs of disorder in other regions of the world.

In the UK, zero tolerance policing proved initially unpopular and was heavily criticised by the senior management of many Police forces. During the early 1990s, a 'softer' form of zero tolerance was used as a strategy to clean up environments of graffiti, the eponymous 'broken windows' and other environmental degradation. As such the regeneration industry adopted the idea alongside the community safety perspective to argue for improvements in street cleansing and lighting, for housing improvements and, rather than sweep young people off the streets, to fund social programmes which would engage young people in leisure, training and creative opportunities. By the late 1990s, however, a harsher tone could be detected as the problem of crime eclipsed the community safety narrative. This tone was evident in the 1998 Crime and Disorder Act which lowered the age of criminal responsibility in England and Wales from 14 years to 10 and furnished the Police and the courts with an entirely new raft of control measures 'civil preventive orders' and the new (civil) offence of 'anti-social behaviour' (Evans 2003). In the intervening years, the powers of control given over to the Police have been further extended and are now both more fully and more widely utilised. In addition, the Anti-Social Behaviour Order (ASBO) has been joined by other preventive measures such as the Serious Crime Prevention Order, Risk of Sexual Harm Orders and Terrorism Prevention and Investigation Measures (TPIMs) (Ashworth and Zedner 2014).

The adoption of zero tolerance policing tactics has not gone unchallenged. Young (1999) spends considerable time in *The Exclusive Society* debunking the myths which built up around these techniques. He points out that the dramatic drop in crime which New York City experienced during this period was mirrored in 17 out of the 25 largest cities in the US and that the drop in crime experienced by New York City was part of a general decline in recorded crime in the US and in many other countries, a decline which has continued and for which there is no agreed explanation. Young also challenges the view that zero tolerance policing has ever been used, given that it 'would stretch the resources of any foreseeable police budget' (Young 1999:125). Instead, he argues, what *has* emerged is an intolerance towards individuals, disorder and the signs of poverty and neglect which has fed into aggressive policing and policy-making against the poor and which has excluded them further from the possibility of engaging fully in society. The state has instigated a 'quick fix' solution, he argues, to problems which are in reality deep-rooted and long-standing. The steady rise in imprisonment to unprecedented levels of incarceration in countries such as the US and the UK has been one outcome of this process. Another is the demonization of those whom society excludes.

The policing of young black men

As I was close to putting the finishing touches to this book in August 2014, the events surrounding young Michael Brown's death at the hands of the Missouri police hit the global headlines. This incident was followed a matter of days later by the death of Kajieme Powell, another young African American man gunned down by the police, this time in broad daylight, on the streets of St Louis. The policing of young black men in the US was once again at the centre of much debate and controversy. Michael Brown's death was met by community protest, and a curfew was imposed. In places the curfew was resisted, and over the ensuing weeks Ferguson's neighbourhoods endured a militarised Police response, which later even involved the National Guard bringing armoured vehicles onto the streets of a city's suburb. Interspersed with heavy-handed and divisive crowd control tactics was the State Police's attempt to quell the protests through community policing tactics – putting officers and the Police Commissioner himself into the public arena to meet the public and to listen to the community's concerns. However, as the *Guardian*'s US correspondent Gary Younge (2014) argued, the state's militarised reaction reflected decades of authoritarian policing of the area which had led to a spiralling of violence and mistrust which could never be overcome by a few appeals to community over a few days.

As Brunson and Miller have stated regarding the African American's experience in the US, 'People of colour living in disadvantaged urban communities have been shown to be the disproportionate recipients of both proactive policing strategies and various forms of police misconduct' (2006:613). At one and the same time, however, they are under-policed as victims, with response times to call-outs slow and an effective service to victims clearly lacking. The areas in which African Americans constitute the majority of the population are still considered as 'dangerous and violent places' (Brunson and Miller 2006:615). Young black men, in particular, Brunson and Miller argue, have been characterised as 'symbolic assailants' by the criminal justice system and within the popular imagination more generally. As a result, they have been subjected to a particularly assertive and confrontational policing style which seeks to control and subdue them. In Europe as well as in America, very similar attitudes can be identified. The consequence is a level of distrust and dissatisfaction in policing which is deeply felt and long held. The stereotyping of black communities as uncompliant, while particularly enduring, has been shown by much research in the US to be a myth. In fact, while research has shown that the more aggressive or disrespectful the police are with citizens, the less compliant these citizens will be when the behaviour of the police is taken into account, 'males and minority citizens are more likely to show compliance' (Mastrofski et al 1996:289). The highest rates of compliance are found in white officer/minority citizen encounters (Anderson 1990 in Brunson and Miller 2006:613). Brunson and Miller go on to explain that disproportionate experiences of surveillance and stop and search, the verbal abuse by Police officers of black males, together with an excessive use of force, including deadly force, explain the young black male's lack of trust of the police. Knowledge that they are likely to experience these negative reactions from the Police is likely to explain their generally compliant demeanour. As the events in Ferguson demonstrate, however, that compliance cannot always be relied upon, and at times obvious frustration spills over into anger and a demand for justice and respect.

In the UK, areas of African-Caribbean settlement have been equally characterised as problematic and have been subjected to disproportionate police attention and surveillance; these areas, too, have intermittently exploded in anger. As explained in Chapter Five, however, the so-called black areas of the UK are actually more diverse in their demographic make-up than those in the US. Nevertheless, the policing of areas of black settlement came into special prominence in the UK in the 1980s. Cowell et al's edited volume *Policing the Riots* (1982), for example, tells a tale of institutionalised racism, discriminatory policing and a lack of accountability which characterised the policing of African-Caribbean males and their communities across the country. A judicial enquiry led by Lord Scarman into the 'Brixton Riots' of 1981 acknowledged this to be the case (though falling short of admitting the Police were institutionally racist), although the Gifford Report, commissioned by the Liverpool City Council in 1988, was unequivocal in its agreement that the police in that city were institutionally racist (Lord Gifford 1989). Lord Scarman's report into the disturbances of 1981 recommended that there should be more formal opportunities for positive contact between the Police and all communities. In the UK, Police Community Consultative Groups (PCCGs) were established in many areas; these were open meetings which typically brought together the Police and community members once a month to discuss policing priorities. Nevertheless, after the racist murder of the black teenager Stephen Lawrence in London in 1993, Lord Macpherson's report into the bungled police investigation revealed not only incompetence but the Police's continuing stereotyping of young black males as potential gang members and criminals, a stereotyping that was still rife in the Metropolitan Police Force (Lord Macpherson 1999). Scarman's hope that PCCGs and more contact between the Police and black communities would break down prejudice and lead to 'colour-blind' policing (Scarman 1982) had certainly not been realised. In August 2011, the death of another young black man, Mark Duggan, at the hands of the Metropolitan Police unleashed a storm of protest which lasted days and involved black and white youth in civil unrest and looting in cities hundreds of miles apart. A report prepared for the government immediately afterwards found young people's perception of the Police's poor attitude and behaviour to be a significant factor in the motivations of the protestors. The report highlighted:

> a lack of respect by the police that was common in the experience of young black people in some parts of London. Outside London, the rioting was not generally attributed to the Mark Duggan case. However, the attitude and behaviour of the police locally was consistently cited as a trigger outside as well as within London.
>
> (Morell et al 2011:5)

Since 2001, members of Muslim communities in the UK, mainly young Muslim males, have faced similar negative police attention. During the 1970s and 1980s, Muslim communities were considered as generally law-abiding and unproblematic in policing terms (Lea and Young 1984). By the early 2000s, however, as detailed in Chapter Five, this view had started to change. The 'war on terror' declared in 2001 and the subsequent use (and abuse) of the new anti-terrorism legislation to police Muslims have had a profound effect, building mistrust between the Police and this community. The result has been 'frictional acts of resistance' which are further tainting the relationship between them, disrupting flows of communication and ensuring the likelihood of confrontational encounters (Pantazis and Pemberton 2011:370). As Treadwell (2014:60) has argued 'The relationship between the state and the public determines the effectiveness of policing'. The examples above reveal a significant gap between certain communities' expectations of the Police and their actual experiences.

A community subjected to over-policing can be negatively affected in various ways. Racial profiling, for example, puts an entire ethnic group under constant suspicion, while age profiling can affect young people's sense of engagement with wider society (James and James 2001) and can lead, as Muncie (1999) has argued, to an institutionalised intolerance of the young. Research by Beth Loftus (2009) in the UK suggests that, in addition, an increasing intolerance of the poorest sections of society has also become more apparent as a key aspect of Police occupational culture. Of course, those individuals perceived as belonging to or who identify themselves as a part of that group which is brought under suspicion may feel a sense of injustice that they are singled out for attention over other groups (Pampel 2004). This sense of injustice may be felt even if an individual is not subject to unwarranted intrusions themselves. For those who are individually targeted for Police attention the injustice takes a more palpable form. According to Pampel, the emotional and psychological effects of such attention should not be underestimated, and the stress of constant, negative contact with the Police can bring on symptoms similar to posttraumatic stress disorder, evoking negative thoughts, nightmares and avoidance behaviour in the victim. Additionally, Pampel continues, many of the groups affected by this profiling are aware and affected by historical injustices, which only compounds their feelings of alienation and distrust of the law and enforcement agents.

Surveillance, security and the militarisation of policing

At the same time as models of community policing were being planned and implemented, concern was growing that the Police in various countries were also developing militarised units. This concern was articulated in Kraska's work, together with Cubellis and Kappeler in the US (1997). This work revealed that Police forces in cities across the US were acquiring military weapons, using military training techniques to train officers and beginning to develop a confrontational style in handling suspects; they were treating them more like enemy combatants than citizens with rights (den Heyer 2014). According to Hall and Coyne (2013), both state and local law enforcement agencies across the nation have created Police Paramilitary Units (PPUs), which by 1995 could be found in 89 per cent of all Police departments. These units are equipped with hundreds of millions of dollars of military equipment ranging from wiretaps to assault rifles, grenade launchers and armoured vehicles. This engagement with military tactics has been argued to have arisen as a consequence of popular criticism and resistance to government policies in the 1960s (den Heyer 2014) and has been exacerbated by 'the war on drugs' in the 1980s and 'the war on terror' at the turn of the new century (Hall and Coyne 2013). The militarisation of the police was initially concentrated in PPUs, but it has since reached into everyday policing styles and become a significant policing style. Den Heyer notes that this trend was not limited to the US and that it now extended to the UK, Canada, New Zealand and Australia, all of which are generally considered non-militarised and democratic domains which govern by consensus rather than coercion, nevertheless, 'all established similar police response units from the early 1960s to the mid-1970s' (2013:350). Whilst each of these countries may have articulated a different rationale for their adoption, and each would have deployed differing techniques for the scenarios which affected their own nation, the adoption of armed response units, the deployment of riot equipment and the increased use of surveillance techniques in policing have become more routine and acceptable.

Over the last twenty-five to thirty years, the surveillance of different populations has become an everyday fact of life. It has become so 'commonplace' that it is little questioned and indeed is considered to be a 'public good' or has become 'banal', 'taken for granted' and 'rarely subject to attention or concern' (Goold et al 2013:978). We have already seen in Chapter Six that the populations more likely to come under intense surveillance are those considered as 'suspect'. As new 'threats' arise, new objects of surveillance are created. However, the old suspect communities are not always replaced by the new; instead additional 'suspect groups' are created. As a consequence, surveillance practice has increased, the surveillance gaze has widened to incorporate a greater number of 'problems' and the practice of surveillance has become normalised as a policing tool. Concerns over the increased use of surveillance have been raised, but here the context is important. In the UK, which is often said to be the highest user of CCTV systems in the world, there has been very little opposition to their proliferation, whereas in other countries the use of surveillance cameras on public streets, monitoring everyday behaviour, has been considered a breach of a citizen's right to privacy. The widespread acceptance of cameras in the UK has been explained by the national fixation on crime prevention at the time that the government released millions of pounds of funding for cameras through its CCTV Challenge competitions in the mid-1990s and by the absence of a legal framework by which the growth of these systems might be challenged (Goold et al 2013). In the US, support for crime profiling in law enforcement, the practice of identifying characteristics of offenders and their modus operandi, and using these to identify individual suspects, morphed into the practice of 'racial profiling' as early as the 1970s when it was used to justify the disproportionate searches of African Americans in the so-called war on drugs (Suh 2009). Such profiling, Suh maintains, has led to increased surveillance of African Americans since the time of slavery; the monitoring of Hispanic populations (especially in the border states of the US) in the name of policing immigration; and the over-policing of poor communities considered more prone to criminality. Profiling is also in widespread use in anti-terrorism policing.

The high-profile security agenda which has dominated the first years of the twenty-first century has increased the use of selective surveillance. A poll conducted in the US in 1999 showed that 81 per cent of individuals disapproved of racial profiling in traffic enforcement. Another poll conducted two years after the September 11 attacks showed a majority in favour of using racial profiling to monitor people from Arab backgrounds in airports and on planes (Suh 2009). However, following Edward Snowden's revelation of the use of mass surveillance techniques by national governments, it has been argued that surveillance has penetrated into everyday life. In addition, Lyon (2014) contends that surveillance destroys the presumption of innocence when it is used as a tool in the technique of 'pre-emptive prediction' which seeks to identify individuals who may become threats to national security before they have committed any offence. Ashworth and Zedner (2014) describe the emergence of the concept of 'the preventive state', a new paradigm in social control which seeks to deprive 'dangerous individuals' of their liberty before they have the opportunity to harm others. This paradigm has serious implications for human rights and liberties. It places the state firmly in control of the definitions of 'harm', and it allows for a criminal justice process which lies outside of the usual framework employing preventive detention, closed courts and control orders.

Some concluding comments and questions

This chapter has explored the policing of communities. It has looked at the formal policing role and the ways in which this role has been described as either consensus or conflict-based. The chapter interrogates the concept of community policing and the techniques which have been employed to incorporate community as a partner in policing. At the same time, however, the employment of profiling, preventive policing and the categorisation of entire social groups as suspect populations have meant that the gap between police authorities and targeted communities is widening and is likely to continue to do so if a change in policing policy and priorities is not made evident. As Lea and Young first explained, conflict policing is more likely where relationships of mutual trust have broken down. This would explain the increasing use of militarised policing techniques against communities and publics which have, in turn, lost their trust in figures of authority. Consider the following questions:

1. Is policing by consent a possibility, or will there always be conflict between the Police and the policed?
2. Is surveillance a public good?

Further reading

Many interesting and engaging works have been published on the role of policing in society. To see how this role has changed, it would be useful to take a look at Banton's *The Policeman in the Community* (1964) and to compare it to Lea and Young's *What Is to Be Done About Law and Order?* (1984). These classic books are written from a very different perspective and therefore reveal much about the policing problem. To understand the background to the militarisation of the state's response to crime, Harvey's article 'NeoLiberalism as Creative Destruction' (2007) gives a flavour of the formation of neo-liberal discourses, and Cohen's article 'Policing the Working-Class City', while written in 1979, still rings true today.

References

Allen, W., and Barzel, Y. (2011) 'The Evolution of Criminal Law and Police during the Pre-modern Era' *Journal of Law and Economic Organisation* 27(3) pp. 540–67.

Ashworth, A., and Zedner, L. (2014) *Preventive Justice* Oxford, UK: Oxford University Press.

Banton, M. (1964) *The Policeman in the Community* London: Penguin Books.

Braga, A. A., and Weisburd, D. L. (2019) *Policing Problem Places: Crime Hot Spots and Effective Prevention* New York: Oxford University Press.

Bratton, W. (ed) (1997) *Zero Tolerance: Policing a Free Society* London: The IEA Health and Welfare Unit.

Brogden, M. (1982) *The Police: Autonomy and Consent* London: Academic Press.

Brunson, R. K., and Miller, J. (2006) 'Young Black Men and Urban Policing in the United States' *The British Journal of Criminology* 46(4) pp. 613–40.

Bullock, K., and Tilley, N. (2009) 'Born to Fail? Policing, Reform and Neighbourhood Problem-Solving' *The Police Journal* 83(2) pp. 117–30.

Bunyan, T. (1977) *Political Police in Britain* London: Quartet Books.

Burke, A. (2013) 'Policing, Protestors, and Discretion' *North Carolina Law Review* 91(2) pp. 606–60.

Christian, L. (1983) *Policing by Coercion* London: GLC Police Committee Support Unit.

Cohen, P. (1979) 'Policing the Working-Class City' in Fine, B., Kinsey, R., Lea, J., Picciotto S., and Young, J. (eds), *Capitalism and the Rule of Law* (pp. 118–36) London: Hutchinson.

Cowell, D., Jones, T., and Young, J. (eds) (1982) *Policing the Riots* London: Junction Books.

Crawford, A. (2002) 'The Growth of Crime Prevention in France as Contrasted with the English Experience: Some Thoughts on the Politics of Insecurity' in Hughes, G., McLaughlin, E., and Muncie, J.(eds), *Crime Prevention and Community Safety. New Directions* London: Sage.

Crawford, A. (1999) *The Local Governance of Crime: Appeals to Community and Partnerships* Oxford, UK: Oxford University Press.

Crawford, A. (1998) *Crime Prevention and Community Safety* Harlow, UK: Longman.

Crawford, A. (1997) *The Local Governance of Crime: Appeals to Community and Partnerships* Oxford, UK: Oxford University Press.

den Heyer, G. (2014) 'Mayberry Revisited: A Review of the Influence of Police Paramilitary Units on Policing' *Policing and Society: An International Journal of Research and Policy* 24(3) pp. 346–61.

Evans. K. (2003) 'Out of Control – Community Responses to Crime' in Boran, A. (ed), *Crime. Fear or Fascination?* Chester: Academic Press.

Evans, K., Fraser, P., and Walklate, S. (1996) 'Whom Can You Trust? The Politics of "Grassing" on an Inner-City Housing Estate' *Sociological Review* 44(3) pp. 361–80.

Finegan, S. (2013) 'Watching the Watchers: The Growing Privatization of Criminal Law Enforcement and the Need for Limits on Neighbourhood Watch Associations' *UMass Law Review* 8(1) pp. 88–136.

Fyfe, N. (1995) 'Law and Order Policy and the Spaces of Citizenship in Contemporary Britain' *Political Geography* 14(12) pp. 1–189.

Garland, D. (1996) 'The Limits of the Sovereign State. Strategies of Crime Control in Contemporary Society' *The British Journal of Criminology* 36(4) pp. 445–71.

Gilling, D. (2007) *Crime Reduction and Community Safety* Cullompton, Devon, UK: Willan Publishing.

Gilling, D. (2001) 'Community Safety and Social Policy' *European Journal on Criminal Policy and Research* 9(4) pp. 381–400.

Goold, B., Loader, I., and Thumala, A. (2013) 'The Banality of Security. The Curious Case of Surveillance Cameras' *British Journal of Criminology* 53(6) pp. 977–96.

Grover, C. (2008) *Crime and Inequality* Cullompton, Devon, UK: Willan Publishing.

Hall, A., and Coyne, C. (2013) 'The Militarization of U.S. Domestic Policing' *Independent Review* 17(4) pp. 485–504.

Harvey, D. (2007) 'NeoLiberalism as Creative Destruction' *The Annals of the American Academy of Political and Social Science* 610 pp. 21–44.

Hopkins, M., and Wickson, J. (2012) 'Targeting Prolific and Other Priority Offenders and Promoting Pathways to Desistance: Some Reflections on the PPO Programme Using a Theory of Change Framework' *Criminology and Criminal Justice* 13(5) pp. 594–614.

Hughes, G. (2003) *Understanding Crime Prevention* Milton Keynes: Open University Press.

James, A. L., and James, A. (2001) 'Tightening the Net: Children, Community and Control' *British Journal of Sociology* 5(2) pp. 211–28.

Jamieson, J. (2012) 'Bleak Times for Children? The Anti-Social Behaviour Agenda and the Criminalisation of Social Policy' *Social Policy and Administration* 46(4) pp. 448–64.

Kelling, G. L., and Wilson, J. Q. (1982) 'Broken Windows. The Police and Neighborhood Safety' *Atlantic Monthly* March.

Kraska, P. B., and Cubellis, L. J (1997) 'Militarizing Mayberry and Beyond: Making Sense of American Paramilitary Policing' *Justice Quarterly* 14(4) pp. 607–29.

Kraska, P. B., and Kappeler, V. E. (1997) 'Militarizing American Police: The Rise and Normalization of Paramilitary Units' *Social Problems* 44(1) pp. 1–18.

Lea, J. (2002) *Crime and Modernity. Continuities in Left Realist Criminology* London: Sage.

Lea, J., and Young, J. (1984) *What Is to Be Done About Law and Order?* London: Penguin Books.

Lister, S. C. (2006) 'Plural Policing, Local Communities and the Market in Visible Patrols' in Dearling, A., Newburn, T., and Somerville, P. (eds), *Supporting Safe Communities: Housing, Crime and Communities.* London: Chartered Institute of Housing.

Loftus, B. (2009) *Police Culture in a Changing World* Oxford, UK: Oxford University Press.

Lord Gifford QC, Brown, W., and Bundey, R. (1989) *'Loosen the Shackles' First Report of the Liverpool 8 Inquiry into Race Relations in Liverpool* Liverpool, UK: Biddles Limited.

Lord Macpherson (1999) *The Stephen Lawrence Inquiry Report of an Inquiry by Sir William Macpherson of Cluny* London: HM Government.

Lyon, D. (2014) 'David Lyon speaks on Contemporary Surveillance' *Routledge Textbooks* https://www.youtube.com/watch?v=Ov05EgnjMy0&feature=youtu.be&utm_source=Adestra&utm_medium=Email&utm_campaign=SBU3_SJO_4MX_1em_5SOC_57737_SSC [Accessed 29.08.14]

Marx, K. (1983) *Capital Volume One* London: Lawrence and Wishart.

Mastrofski, S. D., Snipes, J. B., and Supina, A. E. (1996) 'Compliance on Demand: The Public's Response to Specific Police Requests' *Journal of Research in Crime and Delinquency* 33 pp. 269–305.

Morrell, G., Scott, S., McNeish, D., and Webster, S. (2011) *The August Riots in England: Understanding the Involvement of Young People* London: Cabinet Office.

Muncie, J. (1999) 'Institutionalized Intolerance; Youth Justice and the 1998 Crime and Disorder Act' *Critical Social Policy* 19(2) pp. 147–75.

Muncie, J., and Hughes, G. (2002) 'Modes of Youth Governance: Political Rationalities, Criminalization and Resistance' in Muncie, J., Hughes, G., and McLaughlin, E. (eds) *Youth Justice: Critical Readings* (pp. 1–18) London: Sage.

Pampel, F. C. (2004) *Racial Profiling* New York: Facts on File Incorporated.

Pantazis, C., and Pemberton, S. A. (2011) 'Re-stating the Case for the Suspect Community: A Reply to Greer' *British Journal of Criminology* pp. 1054–63.

Reiner, R. (2010) *The Politics of the Police* Oxford, UK: Oxford University Press.

Scarman, L. G. (1981) *The Scarman Report: The Brixton Disorders, 10–12 April 1981: Report of an Inquiry* London: Penguin Books.

Shapland, J. (ed) (2008) *Justice, Community and Civil Society* Cullompton, Devon, UK: Willan Publishing.

Sharp, D., Atherton, S., and Williams, K. (2008) 'Civilian Policing, Legitimacy and Vigilantism: Findings from Three Case Studies in England and Wales' *Policing and Society: An International Journal of Research and Policy* 18(3) pp. 245–57.

Sharpe, J. (2001) 'Crime, Order and Historical Change' in Muncie, J., and McLaughlin, E. *The Problem of Crime* London: Sage.

Sherman, L. W., and Weisburd, D. (1995) 'General Deterrent Effects of Police Patrol in Crime Hot Spots: A Randomized, Controlled Trial' *Justice Quarterly* (12) pp. 635–48.

Smith, D. J. (2004) 'The Bakassi Boys: Vigilantism, Violence, and Political Imagination in Nigeria' *Cultural Anthropology* 19(3) pp. 429–55.

Squires, P. (ed) (2006) *Community Safety: Critical Perspectives on Policy and Practice* Bristol, UK: Policy Press.

Suh, R. (2009) 'Racial Profiling' *Research Starters Sociology* (Online Edition).

Taylor, I., Evans, K., and Fraser, P. (1996) *A Tale of Two Cities. Global Change, Local Feeling and Everyday Life in the North of England, A Study of Manchester and Sheffield* London: Routledge.

Treadwell, J. (2014) 'Controlling the New Far Right on the Streets: Policing the English Defence League in Policy and Praxis' in Chakraborti, N., and Garland, J. (eds), *Responding to Hate Crime: The Case for Connecting Policy and Research* Bristol, UK: Policy Press.

Tufail, W. (2013) *'Partnership Policing' in Three Marginalised Communities: An Ethnographic Study'* Unpublished PhD thesis submitted to the University of Salford.

Van Swaaningen, R. (2008) 'Sweeping the Street: Civil Society and Community Safety in Rotterdam' in Shapland, J. (ed) *Justice, Community and Civil Society: A Contested Terrain* Devon, UK: Willan Publishing.

Young, J. (1999) *The Exclusive Society* London: Sage.

Younge, G. (2014) 'In Ferguson the Violence of the State Created the Violence of the Street' *The Guardian* http://www.theguardian.com/commentisfree/2014/aug/18/ferguson-violence-martin-luther-king-michael-brown [Accessed 18.04.14].

8

THE PROBLEM OF COMMUNITY

The problem of criminology and the control of crime

To see the world through the problem of crime is to see it through a divisive frame-work. The ways in which the problem of crime has been constructed sets victims against offenders, the harmed against those who have committed the harmful acts and the state against the law-breaker. Over the last fifty years, however, the problem of crime has attained an almost iconic status which has gradually predominated and overwhelmed significant areas of concern around poverty, inequalities of power and human rights. These issues demand a social justice response which opens up the possibility for unity in action to achieve positive social outcomes across society. In contrast, the focus on crime constructs the problem as the criminal, the offender, and, increasingly in the twenty-first century, the terrorist, operating outside of the social boundaries and an element that must be isolated and condemned. Although a social justice model would look to understand the harmful behaviour of others and to place it into a fully social context, this is too often ruled out as utopian and unat-tainable by those who seek to reestablish social order through the control of crime. As a consequence, we are increasingly governed through the lens of crime control (Palmer 2000), with the exclusionary discourses of criminality and difference hav-ing driven their way even into the heart of the so-called liberal establishment. The Labour Party in the UK declared that it would be 'tough on crime' and when in office enacted a Crime and Disorder bill which significantly widened the net of crime control; similarly, it was a Democrat administration led by Clinton which rolled out 'three strikes and you're out' legislation in the US; exclusionary practices in the policing and management of public space in Australia grew in evidence under Labour-led governments in the 1980s and 1990s (White and Sutton 1995); and in New Zealand it was a Labour government which initiated the public-sector reforms which drove the crime control agenda onto responsibilised communities (Bradley and Walters 2002). Rather than tackling the causes of crime, governments of all political persuasions in the Anglophone world have looked to eliminate the signs of economic and social decline rather than to reverse these trends and to control and contain their excluded and marginalised populations, not to include and involve them.

It is not surprising that the rhetoric of the policy-makers has found its way into popular discourse and understanding. Social interventions have increasingly been built around the framework of crime and its control. This criminalization of social policy has not been resisted as much as it has been embraced by populations keen to minimise the impact of crime on local areas and to work with relevant authorities to find a solution that might work for their neighbourhoods. Examples abound of community organisations joining up with crime control agencies in crime prevention and community safety partnerships, but as Tufail (2013) and others before him have demonstrated (Crawford 1998; Whyte 2002), the dynamics of power are likely to drive the discourse of control downwards rather than that community understandings, tolerances and inclusionary practices are driven upwards.

The appeal to 'community' in crime prevention policy has proved to be rather limited in scope, co-opting residents of high-crime neighbourhoods into the state's agenda to reduce crime and victimisation using the tried and tested techniques embedded in situational and social crime prevention measures evaluated as those 'that work'. This approach has severely limited the options available to the communities involved. More ambitious, innovative and perhaps risky possibilities and those which look outside the problem of crime to the social, economic and environmental issues which affect a community's safety and security have rarely been attempted, let alone supported. Criminology's relationship with 'community' has proved problematic and in many ways exclusionary too. Mainstream criminology has characterised areas of high crime as exhibiting unusual traits; as outside the bounds of 'normal society'; as problems to be solved; and as places to be avoided. The suggestion that areas of high criminal victimisation include within them the source and seed of their own problems has created a particular view of these areas and of the people who live within them as places and people to be worked upon, altered in their physical and social nature and controlled and coerced into acceptable standards and behaviours. Their perspective has mirrored the moral authoritarian agenda of the state which has been successful in mobilising the 'good' and 'law-abiding communities' against the 'problematic' and 'criminal' (Hughes 2007). Back in 1978, Hall et al revealed the success of this approach in defining, representing and then controlling the crime of 'mugging'. The authoritarian state which they describe has continued to control the conversation, to define both the problem of crime and the solution in the intervening years. Indeed, Hancock (2009:159) has concluded that the dominance of state-centred discourses has 'become commonplace in the politics of crime control'. She draws parallels with contemporary discourses around anti-social behaviour which have been similarly redrawn by the state. Hancock et al (2012) have since extended this insight to consider the ways contemporary understandings of poverty and need have been similarly shaped through the lens of the neo-liberal state and have been successfully represented as problems of idleness and entitlement.

Of course, criminology has not been without its critical voices which have achieved some success in turning the monolith away from its traditional course but arguably only at the margins. Both democratic and more authoritarian states have distinguished between 'proper' criminology, which pretends a scientific basis for its findings and legitimates their agenda of crime control, and 'deviant' criminology, which challenges in its approach, methodology and conclusions (Schuman 1978 in Gilmore et al 2013; Hope 2004). In the area of crime and community, it is perhaps the left realist perspective which appeared able to wrest control of the subject from the hands of the administrative criminologists for some period of time. The intervention of left realism underpinned a turn away from the narrow confines of crime prevention and towards what, in the English-speaking world we have come to know as community safety. Outside of the Anglophone world, reference to the concept of 'community' has remained more problematic. The term 'community' has not been commonly employed, yet the approach which steered practitioners towards a more social understanding of the problem of crime did find favour in other nations' approaches. Following the tradition set by Durkheim and Weber, the countries of continental European have considered appeal to 'community' as backward-looking, exclusionary and parochial, whereas the concepts of social inclusion, citizen empowerment and social justice have been more easily absorbed, if not always implemented (Crawford 2002). It is not only an issue of semantics, however. Where neo-liberal logics have been slower in gaining ascendancy, the politics of 'revanchist urbanism' (a policy approach which punishes the poor for their disorderly and law-breaking conduct by removing their rights to public space and support) have been slower to catch on but are emerging nevertheless (van Swaaningen 2005). It is in these spatial and temporal interstices, however, that examples might be found which can point to the possibility of engaging with communities in a way which allows for more inclusive and egalitarian relationships to develop.

The enduring significance of community

An 'enduring nostalgia for the idea of community as a source of security and belonging in an increasingly insecure world' (Delanty 2003:1) has been noted by a number of writers as a significant social response to the risky and uncertain conditions of the current period (Baumann 2001; Beck 1992; Giddens 1991). Their characterisation of the quest for 'community' as nostalgic, however, betrays a certain contempt for the concept of community as somehow anti-modern and by implication anti-progressive. It also reveals a lack of understanding of how community may be used as a resource in contemporary society. Certainly, the objective conditions which can sustain residential 'community' are under threat or have been all but wiped out in many places at the beginning of the twenty-first century. The dominant economic model requires a level of mobility from the workforce which must be truly unprecedented and which individualises and atomises social relations to a greater extent than ever before. Individuals are now expected to move away from family and social support networks to look for work, and the international market for employment (notwithstanding the rise of the anti-immigration agenda internationally) continues to grow, with intercontinental movement of labour no longer a rare and exotic career choice. Once in work the demands for what has become known as 'flexible labour' require long working hours and a commitment to work which extends into the time which was once carved out as a separate private sphere for family, friends and interests outside of the workplace. Under such circumstances the space for 'community' and for 'civic engagement', as Putnam realised, is severely contracted and in danger of disappearing altogether. However, to base an understanding of the salience of community today solely or mainly on the emergence of this particular form of labour would be to exclude and ignore the millions who live in very different economic and social circumstances and also to forget that people, however constraining their employment, still look for meaningful relationships outside of the world of work. It is also important to remember that the working-life for most of us is bracketed by childhood and retirement and that community may take on more relevance and meaning at certain periods of an individual's life. Whether absorbed in work and career progression or without employment people still turn to others to find relations of attachment and a sense of belonging. While in the contemporary world this might be more difficult to find, especially in residential settings, than it has previously been, it would not be true to say that the idea of community itself is dead or that it is no longer considered an attractive state in which to be engaged.

CASE STUDY – KEEPING SAFE IN UNSAFE COMMUNITIES: DUBOIS TOWERS, PHILADELPHIA

'DuBois Towers' in Philadelphia was an archetypal dangerous estate, considered one of the most dangerous in the city. It consisted of four high-rise buildings built around a shared public space where children played and neighbours congregated, but also where adults gambled, gun fights broke out and drugs were openly sold on the streets. The high-rises were dilapidated, daubed with graffiti and attracted a steady stream of strangers, unknown to the residents, who were drawn there by the easy availability of illegal drugs. At the end of the 1990s, the Department of Housing and Urban Development in Philadelphia

(Continued)

made billions of dollars available to tackle their problem estates, demolishing many and relocating their residents to less dangerous social housing units across the city. Sometimes the demolished areas were rebuilt and the residents moved back in, but in most cases their relocation became permanent.

DuBois Towers was demolished in 1999. Two to three years after the demolition, Clampet-Lundquist interviewed forty-one families with children under 18 which had been relocated and twenty-two teenagers living in those families, in order to explore their experiences and feelings regarding their new neighbourhoods. Many of those who were moved reported feeling less safe, less confident and more vulnerable in their new surroundings, which, although ostensibly 'safer' with lower rates of crime and victimisation, were unfamiliar surroundings in which the new arrivals were not embedded and could not negotiate their own safety and security.

Clampet-Lundquist concluded that the disruption to local social ties and community networks had disoriented and disrupted the residents' lives. However manifestly unsafe their former neighbourhood had been, the residents had 'learned a cultural repertoire' and had attained a situated knowledge which allowed them to manage the risks of daily life in DuBois Towers. This knowledge was specific to that neighbourhood and the community networks which had been built up over a considerable period of time. It allowed the residents to avoid situations which were unsafe and to protect themselves against violence. As Clampet-Lundquist understands it, residents 'used their social and cultural capital to gain security and predictability in their daily encounters with people and situations. This capital was necessary for their basic survival', but it was also 'community-specific' (2010:103) and could not be replicated in their new surroundings.

Adapted from Clampet-Lundquist 2010

The relations of solidarity and belonging which the early theorists associated with community are most likely to be found in the residential setting where the movement of people through the neighbourhood is slow and residential patterns are more fixed. These are the areas where it is more likely that neighbours will know each other by sight, if not by name, and there is an increased likelihood that closer connections and relationships with neighbours can form. Community-based research conducted by criminologists, especially that inspired by the left realist perspective in the 1980s and 1990s, is replete with examples of close connection and the existence of shared values and experiences between the residents of areas which, to the outsider may appear to be stagnant and economically marginal but to the resident insider offer affection, solidarity and support between neighbours. Even under difficult social circumstances, indeed in some cases precisely because of shared difficulties, individuals have reported that they felt connected to community concerns and willing to work with others to improve their lives. These studies have revealed the existence of local networks and connections which have bound people together in relationships of inclusion which were highly significant to their lives (Evans 2004). As the economic backdrop to the lives of residents in such areas is likely to have worsened and as the state has withdrawn from areas of social provision in recent decades, informal networks of mutuality and support will likely have become more important. In the US and UK especially, research has shown that voluntary organisations, both secular and religious, have had to step in to fill the void left by the hollowed-out state, recruiting unpaid service providers to ensure some continuity in provision (O'Dowd 2013).

There are other arenas, apart from the residential setting, in which community is experienced and can be felt deeply in contemporary society. Candland (2001) has suggested, for example, that the significance of religion in people's lives is vastly underestimated in the largely secular West. He criticises the generally held presumption that individuals are always self-serving and pursue competing interests. He suggests instead that the affective bonds of loyalty and religious sentiment can often lead to significant collective action. Candland further contends that religious association offers not only a source of spirituality and comfort but also key social capital which can confer significant mutual benefits arising from exploiting trusting and co-operative relationships. It is not even necessary, he argues, for face-to-face interactions to take place before this trust is conferred; shared religious values may be enough for important links to be solidified. Where other forms of social capital are difficult to access, for example, through economic or cultural exclusion, then networks of religion, kinship and community may provide the necessary connections to finance, advice and opportunities which are otherwise lacking. It should come as no surprise therefore that, in times when the state is rolling back its support of the community, the solidarity and connections found through religious affiliation would take its place.

Within the realm of politics there has also been a much vaunted return to consideration of community as a significant site of organisation and action. The globalisation of economic relations and the prominent role international markets play in setting the scene in which national politics can take place and influence the decision making of national governments wary of upsetting such markets have, it is argued, severely limited the options open to national politicians and diminished the power of the nation-state (Rose 1996). In consequence, it is further argued, affiliation to national politics has diminished, and local spaces have taken on more significance and meaning, with a consequent push towards local autonomy and locality as a site of political action. This thesis has consequently been employed to valorise the national governments' turn towards community, presenting them with a third way and another arena in which to influence and engage the voting public. There is little concrete evidence, however, to suggest that community has played a more significant role in recent decades as a consequence of the demise of the nation-state. Indeed, the end of the twentieth century saw a surge in the politics of internationalism and the rise of social movements such as the anti-capitalist Global Social Forums and Occupy which sought to challenge the power of the international markets (Sen 2004). At the same time, nationalist sentiments have become more important to some political groups, especially those of the far right, which have reacted to the loss of national power and identity by proclaiming the importance of the resurgence of the same. While there have certainly been community-based groups which have seen local residents take action on a range of political fronts, protesting the effects of 'austerity' economics, there is no evidence that these groups have proliferated or taken a different direction than community-based organisation in the past. If anything, the global nature of the economic collapse of 2008 suggests that community-based responses will have less effect and power to change social conditions for the better.

The exclusive community

At the edges of networks of inclusion and support are the boundaries at which community ends and exclusion begins. However large and wide-ranging the community, or however small and tight-knit it appears, inclusion necessarily implies the exclusion of others, and it would be both naïve and dangerous to suggest that this was not the case. The actual form and impact which inclusion and exclusion take will vary widely, and chroniclers of community have rightly stressed the importance of carefully observing and responding to these particularities if meaningful engagement is to be achieved and communities are to be fully included in conversations and decision making which impact their lives (Walklate and Evans 1996). It is important that the knowledge so gained, however, be used to positive effect in order to advance a progressive agenda which improves local relations within an inclusionary framework. Carson (2004) has warned of the dangers of communalism and the divisive outcomes which an over-reliance on community voices can deliver. He uses Hancock and Matthews' (2001) concern that urban networks can just as easily form around neo-tribalist discourses which may be transient and fragile, although no less harmful as a consequence, to warn of the dangers of basing social policy on a muddled and muddied notion of community. In addition, Carson considers the dangers of continuing to base key crime prevention (or indeed any other) policy and decisions on ill-defined notions of community in multicultural and diverse social settings, especially given the current impact of the 'war on terror' in racialising and demonising 'the other'.

At certain times, when individuals feel under threat as a consequence of their religious beliefs, they may cohere as a group in a defensive reaction from which other groups may be perceived as opponents rather than as potential allies. While

Candland has described the significant relationships of trust which can be forged within religious communities, he also acknowledges that in each of the countries in which he has researched the positive benefits of belonging to a particular religion (Indonesia, Pakistan and Sri Lanka) 'militant religious ideologies have also played a part in promoting horrific violence against religious minority communities and atheists, especially communists' (2001:356).

Evidence has also emerged more recently showing that the appeal to community governance of crime and disorder can have divisive outcomes. Hughes and Edwards (2002) have raised concerns that the replacement of a universal provision of welfare and support services with a targeted devolvement of support to the needy has inadvertently eroded collective solidarity and the idea that a sense of security should be assured throughout society. Instead, the needs of communities are pitted against each other, with each having to make the claim that its particular circumstances justify access to an increasingly smaller pot of money which is no longer shared equally. Cain and Yuval-Davis (1990) have collected evidence which reveals that these funding strategies have exacerbated tensions between communities in the UK, especially in areas where BME communities appeared to be more successful in obtaining funding than their majority white counterparts and neighbours. As we have seen in earlier chapters, the response to these increasing tensions has (in contradiction to the stated claim that communities of difference must be celebrated and that communities should set their own local agendas) been a reassertion of the sovereign authority of the state and a top-down re-imposition of the requirement to assimilate to a national identity which is defined by the state alone.

CASE STUDY – THE PROMISE OF INCLUSION AND THE MAINTENANCE OF EXCLUSION: THE GOVERNANCE OF PUBLIC SPACE IN BOGOTA, COLOMBIA

Planners for the city of Bogota, Colombia, have signed on to an approach to provide open space which is egalitarian and inclusive. They have claimed that the particular approach they have taken stands in contrast to the exclusive urbanism found in much of Latin America and in its stead serves as an example of 'post-revanchist' political engagement. Bogota's Plan Maestro de Espacio Publico (PMEP) attempts to put public space at the heart of policies which will promote innovation in inclusionary community governance and equality in the use of the city's public spaces. By 2010, as many as eighty-seven organisations were involved in the management of 427 public spaces ranging from parks to community centres, and the policy was hailed as a success and a method of achieving harmonious social relationships and

(Continued)

across the city's neighbourhoods as well as contributing to the regeneration and revitalisation of areas of the city which had become neglected and rarely used. The PMEP set out to encourage citizen participation in the daily governance of public space in the city through educational and community-run activities based in public space, designed to encourage citizens of Bogota to appropriate public space as their own. As a mechanism of participation, local residents and businesses were encouraged to get together in 'social promotion networks' which would design and manage the use of particular areas of public space. These networks were considered as an opportunity for local people from different class backgrounds and experiences to work together to bring about positive changes in the city's social and physical landscape.

In their practice, the networks promoted and supported through the PMEP did not result in innovative or inclusionary practices on the ground. Instead, existing exclusionary policies were replicated by the social promotion networks. The result looks very much like the zero tolerance policies of Bratton's New York. While the citizen groups themselves did not act as Police in the place of state authorities, they were active in designing policies which tightly policed and restricted the kinds of activities allowed to take place in public space. Some organisations used revenue from car parking in their public space to finance private security patrols which would monitor use of the space and enforce these policies on a daily basis. Those without such resources would inform the relevant authorities, who would respond rapidly to their calls to attend and deal with groups of people perceived to be acting outside of the community's accepted norms. The kind of activity which these networks tended to outlaw were the drinking of alcohol, and in some places the use of the public spaces for demonstrations; dissemination of political ideas or literature was also frowned upon. Unwelcome, too, were groups of young people considered to be too large or noisy, street vendors and the homeless.

In the end, Galvis (2013) argues that the communities involved in the officially sanctioned networks proved to act in as conservative and exclusionary a manner as state authorities had done before them. The experiment reveals that exclusion does not have to be enforced from the top-down. Instead, local groups can be similarly influenced by a politics of class and can take on official definitions of inclusion and exclusion and make them their own. The conservative and state-centred response of local community groups reflected the fact that the authorities controlled the groups which were considered as suitable partners, and the design of the strategy was top-down rather than arising from a grassroots campaign and frame of reference.

Adapted from Galvis (2013)

Uses (and abuse) of community

The social complexities of twenty-first century living in economically developed societies mean that the concept of 'community' is not easily applied to current social arrangements yet the term has not lost its power altogether. The presence of 'community' is still generally considered asa social good and its absence as signalling possible or actual social breakdown. Paradoxically, the idea that community could be invoked 'as an alternative to the state as a basis for politics' (Delanty 2003:1) found favour just as powerful economic forces were pushing a realignment of social and economic policy which preferred to organise society through the invisible hand of market forces rather than through any collective provision of services. Those governments which appeared most enamoured with the concept of 'community' and most insistent that it remain an organising social concept were the very bodies which were also dismantling frameworks of collective action foregrounding a particularly individualistic and self-oriented approach to survival in contrast to the development of a social consciousness. As a consequence, crime control policy under neo-liberal governance has attempted to co-opt community less as a local resource offering situated knowledge and expertise but more as a source of disciplinary power to manage and control behaviour deemed unacceptable by 'respectable society' (Squires 2006).

The newfound enthusiasm for rebuilding community, civil society and social capital has been copied in various guises across the globe and heralded as the solution to many social ills (Carson 2004), but this approach to community has not been without its problems. As I have argued elsewhere, appeals to community and to active citizen engagement have gone hand in hand with an intensification of social control which has not always been welcome (Evans 2011). Appeals to community have sought to engage with the 'moral voice' of the 'law-abiding community', and only those communities which appear to be participating 'constructively, co-operatively and reasonably' (Karn 2006:199) with this moral authoritarian agenda are considered as truly representative. Policy-makers have implemented this agenda as though there is indeed one community of interest which can be harnessed for positive effect, and that this community of interest accords with state directives on any particular issue. Those who, for whatever reason do not co-operate with the process as it is set out for them by the professionals have been, as Karn reveals, considered uncooperative or even destructive and funding and support have been withdrawn, or such withdrawal threatened, from those communities which are off-message. Communities have been used as objects of policy-making and seen as projects to be worked upon rather than truly worked with and listened to (Imrie and Raco 2003).

Concerns have also been raised that community involvement on the ground can be tokenistic rather then truly participative. As Hancock has outlined, many of the strategies for public and community involvement which have been devised as government-inspired initiatives in the UK have been perceived by the targeted communities as 'cynical attempts to secure, or re-secure, the legitimacy of the police following urban unrest' (2009:168) and as a form of gesture politics rather than a committed attempt to allow communities to guide government thinking. Hancock maintains, however, that under the influence of the communitarian philosophies and third-way politics which emerged in the 1990s, government attempts to engage community should not be seen in such simplistic terms. Rather, she argues, the proponents of third-way communitarianism were genuine in their desire to increase the accountability of the state, to make 'better decisions' and to promote active citizenship (Hancock 2009:168). What communitarianism philosophy has not acknowledged, however, are the inequalities of power between the governed and the governing bodies that make the key decisions which impact on their lives. Nor has it acknowledged the inequalities of wealth and class which set the needs of the entrepreneurial and responsible against the 'ungovernable' urban poor (Coleman 2009). The imaginary of self-governing communities choosing their own boundaries, setting their own limits and tolerances, has not been the observed reality.

Under the post-crash politics of 'austerity' which have dominated the discourse of welfare benefits and the right to social support since 2008, the appeal to community has taken another turn. The fiscal crisis which ensued following the bail-out of the global banking system, rising national debts and shrinking economies which have eroded the tax base of many national economies has been used as justification for savage cuts in state-provided services and for the call for 'community' and 'society' to step in to fill the yawning gap in provision which has resulted. At the same time, many services which were formerly provided by the state have been passed on to private organisations and companies. This shift has often been rationalised as returning power and responsibility to the 'community'. Accompanying this trend then has been a concomitant growth in policies and projects which claim some form of community ownership and provision but which in effect are pulling in the voluntary sector and non-governmental providers into the provision of social services. The rhetoric accompanying this significant shift is that the community should be given more powers to determine their own futures, that decision making should be devolved downwards, that communities should be given the right to take over state-run services and that there should be an expectation that people will get involved in volunteering and community activities (Cabinet Office 2010). Posed as a radical alternative to big government and ensuring the empowerment of millions of ordinary people, the shift of responsibility away from the state actually masks a reduction in the size and spending limits of government departments.

In the face of exclusion or in the absence of an agenda of real inclusion, communities are likely to withdraw their trust in others, in authority and in participative infrastructures. At the other extreme, excluded communities may make their voices heard through loud and sometimes violent outrage. Once this anger has spilled out into the public arena, then real attempts must be made to heal the rifts which have been made, or they can simmer unattended and unresolved. The arguments presented in Chapters Six and Seven revealed how the treatment of communities perceived as 'suspect' or profiled as potentially 'criminal' by persons in authority can contribute to a breakdown of relationships of trust between the public and representatives of the state. This further leads to the institutionalisation of a style and degree of coercive (over)policing which is socially harmful in the present and which also affects the possibility of building relationships of trust in the future. It is telling that at the same time, as governments have exhorted communities to act in their common interests, when the marginalised, the colonised and the excluded demand that their voices be heard they have so often been silenced.

CASE STUDY – WHEN TESCO CAME TO TOWN: COMMUNITY PROTESTS AGAINST CORPORATE POWER

In April 2011, in the inner-city Stokes Croft area of Bristol, a riot broke out triggered by the heavy-handed policing of a sustained campaign opposed to the building of a Tesco store in the area. The background to the 'Tesco riots' included urban gentrification, pressure on housing and rising levels of inequality – all of which created a feeling that the local nature of the community was under pressure from corporate power, control and market logics. It was because Tesco epitomises the ever-mighty power of corporations in the twenty-first century that it was so violently opposed by local people. The campaign against the store began with a lobby of the council's planning meeting by over 300 people, mostly young, in the summer of 2010. Despite a number of regeneration initiatives, and maybe because these initiatives have focused on building homes for sale rather than social housing, there is a marked lack of affordable housing in the area. This shortage has resulted in the growth of the number of occupied empty properties and a relatively new community of squatters in a process that has been termed the 'do-it-yourself regeneration'. This development has been accompanied by a vibrant culture of local enterprise breeding a 'creative' ambience in the area's galleries and cafés, pubs and nightclubs. The area has developed a countercultural vibe which has attracted students and young workers and turned the fortunes of the area around. The arrival of Tesco was seen as threatening this way of life and as an attempt by a large corporation to profit from the community's energy and activity.

By the time Tesco opened its doors in April 2011, campaigners had spent several months conducting low-level resistance of leafleting, petitions and public protest. Activists believe that Tesco's management was infuriated by this continuing dissent and disruption and may well have encouraged the police to take action. On Thursday, April 21, 2011, 160 officers of the Avon

(Continued)

and Somerset, Wiltshire and South Wales Police forces cordoned off the upper half of Stokes Croft, closing off access to this major trunk road for several hours. Having 'secured the area', the Police then moved in to clear a prominent squat. Dozens of bystanders began to resist by using street furniture and anything to hand to hurl at the Police and block off their advance. Rather than using their recent practice of 'kettling' (encircling) people, the police tactics meant that they themselves became kettled and were unable to resist the incursions of protestors at either end of the A38 cordon. Police charged back and forth, and protestors resisted and reoccupied the squat over several hours.

The mood was riotous at this point, and the Tesco store was thoroughly looted. Symbolic anti-capitalist protestors were joined by local youth keen to join the resistance (and make some gains in the process – all the store's cigarettes disappeared). This action was repeated one week later. This time, the police were amassed to make a series of arrests related to the events of the week before. The effectiveness of the first riot had sparked more interest from local youth, who were keen to participate in a powerful expression of their 'right to the streets'. The focus had moved beyond only the Tesco store by this point, with marchers setting off to find a suitable multinational target in the nearby city centre, thus keeping the police occupied in tracking them. The composition of the group of several hundred people had now become more multicultural, more representative of St. Paul's in general, where there are fewer squats, but, rather, a well-established multicultural community experiencing rising unemployment and insecurity.

Adapted from Clement (2014)

Working with community – learning the lessons

Anyone working in the area of criminology, crime prevention and crime control over the last twenty or so years will have observed the increasing politicisation of the subject and a ratcheting up of popular fears about crime and victimisation. Many behaviours that formerly were only perceived as troublesome or anti-social and were dealt with as social issues which should be addressed or civic violations which could be dealt with outside the criminal justice system have now been criminalised and are subject to the full weight of criminal justice sanctions. In the case of anti-social behaviour orders, these sanctions are even 'tailor-made' for the individual, and where more serious violations are suspected, anti-terrorist legislation has been invoked to individually tailor control orders and measures in order to restrict the movement and conversations of suspects. Such harsh and punitive treatment is meted out by the state and is justified on the grounds that it ensures the safety of the wider community. The safety of the community, however, may be better addressed through forms of social rather than criminal justice.

The concept of community safety, as it was developed in the 1980s as an alternative to crime prevention and control perspectives, was focused on the locality, informed by local knowledge and was concerned with the safety of the local neighbourhood. In its most progressive guise, community included in its remit a wider concern to achieve safety within local neighbourhoods, not just ensuring safety from crime but also enhancing safety on the roads, providing cleaner environments, increasing the confidence of women and girls to combat the effects of gender equalities and working with men to understand and reinterpret masculinity and its impacts. This focus on community safety was also a focus on community, on understanding local social formations, respecting local connections which might have been built up over generations and the local knowledge situated in a neighbourhood's streets. It involved exploring local histories as well as presently lived experiences, and it used these to attempt to build better futures. During the period in which community safety work existed as an oppositional movement, outside of national government frameworks, it remained semi-autonomous and could take on progressive agendas. It relied for funding on a variety of sources which could be locally, nationally or internationally generated (for example, European funding from EU programmes) and was therefore unattached to any specific agendas. However, as national governments have co-opted the agenda of community into their repertoire of governance, this has, paradoxically, led to an abandonment of local voice and an imposition of centralised and controlling discourses.

Contemporary practices of community governance and community-focused policies come from a very different place. The more benevolent aspect which the community safety perspective imagined has been replaced in practice with what many experienced as oppressive practices involving the over-policing of certain neighbourhoods, the stigmatisation of entire social groups, the use of military-style methods of control and the invoking of a narrow moral agenda imposed from above. The fear of disorder is so strong that attitudes towards the marginal have hardened (Bowden 2006) and, as the author China Miéville (2012) understands it, 'everyday silliness, adolescent thoughtlessness are treated like social collapse' and consequently detected infringements are likely to be met with an overblown response. Despite the political rhetoric, the direction of policy has shifted from the local to the centre, from safety to risk and from the public service ethos to a privatised and profit-generating provision which undermines the values of inclusion, welfarism and solidarity. The optimism of previous periods informed by a more social democratic zeitgeist, by community development and collective action from below, suggested that the turn to community would result in innovative, progressive and inclusionary policies and practices, whereas in the current context the community itself may well be punitive, risk-averse and focused on security and control.

In the current political climate which is dominated by exclusionary discourses, security agendas, privatised provision and austerity measures, the part 'community' can play is frankly more limited than it has been for many decades. Communities, however, have not remained silent. As the case study above concerning the Tesco 'riots' in Bristol show, there are still many examples of local people coalescing and acting together over issues which are significant in their lives and especially where they feel that the things they treasure most in their local area are subject to external threats. However, the local coalitions do not always serve progressive purposes. As Hughes et al (2002) state, such local activism may also take the form of terrorising 'the other', excluding and marginalising in turn those who appear to act against a local moral order or against local interest and values. If we wish to recapture and reconnect community with a progressive politics and agenda, it is important to step outside the current framework which does so much to prevent a reimagining of the discourse. The form that community action will take in the future will most probably look and feel different from that of the past. Nevertheless, there are lessons we can learn from past practices. We should also explore current engagement with community which lies outside of normative frameworks as well as those drawn from different and currently marginalised traditions. In the following 'lessons' I present some ideas which might help to engage communities in the production of a just society while reconnecting them to the ideas of solidarity, common purpose and attachment to which it has formerly been applied and to a progressive politics of change which might resist the decline into blame (the other side of responsibilisation), exclusion and petty tribalisms. I do not expect that these lessons will be learned under current governance structures. Significant transformations are needed before past mistakes will even be acknowledged, but this should not prevent discussion and debate. This is only the start of a conversation which I hope others will enthusiastically take up.

Lesson 1 – people have a legitimate claim to public resources

Social democratic principles built the public sector and public service after the Second World War, but these principles have been eroded in the very places where they were built. It is important to connect to a value system which defends the rights of the poor and the marginalised, not only to benefit from a national system of support from the cradle to the grave, but also to have their voices heard and their needs understood. The inclusion of these voices in the public arena is as significant as the right of the bodies of the poor and marginalised to occupy public space without condemnation and reprisals. Such a system would distribute available national resources in such a way as to present opportunities for all and especially to those for whom opportunities have previously been denied. Public resources should by definition be owned, managed and controlled by the public. They are not to be given away to private interests , nor should they generate profit for a few. Participatory structures need to be put in place which truly allow for local democratic control and administration from below.

Lesson 2 – let's start with social rather than criminal justice

We need to shift our gaze away from the problem of crime and towards the more inclusive lens of social justice. Even within high-crime neighbourhoods, the communities and the individuals who together make up these social units should be considered as citizens first and foremost and not subject to stigmatising discourses which only marginalise and problematise their lives further. As the social harm theorists remind us, crime is not the only problem experienced in such neighbourhoods (Hillyard and Tombs 2007), but even where crime is considered a significant problem, those who fear and experience crime the most are often those who are least able to deal with its impact. Where we do need to protect this should be accomplished in such a way so as not to compound social problems and divisions. Where crime is a problem, the roots of the problem need to be understood and seriously tackled. We should be intolerant of injustice and the structural conditions which produce alienation and despair.

Lesson 3 – not all communities are the same

It is important that we acknowledge that neighbourhoods have different problems, concerns and fears which will have built up over many years. Local expertise and knowledge is a necessary part of this process and is essential if we are to understand and address the particular problems which manifest locally, even though they may have wider, structural roots. A recent report into the delivery of community safety in Northern Ireland gives a fascinating insight into the ways two very different communities in Belfast have engaged with the idea of community safety. As the authors of the report, Byrne and Topping (2012), have shown, the very different histories of engagement with the state in Northern Ireland which have been experienced by Unionist and Republican communities have translated into unique collaborative projects on the ground. In order to try to heal decades of division, those building community safety partnerships involving these communities had to strip back authoritarian styles of engagement and fully connect with the very differing concerns of both communities. The models of community advocacy, education, mediation and restorative justice which evolved as a consequence look quite different from the community safety practices followed in mainland UK during the same period. Acknowledging local differences allows local voices and community concerns to take centre-stage. It also requires that those who are currently considered 'authorities' take a backseat.

Lesson 4 – the importance of watching the watchers

Power should be held to account, and there is a long history of community-based activism which has set out to achieve this particular purpose. In Britain in the 1970s, grassroots Police Monitoring Groups emerged in many major cities where citizens were concerned about unaccountable Police forces and the increased militarisation of policing methods (Jefferson et al 1988). Independent legal observers are often present today at demonstrations and at disturbances, such as the Tesco Riot, to monitor and report on the behaviour of the Police. Recently, the proliferation of recording devices through smartphones, wearable cameras and digital recorders has meant that there is a real possibility for citizen action and sousveillance (surveillance of the powerful from below), which can turn the gaze on to institutional power structures (Fernback 2013). Fernback has catalogued an increase in sousveillance and countersurveillance communities, driven by critical discourses of resistance, posting video and audio clips to social networking sites in a bid to media and state control of information resources. In my own region, the north of England, local activists and academics have recently revived the concept of monitoring by the community with the setting up of the Northern Police Monitoring Project in 2012. This project has attracted continuing interest from community activists at meetings and also through its own Facebook page. In Georgia, following the protests which followed the shooting of Michael Brown, three teenagers developed an app which encourages people to rate their interactions with local law enforcement officers. All the scores will then be aggregated at county level or even for individual police officers to inform communities and the authorities of policing problems and issues (Independent 2014). These are two examples of many demonstrating how grassroots activism can look for solutions and deliver innovative responses to perceived problems.

Lesson Five – other futures are possible

As Handa et al (2012:449) have remarked, 'Dramatically different beliefs about justice will produce dramatically different methods for achieving justice'. Hand et al's book has engaged with theories and concepts developed in the West and based on Western experiences and perspectives. In recent years, however, the dominance of Western values has been challenged by a number of writers who have looked to different belief systems which have arisen in very different circumstances. Perhaps the most well-known and more widely adopted of these is Braithwaite's championing of restorative justice which he has gleaned from the customs and traditions of the indigenous peoples of Australasia and the emergence of peace-making criminology which challenges the world-view of the mainstream criminology of the West. Such work takes the ideas of more ancient traditions and belief systems seriously and has opened criminology up to a very different agenda, that of non-state justice (Braithwaite 2014). This justice system 'is rooted in notions of relationship and dialogue rather than adversarial dispute, harmony and balance rather than proof and guilt, and renewal rather than punishment' (Peat 1996, quoted in Handa et al 2012:449). These traditional perspectives seek to work with the victims and the perpetrators of harm, and to involve community rather than state in definitions of harmful behaviour, in order to move forward into a more harmonious future. The unique circumstances which societies emerging from state-sponsored and communal conflicts, such as apartheid South Africa or Northern Ireland, have presented have demanded that reconciliation and resolution be foregrounded and that attempts be made to arrest and reverse the mechanisms which have produced previous social harms. The demands of indigenous communities that they receive acknowledgement that they have been harmed by colonial power and for a reorganisation of state and nation to incorporate their ancient knowledge systems and practices have also been based on a return to traditional systems of justice (Short 2008). While these ideas have had some influence on court processes and systems of community justice in some jurisdictions, their impact has remained marginal in the present and vulnerable to withdrawal of funding and support from the state. It is not clear either as to whether all the values underpinning traditional justice would be transferable to the contemporary field or whether they would be welcomed in the future as methods of dealing with all areas of harmful behaviour. What they do remind us, however, is that there are other ways of seeing the world, of respecting and involving community, and that these perspectives do not always have to be dominated by state-led discourses.

Concluding comments and questions

This concluding chapter has explored the limitations of 'community' as an organising concept. It has considered the inherent exclusionary nature of community and the tendency of community to separate as well as to unite. While 'community' is held up as a positive social formation, this chapter uses case studies from the UK and abroad to demonstrate how the building of communities can produce barriers to progressive policy-making. Finally, it has considered how post-conflict discourses of community might be framed and the possibilities this might introduce for crime prevention/community safety in the future. At the final analysis the questions remain:

1. Can community ever act as a progressive force within society?
2. In what ways might the concept of community be differently envisaged in the future?

References

Bauman, Z. (2001) *Community: Seeking Safety in an Insecure World* Cambridge, UK: Polity Press.

Beck, U. (1992) *The Risk Society: Towards a New Modernity* London: Sage.

Bowden, M. (2006) 'Youth Governance and the City' *Youth Studies Ireland* 1(1) pp. 19–39.

Bradley, T., and Walters, R. (2002) 'The Managerialization of Crime Prevention and Community Safety: The New Zealand Experience' in Hughes, G., McLaughlin, E., and Muncie, J. (eds) *Crime Prevention and Community Safety. New Directions* London: Sage.

Braithwaite, J. (2014) 'Traditional Justice' in Llewellyn, J. J., and Philpott, D. (eds), *Restorative Justice, Reconciliation, and Peacebuilding* Oxford, UK: Oxford University Press.

Byrne, J., and Topping, J. (2012) *Community Safety: A Decade of Development, Delivery, Challenge and Change in Northern Ireland* Belfast, UK: Belfast Conflict Resolution Consortium.

Cabinet Office (2010) 'Big Society Speech' Transcript of a speech by the Prime Minister on the Big Society, 19 July 2010 Gov.uk https://www.gov.uk/government/speeches/big-society-speech [Accessed 19.07.10].

Cain, H., and Yuval-Davis, N. (1990) 'The Equal Opportunities Community and the Anti-racist Struggle' *Critical Social Policy* 29 pp. 5–2.

Candland, C. (2001) 'Faith as Social Capital: Religion and Community Development in Southern Asia' *Policy Sciences* 33 pp. 355–74.

Carson, W. G. (2004) 'Is Communalism Dead? Reflections on the Present and Future Practice of Crime Prevention: Part Two' *Australian and New Zealand Journal of Criminology* 37(2) pp. 192–210.

Clampet-Lundquist, S. (2010) '"Everyone Had Your Back". Social Ties, Perceived Safety, and Public Housing Relocation' *City and Community* 9(1) pp. 87–108.

Clement, M. (2014) 'Mobs versus Markets: Bristol's Tesco Riot' in Pakes, F., and Pritchard, D. (eds.), *Riot and Protest on the Global Stage* Basingstoke, UK Palgrave Macmillan.

Coleman, R. (2009) 'Policing the Working Class City in the City of Renewal; The State and Social Surveillance' in Coleman, R., Sim, J., Tombs, S., and Whyte, D. (eds) *State. Power. Crime* London: Sage.

Crawford, A. (ed) (2002) *Crime and Insecurity: The Governance of Safety in Europe* Cullompton, Devon, UK: Willan Publishing.

Crawford, A. (1998) *Crime Prevention and Community Safety* Harlow, UK: Longman.

Delanty, G. (2003) *Community* London: Routledge.

Evans, K. (2004) *Maintaining Community in the Information Age. The Importance of Trust, Locality and Shared Experience* Basingstoke, UK: Palgrave Macmillan.

Evans, K. (2011) *Crime Prevention: A Critical Introduction* London: Sage.

Fernback, J. (2013) 'Sousveillance: Communities of Resistance to the Surveillance Environment' *Telematics and Informatics* 30(1) pp. 11–21.

Galvis, J. P. (2013) 'Remaking Equality: Community Governance and the Politics of Exclusion in Bogotas Public Spaces' *International Journal of Urban and Regional Research* 38(4) pp. 1458–75.

Giddens, A. (1991) *Modernity and Self-Identity* Cambridge, UK: Polity Press.

Gilmore, J. (2011) 'Policing Protest: An Authoritarian Consensus' *Criminal Justice Matters* 82(1).

Hancock, L. (2009) 'Crime Prevention, Community Safety and the Local State' in Coleman, R., Sim, J., Tombs, S., and Whyte, D. (eds), *State, Power, Crime* London: Sage.

Hancock, L., and Matthews, R. (2001) 'Crime, Community Safety and Tolerance' in Matthews, R., and Pitt, J. (eds.), *Crime, Disorder and Community Safety* (pp. 98–119) London: Routledge.

Hancock, L., Mooney, G., and Neal, S. (2012) 'Crisis Social Policy and the Resilience of the Concept of Community' *Critical Social Policy* 32 pp. 343–64.

Handa, C.A., Hankesa, J., and Housea, T. (2012) 'Restorative Justice: The Indigenous Justice System' *Contemporary Justice Review: Issues in Criminal, Social, and Restorative Justice* 15(4) pp. 449–467.

Hillyard, P., and Tombs, S. (2007) 'From "Crime" to Social Harm?' *Crime, Law and Social Change* 48(1–2) pp. 9–25.

Hope, T. (2004) 'Pretend it Works. Evidence and Governance in the Evaluation of the Reducing Burglary Initiative' *Criminology and Criminal Justice* 4(3) pp. 287–308.

Hughes, G. (2007) *The Politics of Crime and Community* Basingstoke, UK: Palgrave.

Hughes, G., and Edwards, A. (eds) (2002) *Crime Control Community. The New Politics of Community Safety* Cullompton, Devon, UK: Willan Publishing.

Hughes, G., McLaughlin, E., and Muncie, J. (2002) *Crime Prevention and Community Safety. New Directions* London: Sage.

Imrie, R., and Raco, M. (2003) *Urban Renaissance? New Labour, Community and Urban Policy* Bristol, UK: Policy Press.

The Independent (2014) 'Ferguson Violence Inspires Tech-Savvy Teenagers to Create App That Tracks Police brutality' *The Independent* 29 September 2014 http://www.indepen dent.co.uk/news/world/americas/ferguson-violence-inspires-techsavvy-teenagers-to-create-app-that-tracks-police-brutality-9688444.html [Accessed 29.09.14].

Jefferson, T., McLaughlin, E., and Robertson, L. (1988) 'Monitoring the Monitors: Account-ability, Democracy and Policewatching in Britain' *Contemporary Crises* 12 pp. 91–106.

Karn, J. (2006) *Narratives of Neglect: Community, Exclusion and the Local Governance of Security* Cullompton, Devon, UK: Willan Publishing.

Miéville, C. (2012) *London's Overthrow* London: Guardian Books.

O'Dowd, A. (2013) 'Half a Million People Using Food Banks in UK as Food Poverty Grows' *British Medical Journal* 346 p. 3578.

Palmer, G. (2000) 'Governing Through Crime: Surveillance, the Community and Local Crime Programming' *Policing and Society* 10 pp. 321–42.

Rose, N. (1996) 'The Death of the Social? Re-figuring the Territory of Government' *Economy and Society* 25(3) pp. 327–56.

Schuman, K. F. (1978) 'On Proper and Deviant Criminology. Varieties in the Production of Legitimation for Penal Law' in Gilmore, J., Moore, J. M., and Scott, D. (eds), (2013) *Critique and Dissent. An Anthology to Mmark 40 Years of the European Group for the Study of Deviance and Social Control* Ottawa: Red Quill Books.

Sen, J. (2004) *World Social Forum: Challenging Empires* New Delhi: Viveka Foundation.

Short, D. (2008) *Reconciliation and Colonial Power. Indigenous Rights in Australia* Aldershot: Ashgate.

Squires, P. (ed) (2006) *Community Safety: Critical Perspectives on Policy and Practice* Bristol, UK: Policy Press.

Tufail, W. (2013) *'Partnership Policing' in Three Marginalised Communities: An Ethnographic Study* Unpublished PhD thesis submitted to the University of Salford.

Van Swaaningen, R. (2005) 'Public Safety and the Management of Fear' *Theoretical Criminology* 9(3) pp. 289–305.

Walklate, S., and Evans, K. (1999) *Zero Tolerance or Community Tolerance? Managing Crime in High Crime Areas* Aldershot: Ashgate.

White, R., and Sutton, A. (1995) 'Crime Prevention, Urban Space and Social Exclusion' *Australian and New Zealand Journal of Sociology* 31(1) pp. 82–99.

Whyte, D. (2002) *Crime Control Partnerships on Merseyside* Liverpool: Centre for Criminal Justice, Liverpool John Moores University.

INDEX

CPSIA information can be obtained
at www.ICGtesting.com
Printed in the USA
BVHW070232131218
535508BV00007B/42/P